SUPERMAN
VOL.3 MULTIPLICITY

PETER J. TOMASI and **PATRICK GLEASON**
writers

JORGE JIMENEZ * **IVAN REIS** * **JOE PRADO** * **RYAN SOOK**
ED BENES * **CLAY MANN** * **TONY S. DANIEL**
SANDU FLOREA * **SETH MANN** * **SEBASTIÁN FIUMARA**
artists

ALEJANDRO SANCHEZ * **MARCELO MAIOLO** * **RYAN SOOK**
DINEI RIBEIRO * **ULISES ARREOLA** * **DAVE STEWART**
colorists

ROB LEIGH * **SAIDA TEMOFONTE**
letterers

IVAN REIS, OCLAIR ALBERT and **MARCELO MAIOLO**
collection cover art

JORGE JIMENEZ and **ALEJANDRO SANCHEZ**
PATRICK GLEASON, MICK GRAY and **JOHN KALISZ**
RYAN SOOK
IVAN REIS, OCLAIR ALBERT and **MARCELO MAIOLO**
SEBASTIÁN FIUMARA and **DAVE STEWART**
original series covers

SUPERMAN created by **JERRY SIEGEL** and **JOE SHUSTER**
By special arrangement with the Jerry Siegel family

EDDIE BERGANZA Editor – Original Series ✳ **ANDREW MARINO** Assistant Editor – Original Series
JEB WOODARD Group Editor – Collected Editions ✳ **SCOTT NYBAKKEN** Editor – Collected Edition
STEVE COOK Design Director – Books ✳ **MONIQUE GRUSPE** Publication Design

BOB HARRAS Senior VP – Editor-in-Chief, DC Comics

DIANE NELSON President ✳ **DAN DiDIO** Publisher ✳ **JIM LEE** Publisher ✳ **GEOFF JOHNS** President & Chief Creative Officer
AMIT DESAI Executive VP – Business & Marketing Strategy, Direct to Consumer & Global Franchise Management ✳ **SAM ADES** Senior VP – Direct to Consumer
BOBBIE CHASE VP – Talent Development ✳ **MARK CHIARELLO** Senior VP – Art, Design & Collected Editions
JOHN CUNNINGHAM Senior VP – Sales & Trade Marketing ✳ **ANNE DePIES** Senior VP – Business Strategy, Finance & Administration
DON FALLETTI VP – Manufacturing Operations ✳ **LAWRENCE GANEM** VP – Editorial Administration & Talent Relations
ALISON GILL Senior VP – Manufacturing & Operations ✳ **HANK KANALZ** Senior VP – Editorial Strategy & Administration
JAY KOGAN VP – Legal Affairs ✳ **THOMAS LOFTUS** VP – Business Affairs
JACK MAHAN VP – Business Affairs ✳ **NICK J. NAPOLITANO** VP – Manufacturing Administration
EDDIE SCANNELL VP – Consumer Marketing ✳ **COURTNEY SIMMONS** Senior VP – Publicity & Communications
JIM (SKI) SOKOLOWSKI VP – Comic Book Specialty Sales & Trade Marketing ✳ **NANCY SPEARS** VP – Mass, Book, Digital Sales & Trade Marketing

SUPERMAN VOL. 3: MULTIPLICITY

Published by DC Comics. Compilation and all new material Copyright © 2017 DC Comics. All Rights Reserved.
Originally published in single magazine form in SUPERMAN ANNUAL 1 and SUPERMAN 14-17. Copyright © 2016, 2017 DC Comics.
All Rights Reserved. All characters, their distinctive likenesses and related elements featured in this publication are trademarks of DC Comics.
The stories, characters and incidents featured in this publication are entirely fictional.
DC Comics does not read or accept unsolicited ideas, stories or artwork.

DC Comics, 2900 West Alameda Ave., Burbank, CA 91505.
Printed by LSC Communications, Owensville, MO, USA. 6/30/17.
First Printing. ISBN: 978-1-4012-7154-1

Library of Congress Cataloging-in-Publication Data is available.

PEFC Certified

Printed on paper from
sustainably managed
forests, controlled
sources

PEFC/29-31-337   www.pefc.org

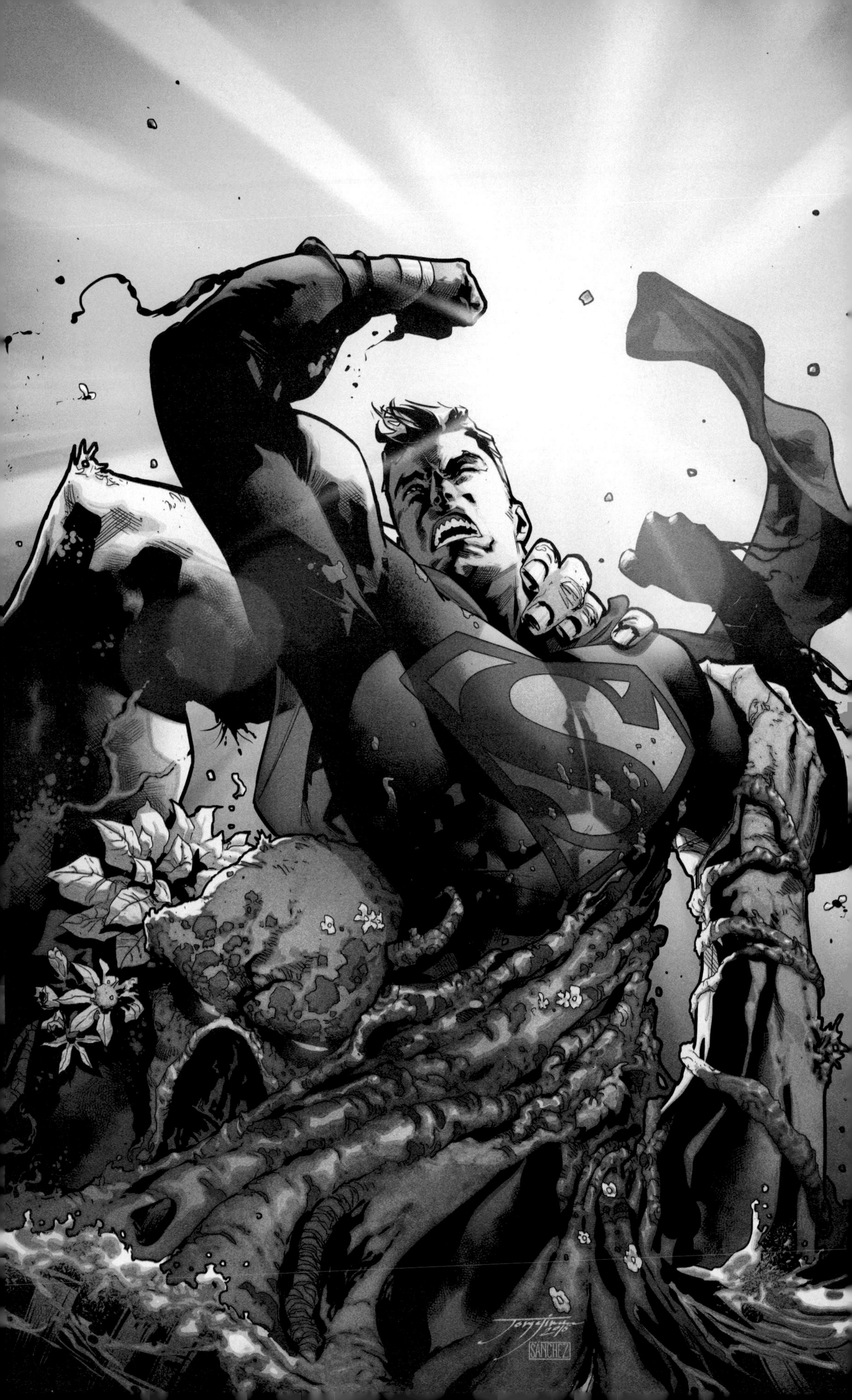
SANCHEZ

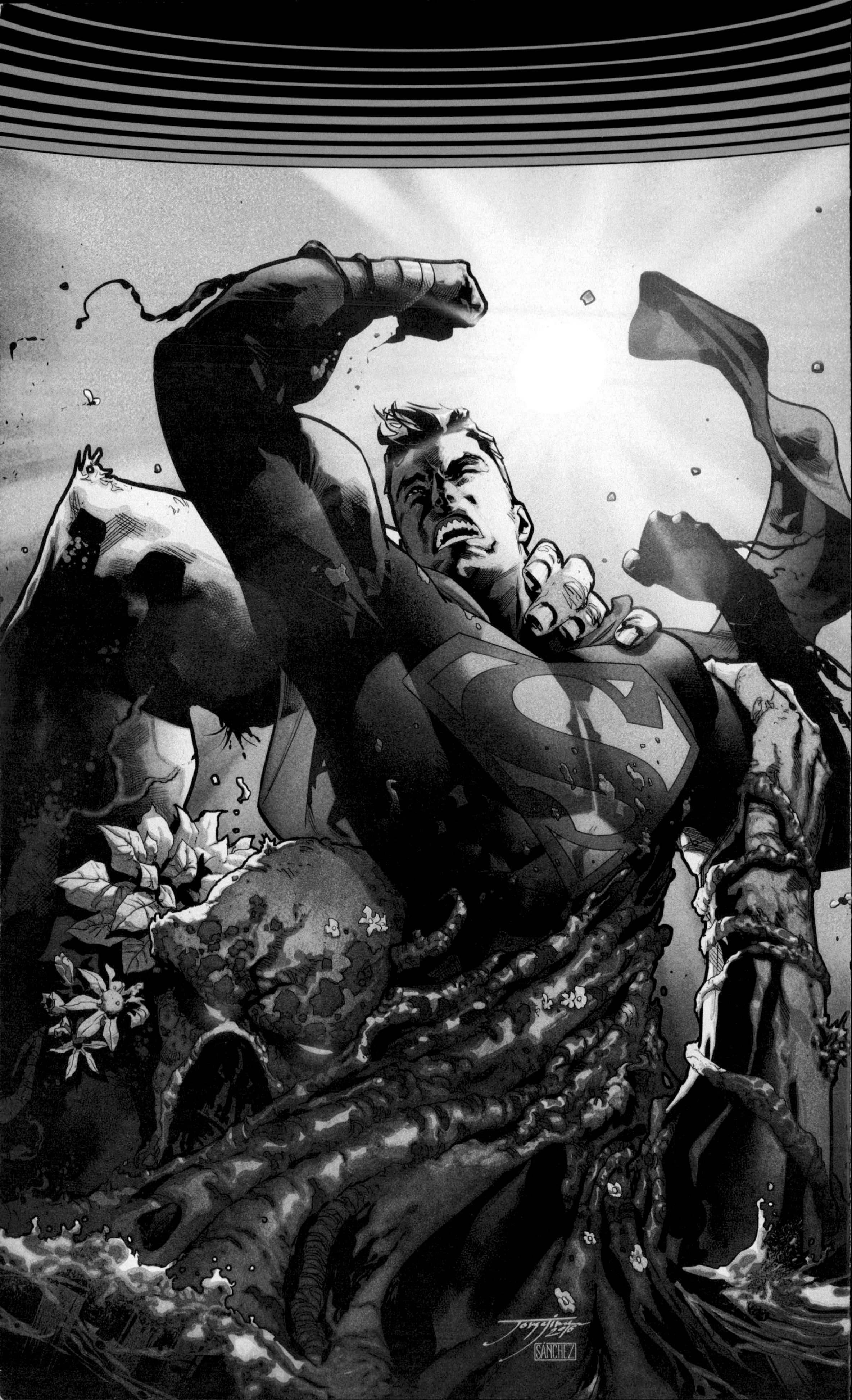
SÁNCHEZ

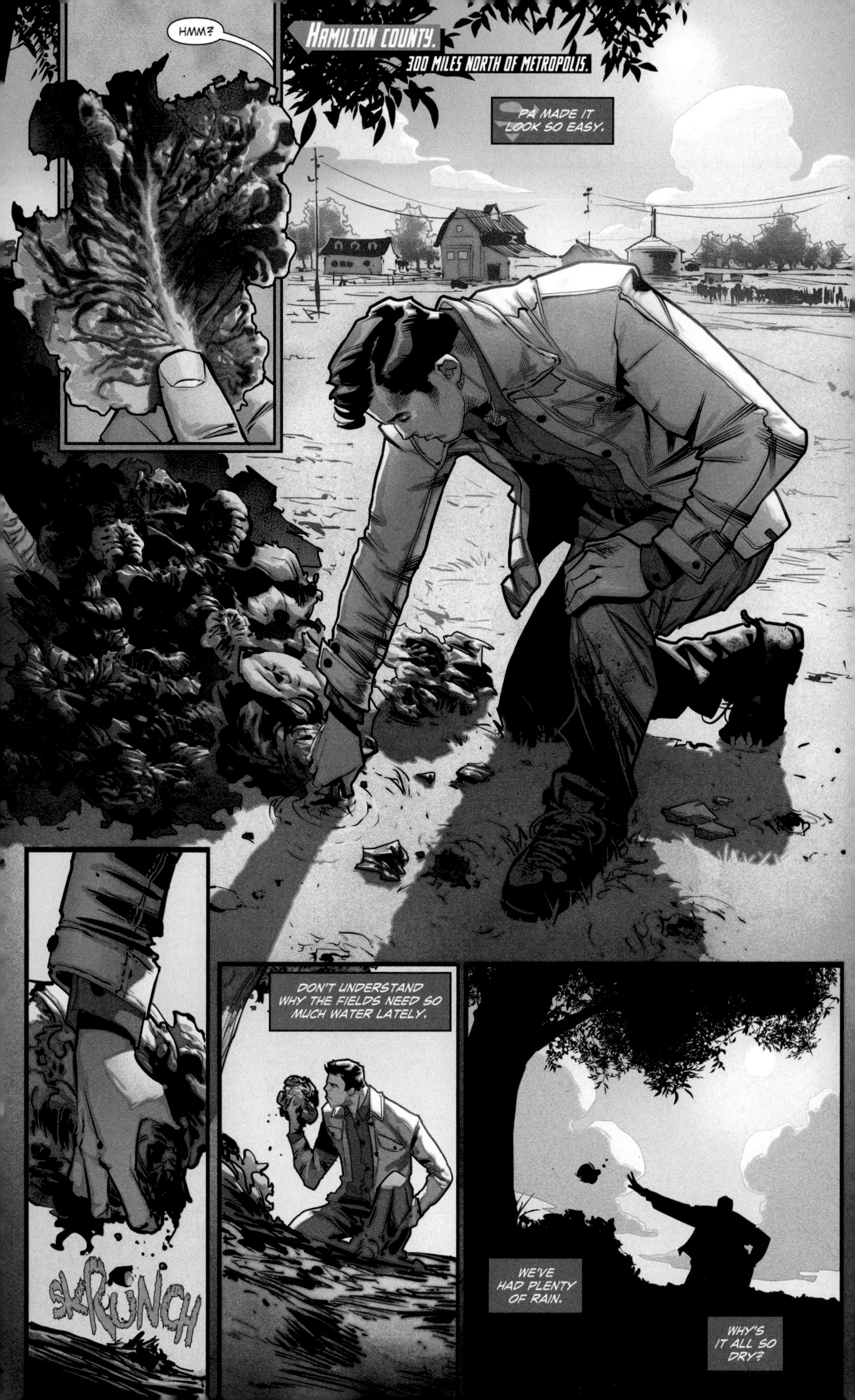
HMM?
HAMILTON COUNTY.
300 MILES NORTH OF METROPOLIS.
PA MADE IT LOOK SO EASY.
SKRUNCH
DON'T UNDERSTAND WHY THE FIELDS NEED SO MUCH WATER LATELY.
WE'VE HAD PLENTY OF RAIN.
WHY'S IT ALL SO DRY?

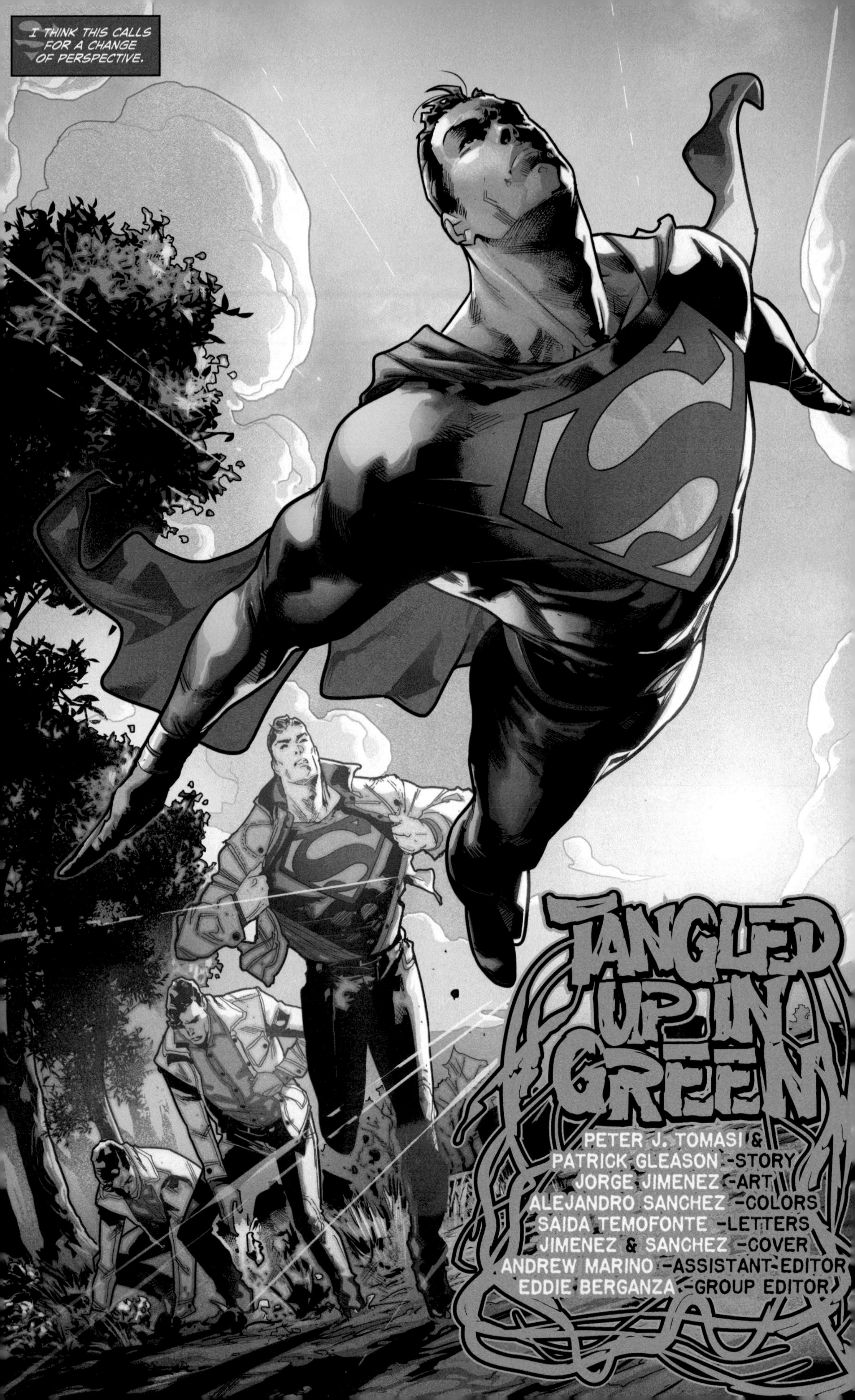
I THINK THIS CALLS FOR A CHANGE OF PERSPECTIVE.
TANGLED UP IN GREEN
PETER J. TOMASI & PATRICK GLEASON -STORY
JORGE JIMENEZ -ART
ALEJANDRO SANCHEZ -COLORS
SAIDA TEMOFONTE -LETTERS
JIMENEZ & SANCHEZ -COVER
ANDREW MARINO -ASSISTANT EDITOR
EDDIE BERGANZA -GROUP EDITOR

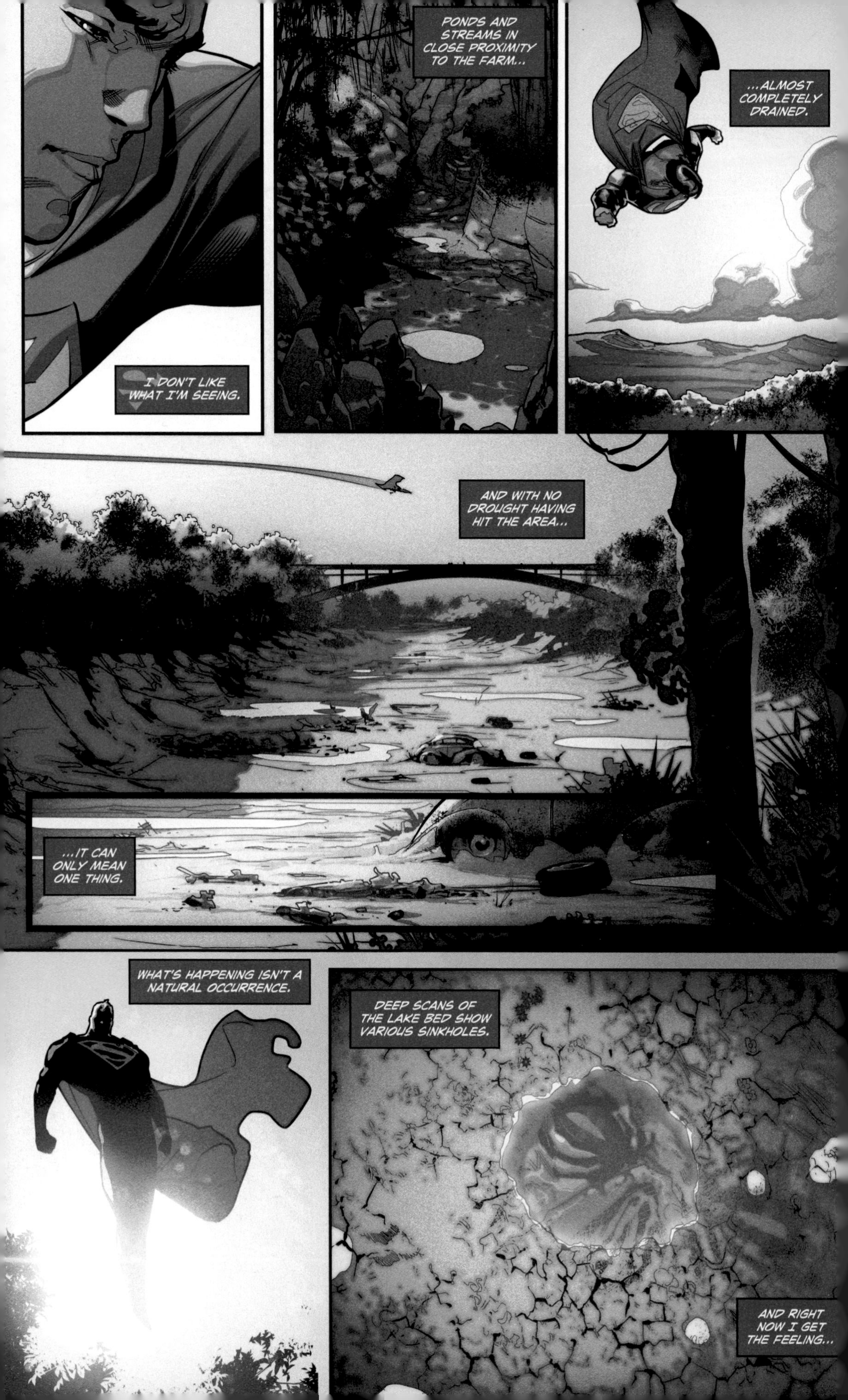
I DON'T LIKE WHAT I'M SEEING.
PONDS AND STREAMS IN CLOSE PROXIMITY TO THE FARM...
...ALMOST COMPLETELY DRAINED.
AND WITH NO DROUGHT HAVING HIT THE AREA...
...IT CAN ONLY MEAN ONE THING.
WHAT'S HAPPENING ISN'T A NATURAL OCCURRENCE.
DEEP SCANS OF THE LAKE BED SHOW VARIOUS SINKHOLES.
AND RIGHT NOW I GET THE FEELING...

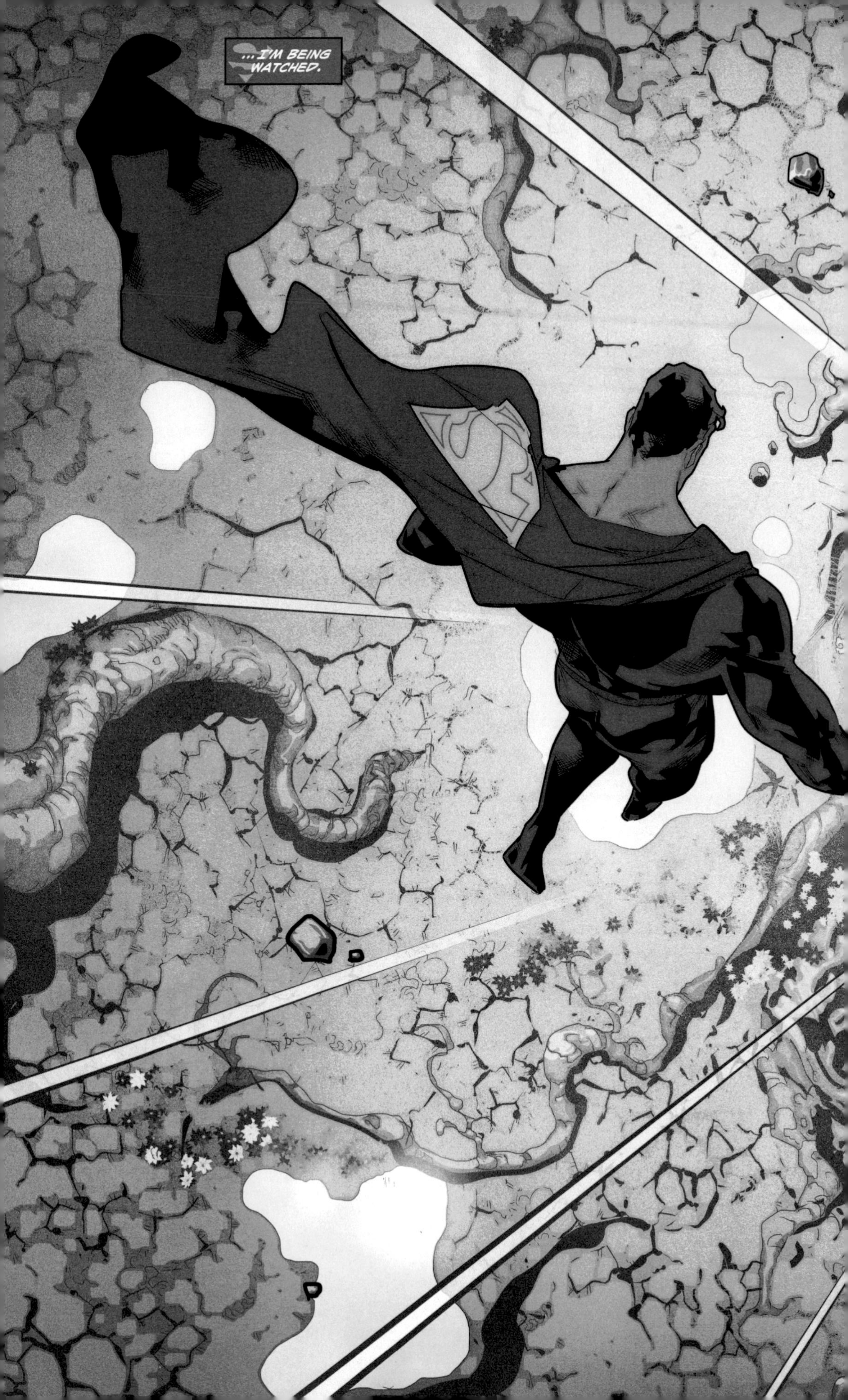
...I'M BEING WATCHED.

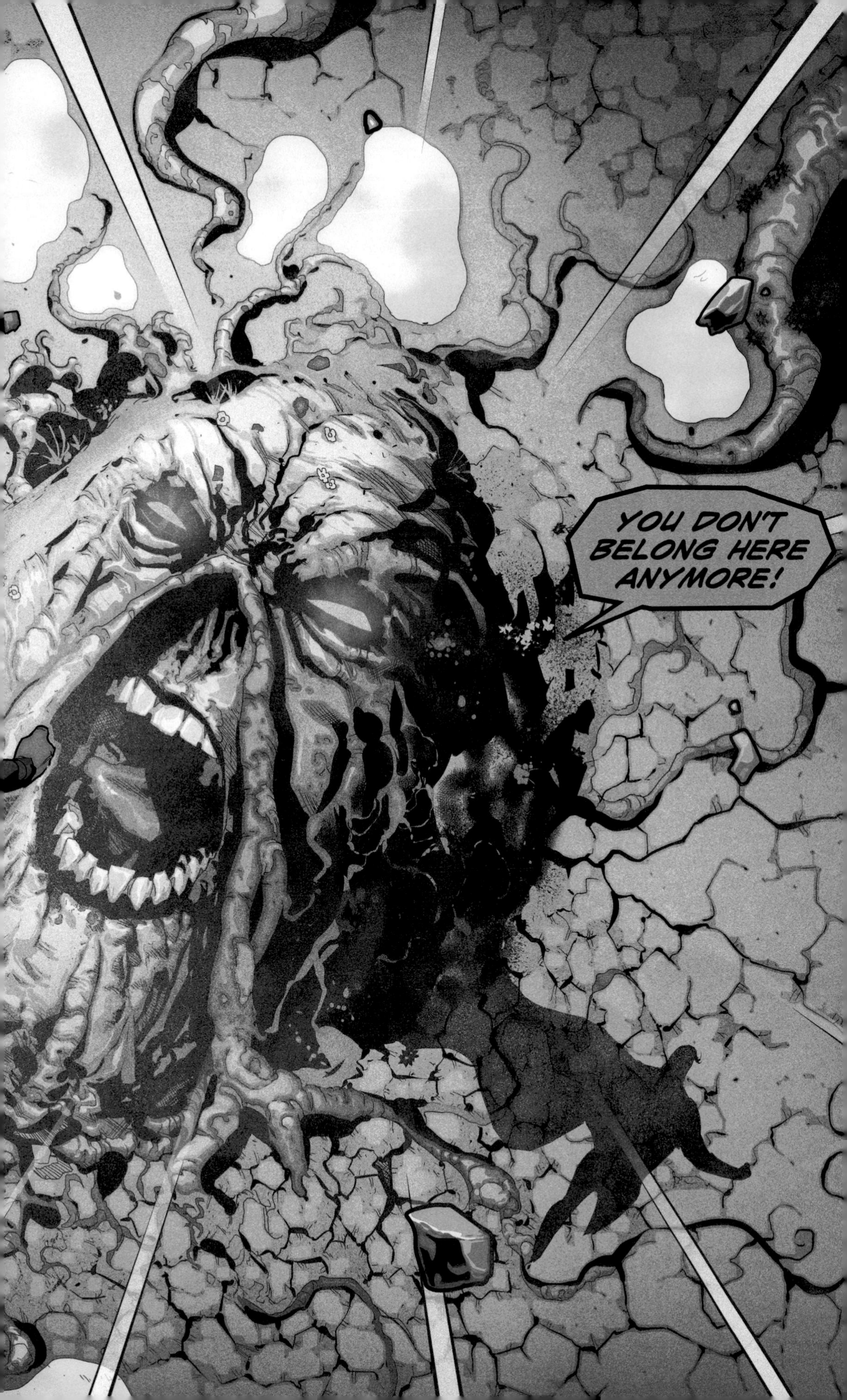
YOU DON'T BELONG HERE ANYMORE!

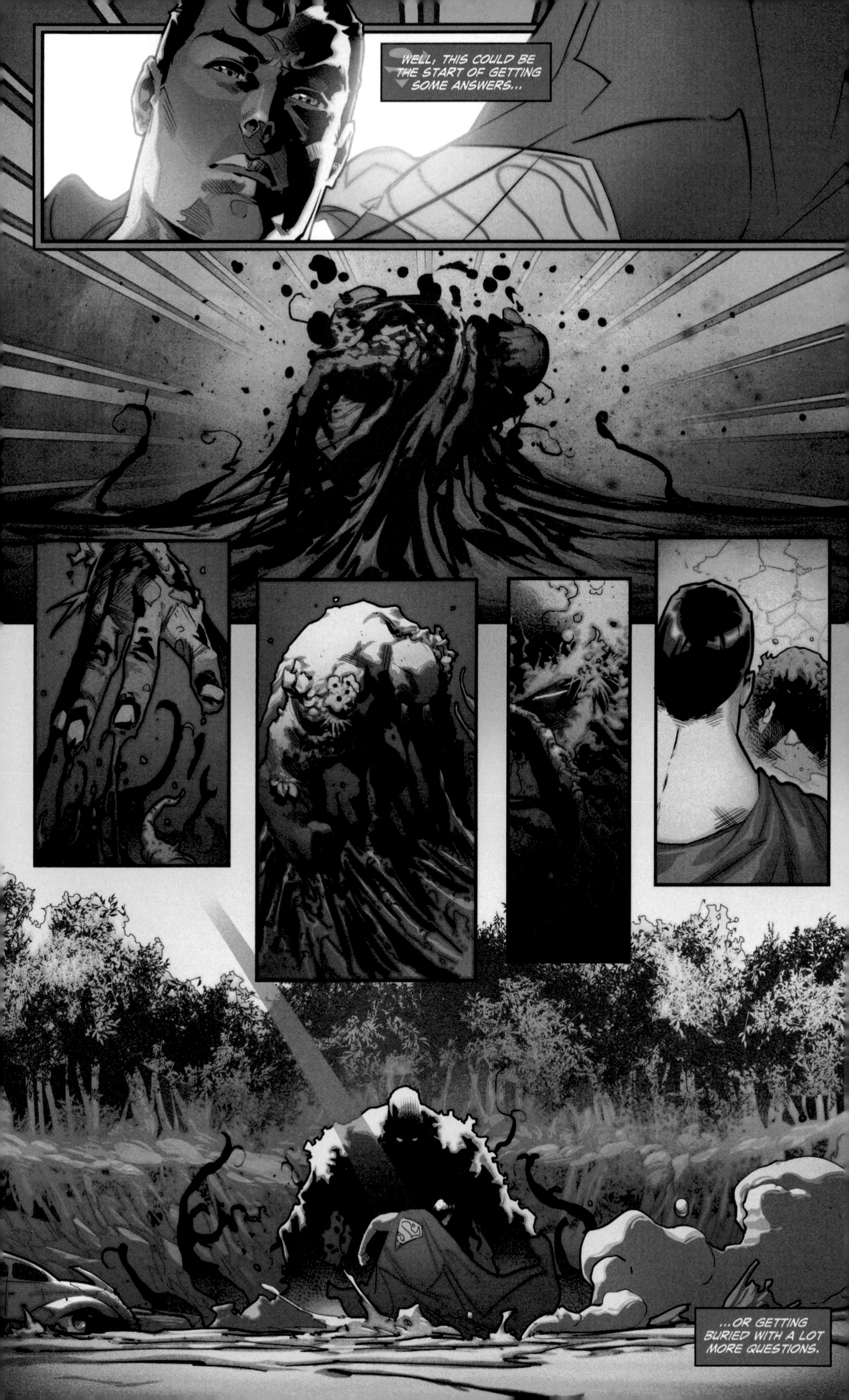
WELL, THIS COULD BE THE START OF GETTING SOME ANSWERS...
...OR GETTING BURIED WITH A LOT MORE QUESTIONS.

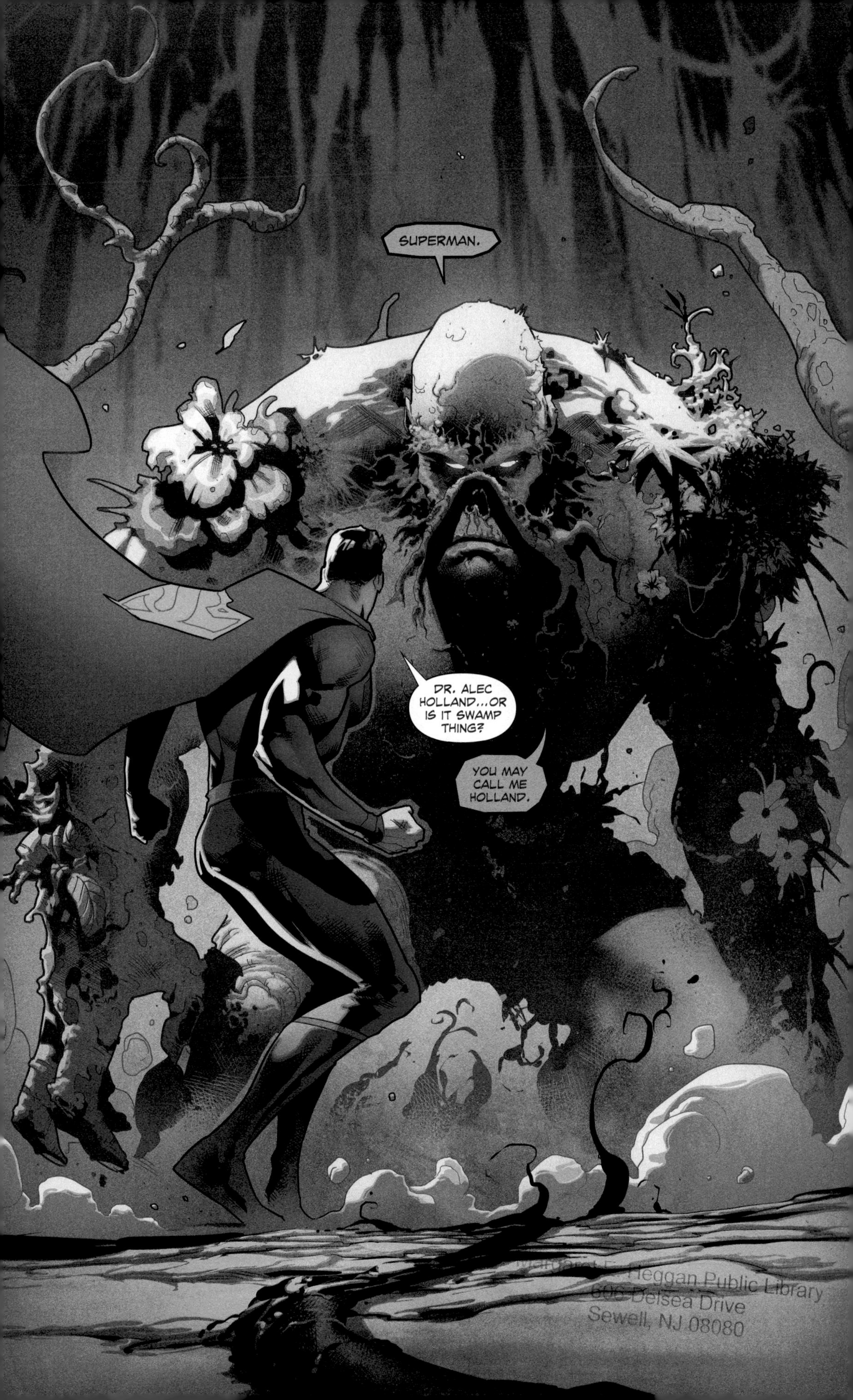
SUPERMAN.
DR. ALEC HOLLAND...OR IS IT SWAMP THING?
YOU MAY CALL ME HOLLAND.

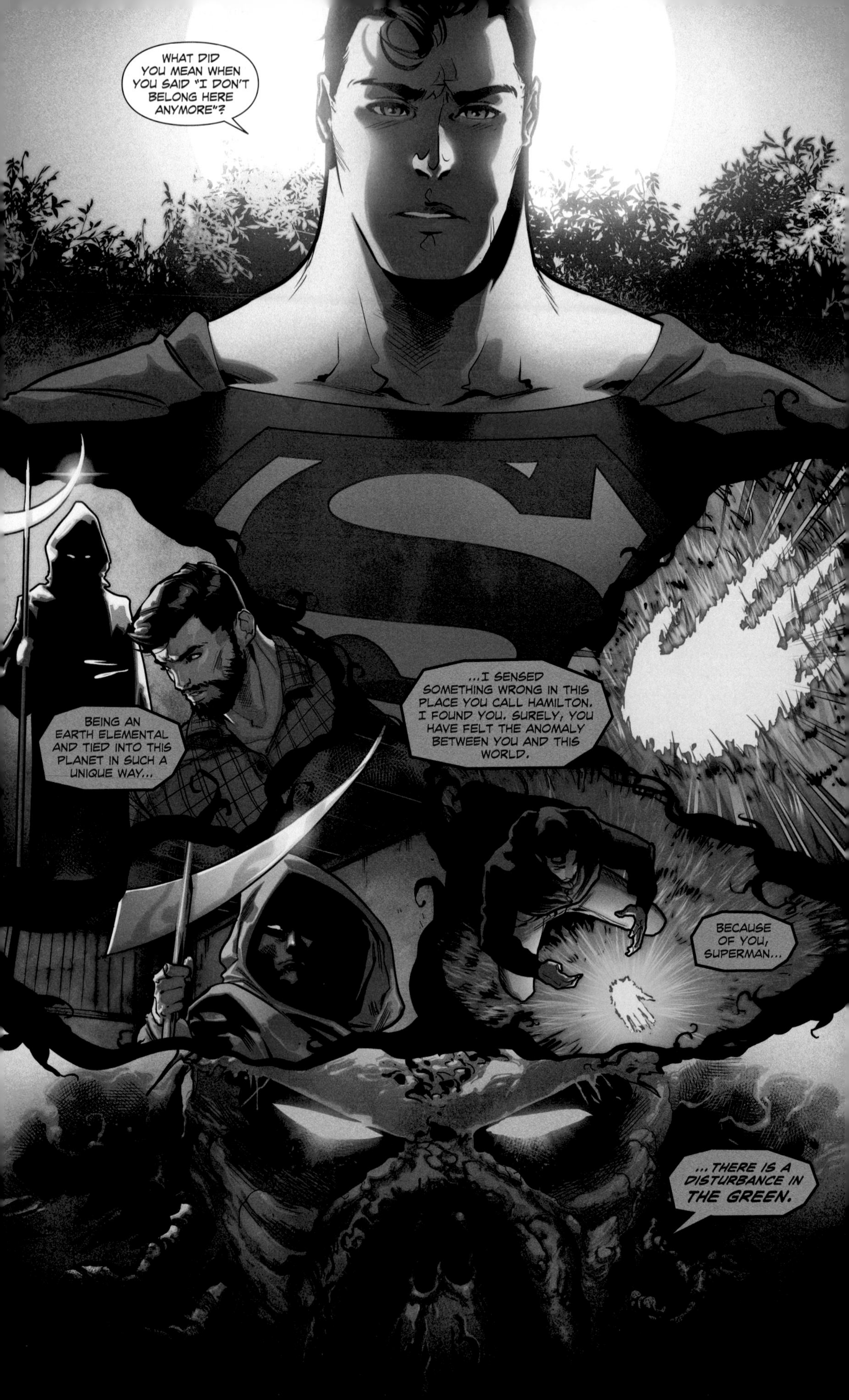

WHAT DID YOU MEAN WHEN YOU SAID "I DON'T BELONG HERE ANYMORE"?
BEING AN EARTH ELEMENTAL AND TIED INTO THIS PLANET IN SUCH A UNIQUE WAY...
...I SENSED SOMETHING WRONG IN THIS PLACE YOU CALL HAMILTON. I FOUND YOU. SURELY, YOU HAVE FELT THE ANOMALY BETWEEN YOU AND THIS WORLD.
BECAUSE OF YOU, SUPERMAN...
...THERE IS A DISTURBANCE IN THE GREEN.

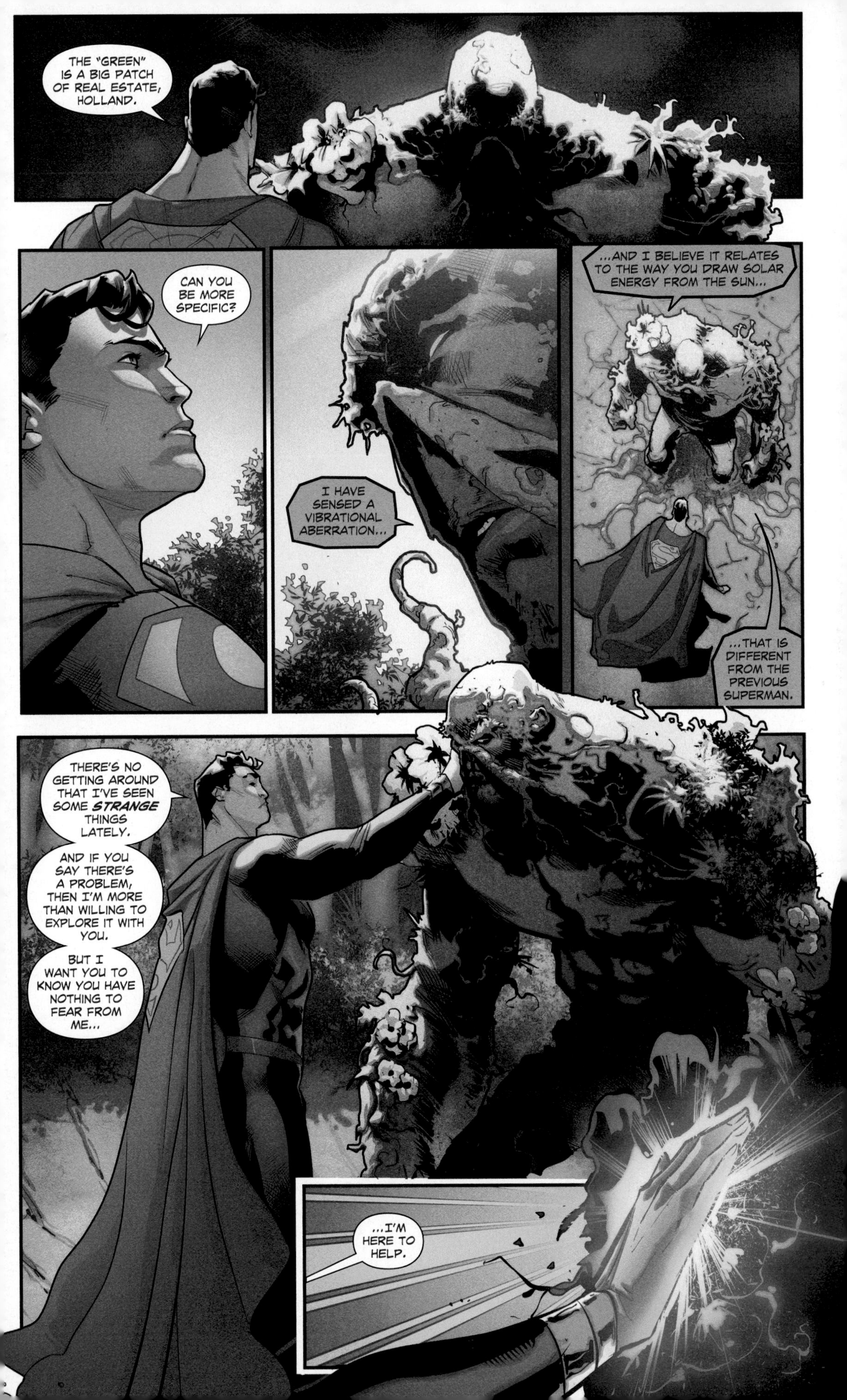
THE "GREEN" IS A BIG PATCH OF REAL ESTATE, HOLLAND.
CAN YOU BE MORE SPECIFIC?
I HAVE SENSED A VIBRATIONAL ABERRATION...
...AND I BELIEVE IT RELATES TO THE WAY YOU DRAW SOLAR ENERGY FROM THE SUN...
...THAT IS DIFFERENT FROM THE PREVIOUS SUPERMAN.
THERE'S NO GETTING AROUND THAT I'VE SEEN SOME STRANGE THINGS LATELY.
AND IF YOU SAY THERE'S A PROBLEM, THEN I'M MORE THAN WILLING TO EXPLORE IT WITH YOU.
BUT I WANT YOU TO KNOW YOU HAVE NOTHING TO FEAR FROM ME...
...I'M HERE TO HELP.

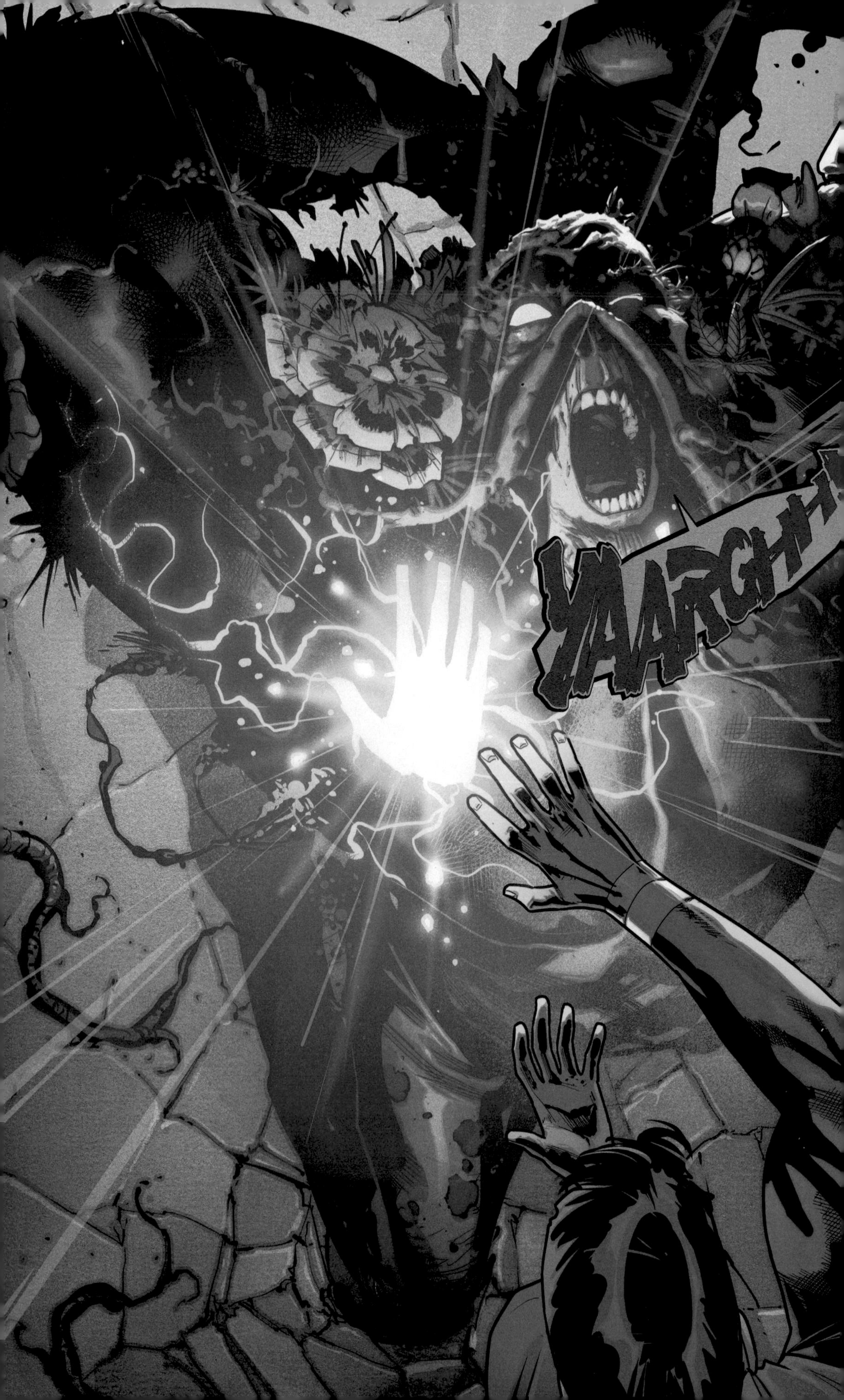
YAARGHH

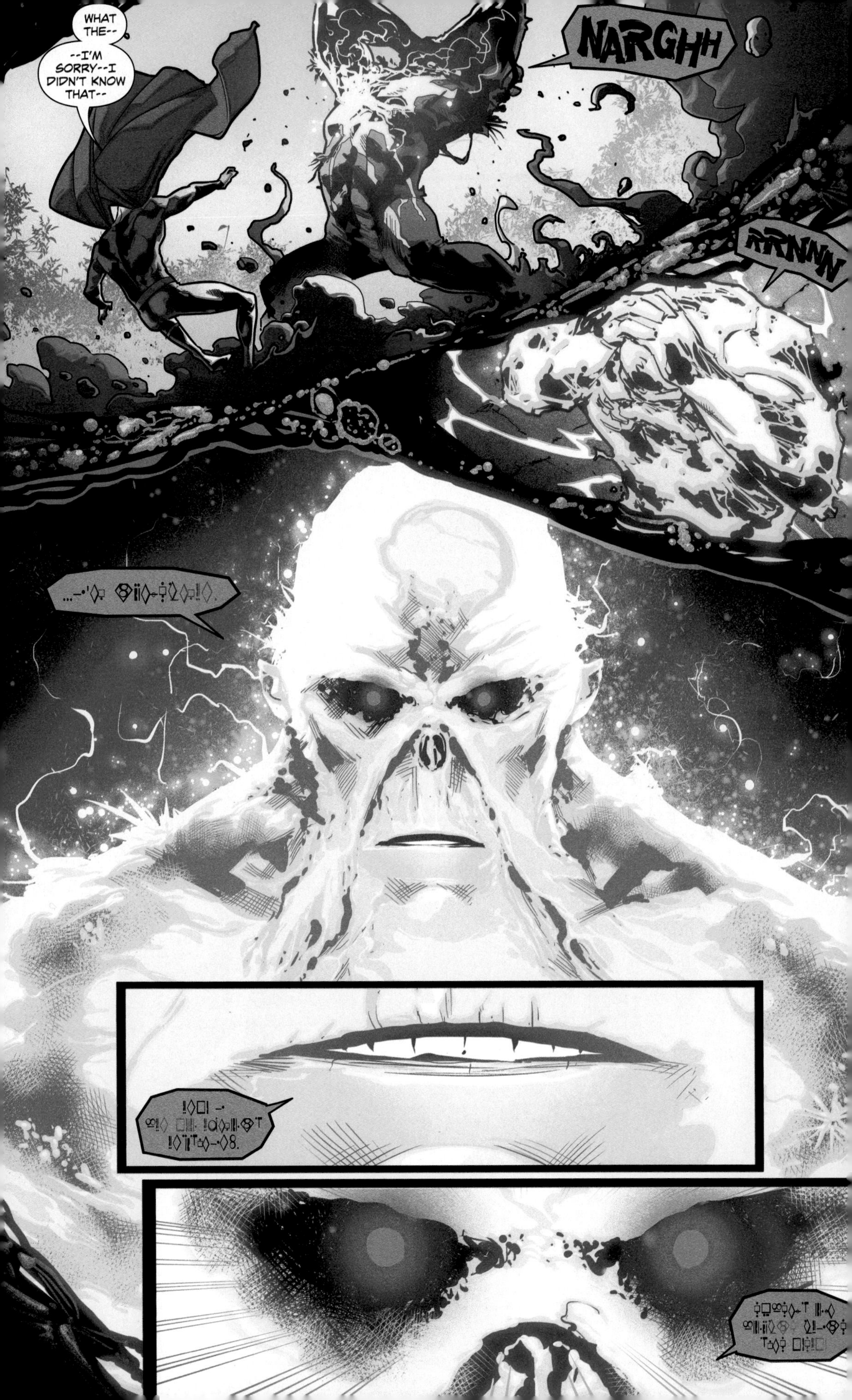
WHAT THE--
--I'M SORRY--I DIDN'T KNOW THAT--
NARGHH
RRNNN

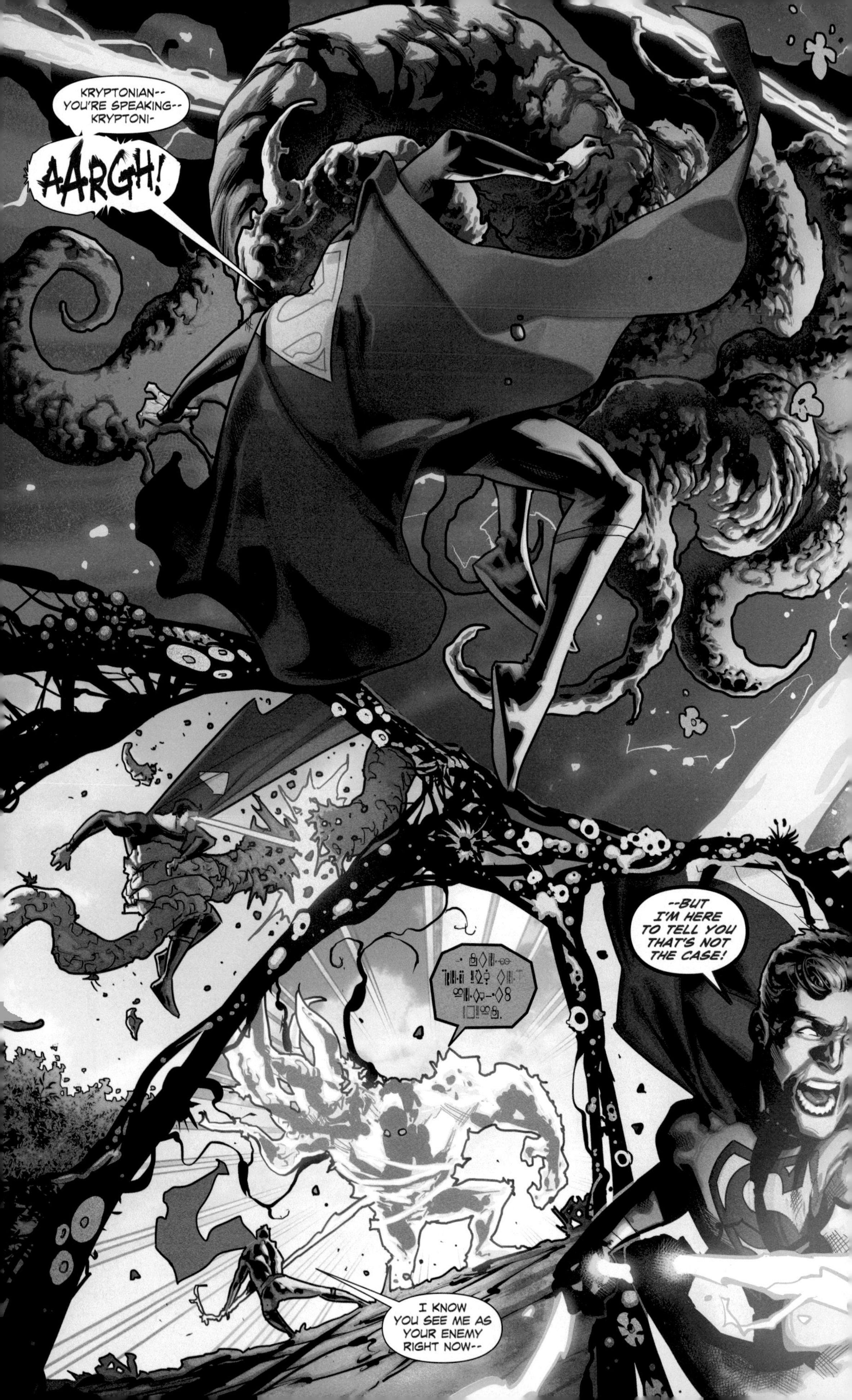
KRYPTONIAN-- YOU'RE SPEAKING-- KRYPTONI-
AARGH!
I KNOW YOU SEE ME AS YOUR ENEMY RIGHT NOW--
--BUT I'M HERE TO TELL YOU THAT'S NOT THE CASE!

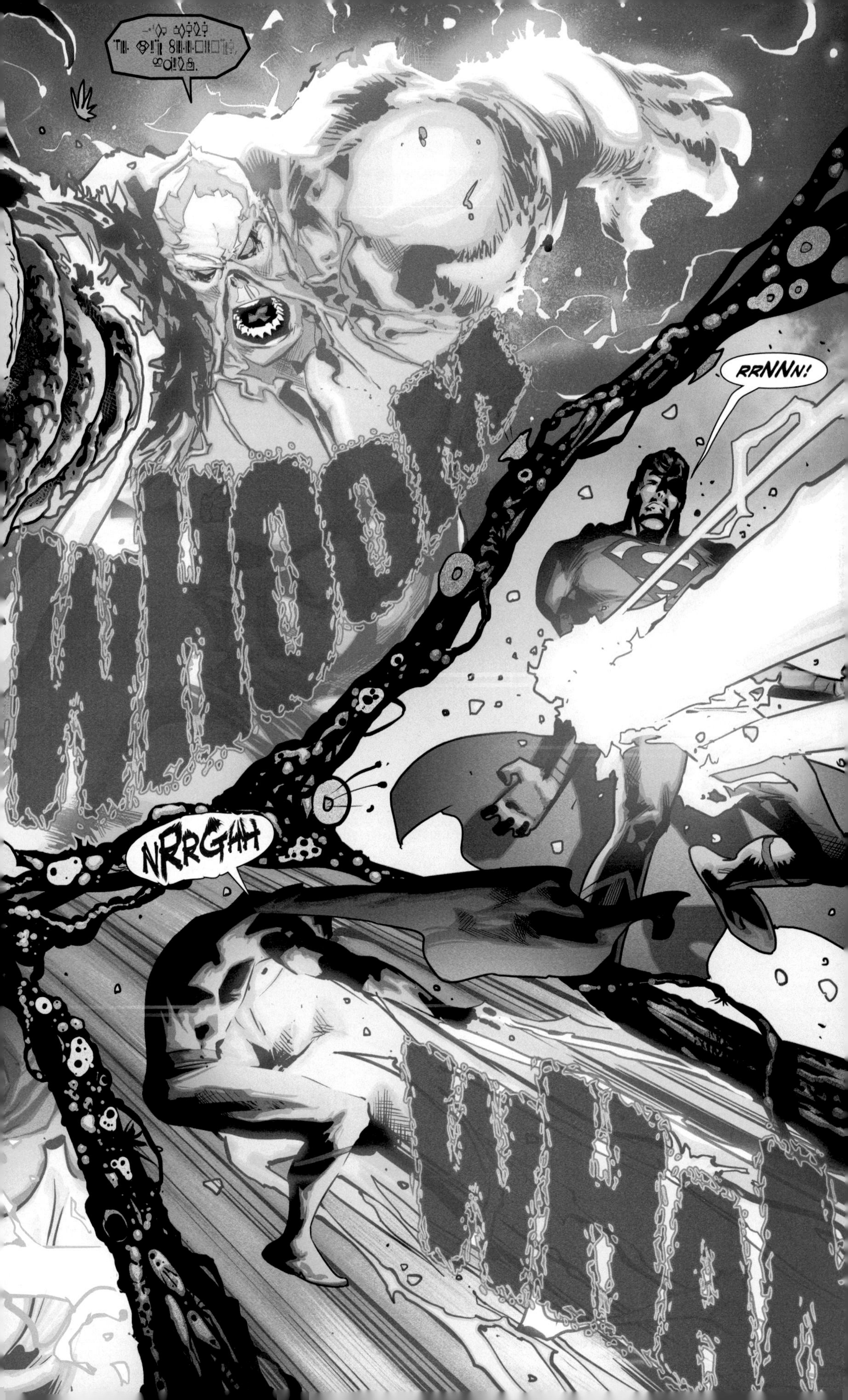
RRNNN!
NRRGAH

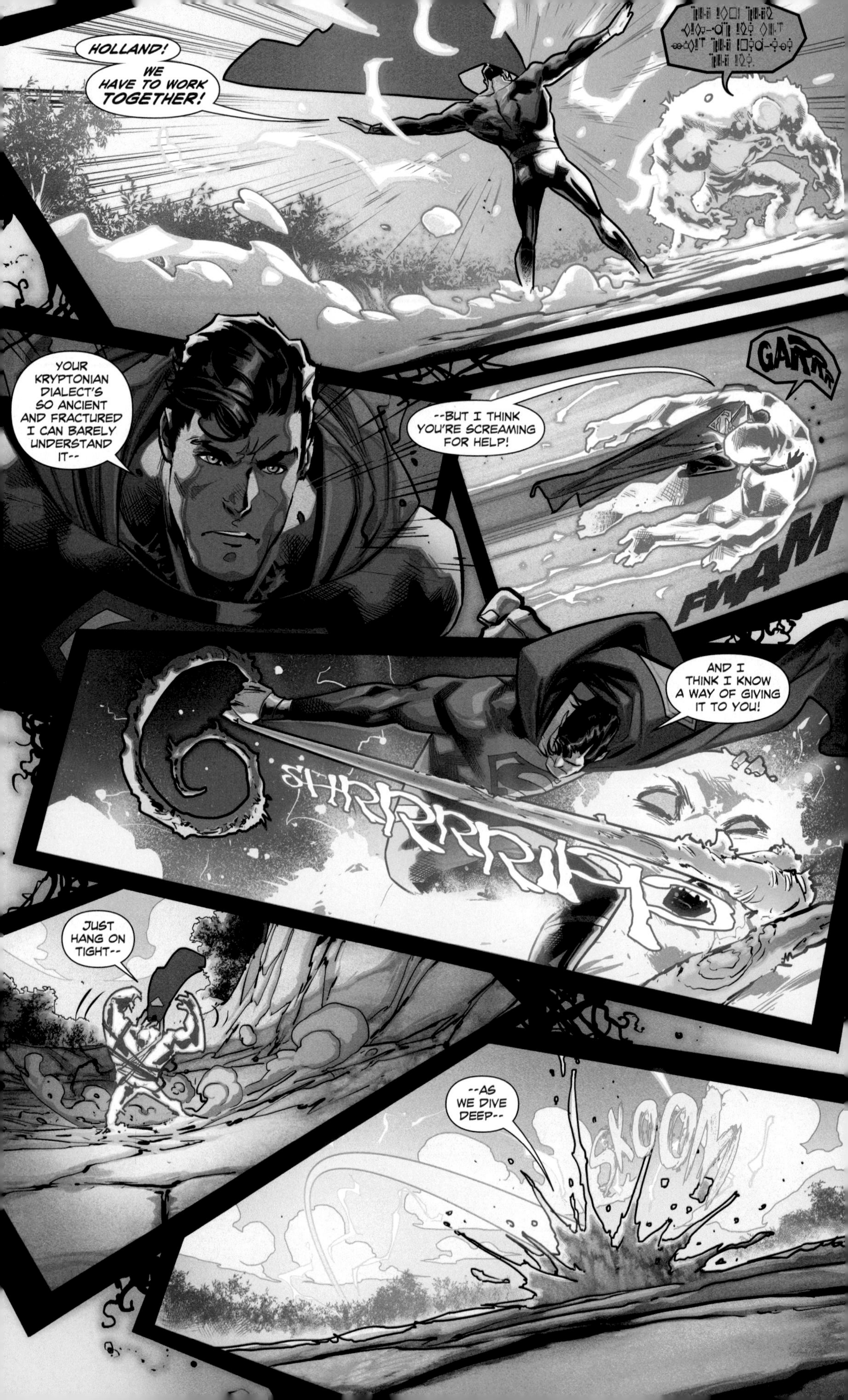
HOLLAND! WE HAVE TO WORK TOGETHER!
YOUR KRYPTONIAN DIALECT'S SO ANCIENT AND FRACTURED I CAN BARELY UNDERSTAND IT--
--BUT I THINK YOU'RE SCREAMING FOR HELP!
GARRRR
FWAM
AND I THINK I KNOW A WAY OF GIVING IT TO YOU!
SHRRRRRIPP
JUST HANG ON TIGHT--
--AS WE DIVE DEEP--
SKOOOM

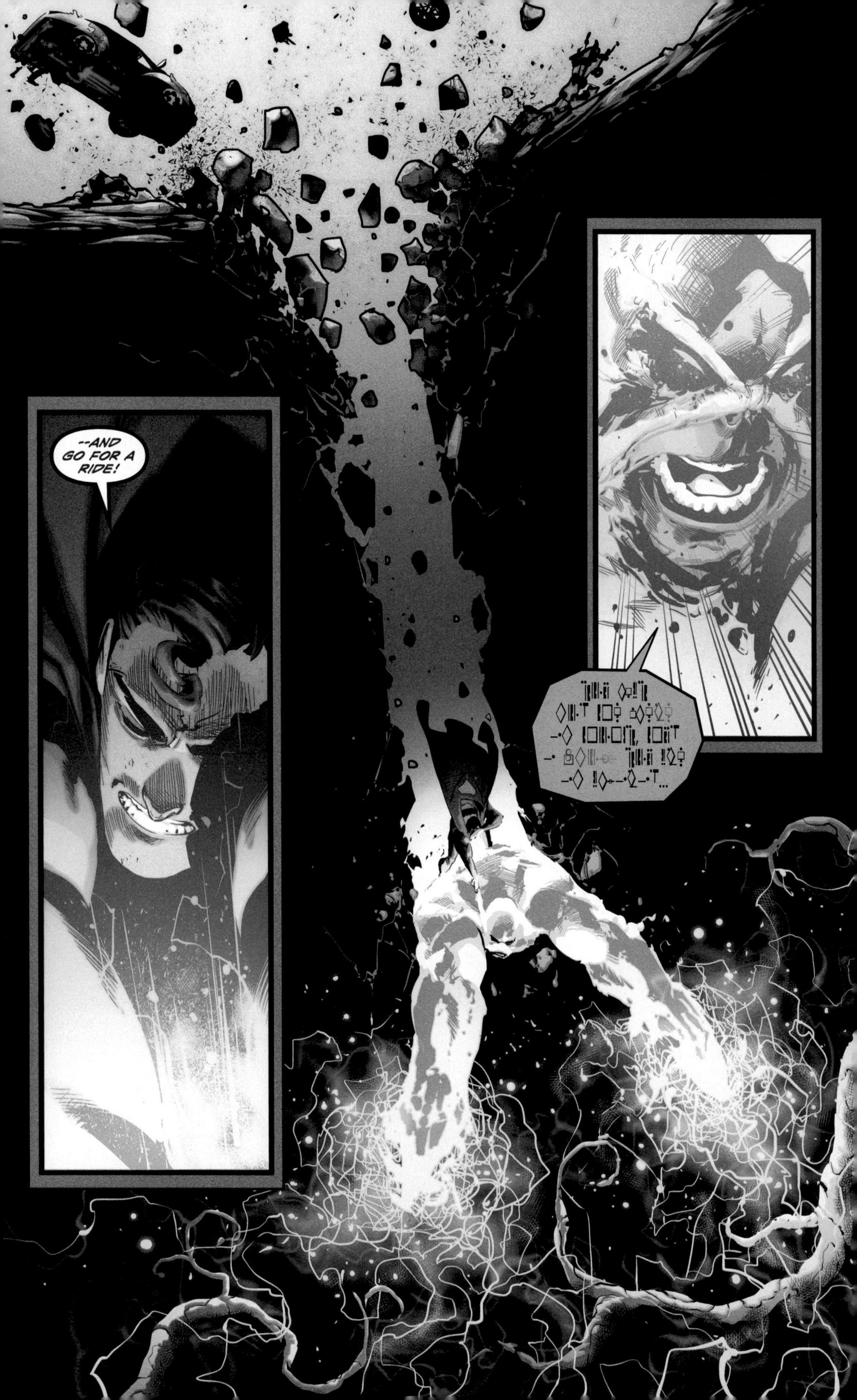
--AND GO FOR A RIDE!

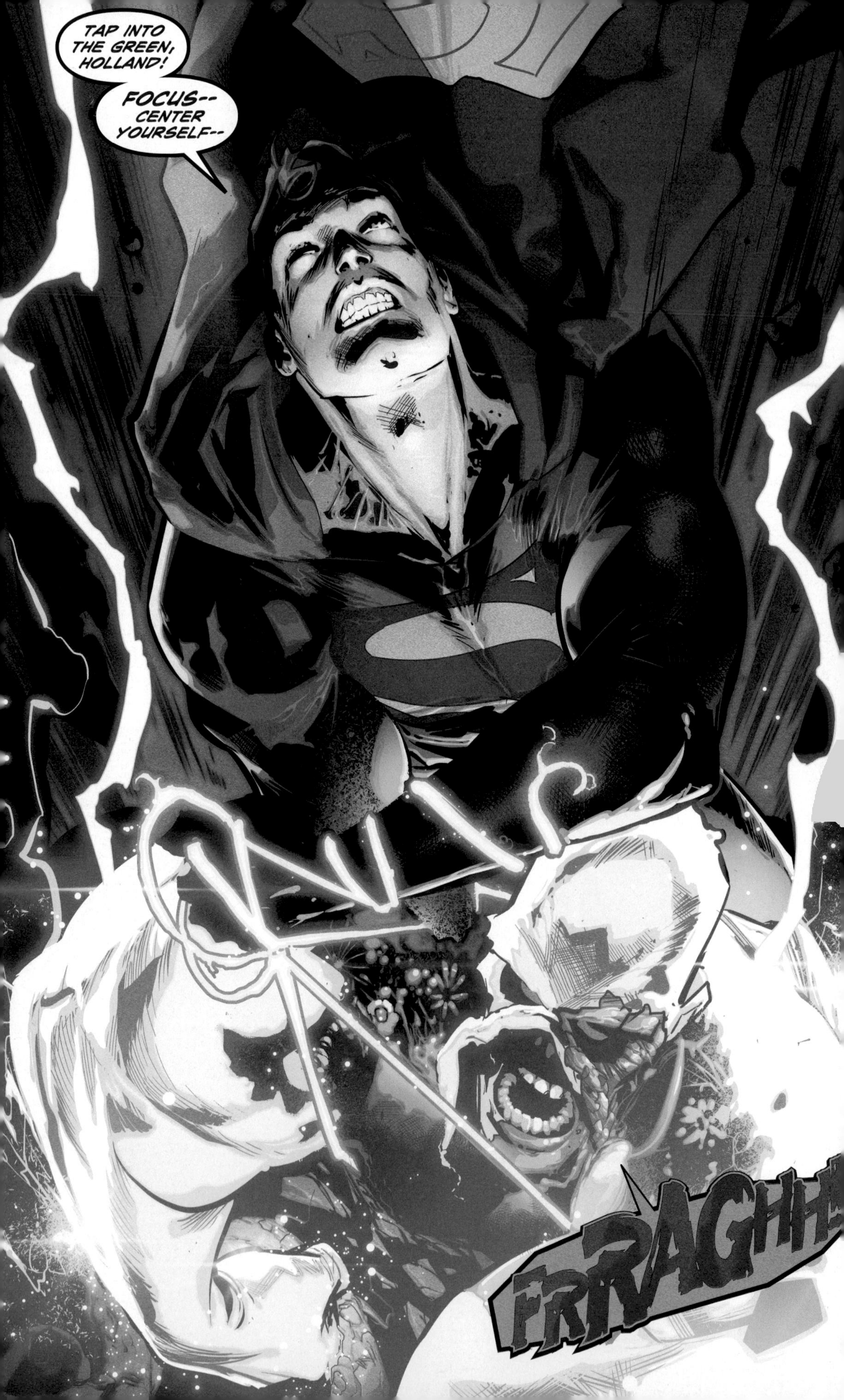
TAP INTO THE GREEN, HOLLAND!
FOCUS-- CENTER YOURSELF--
FRRAGHH

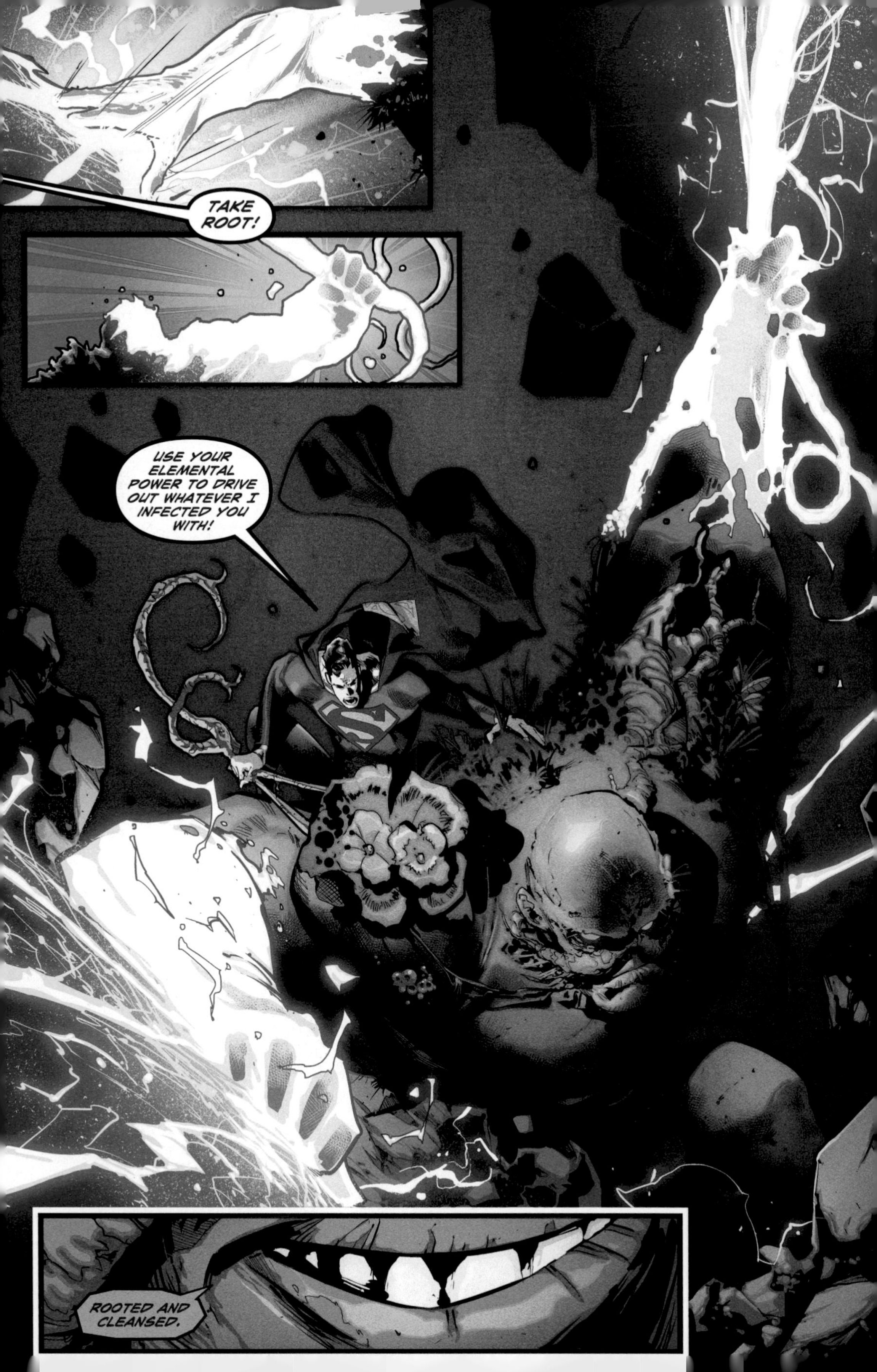
TAKE ROOT!
USE YOUR ELEMENTAL POWER TO DRIVE OUT WHATEVER I INFECTED YOU WITH!
ROOTED AND CLEANSED.

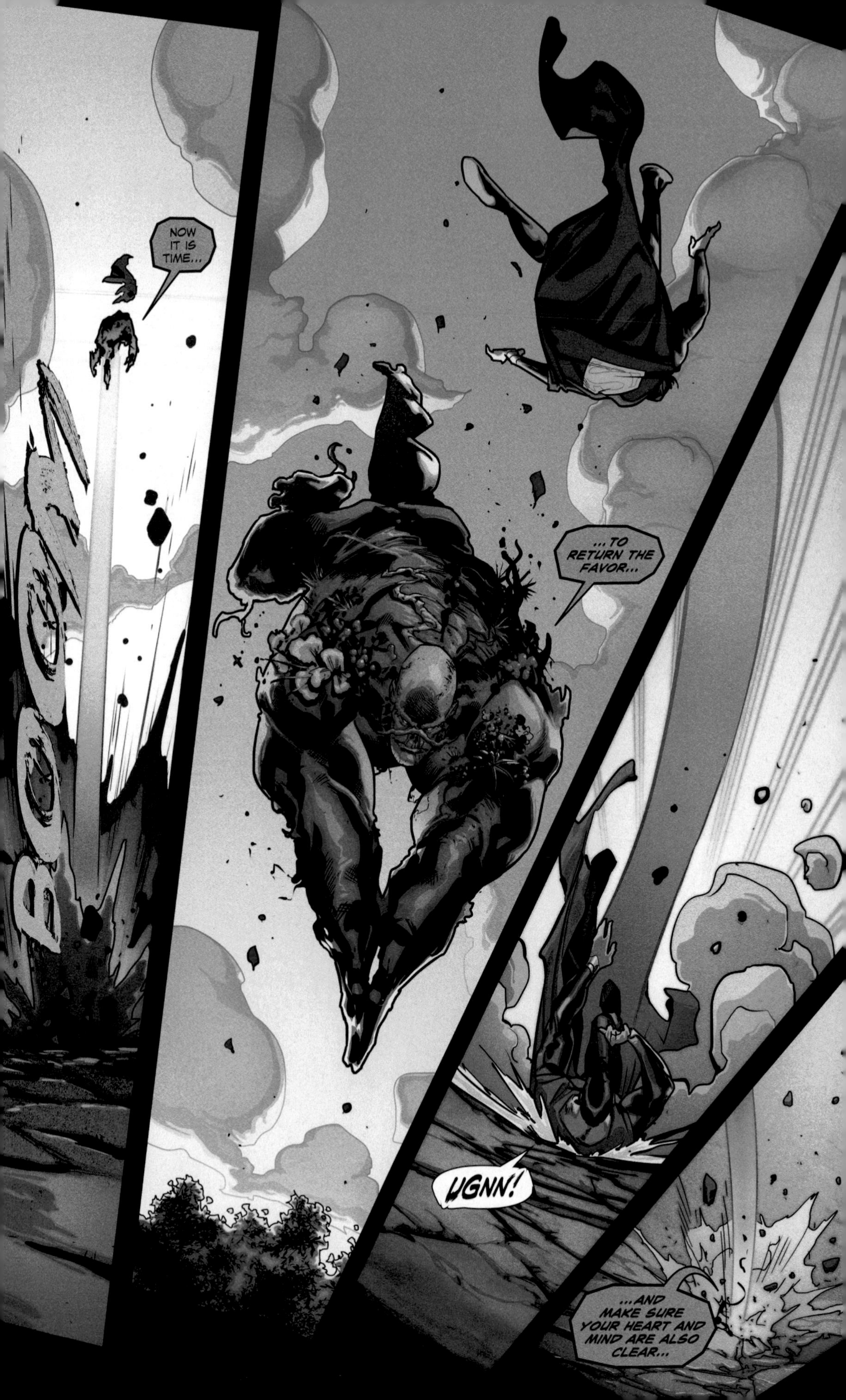
BOOM
NOW IT IS TIME...
...TO RETURN THE FAVOR...
UGNN!
...AND MAKE SURE YOUR HEART AND MIND ARE ALSO CLEAR...

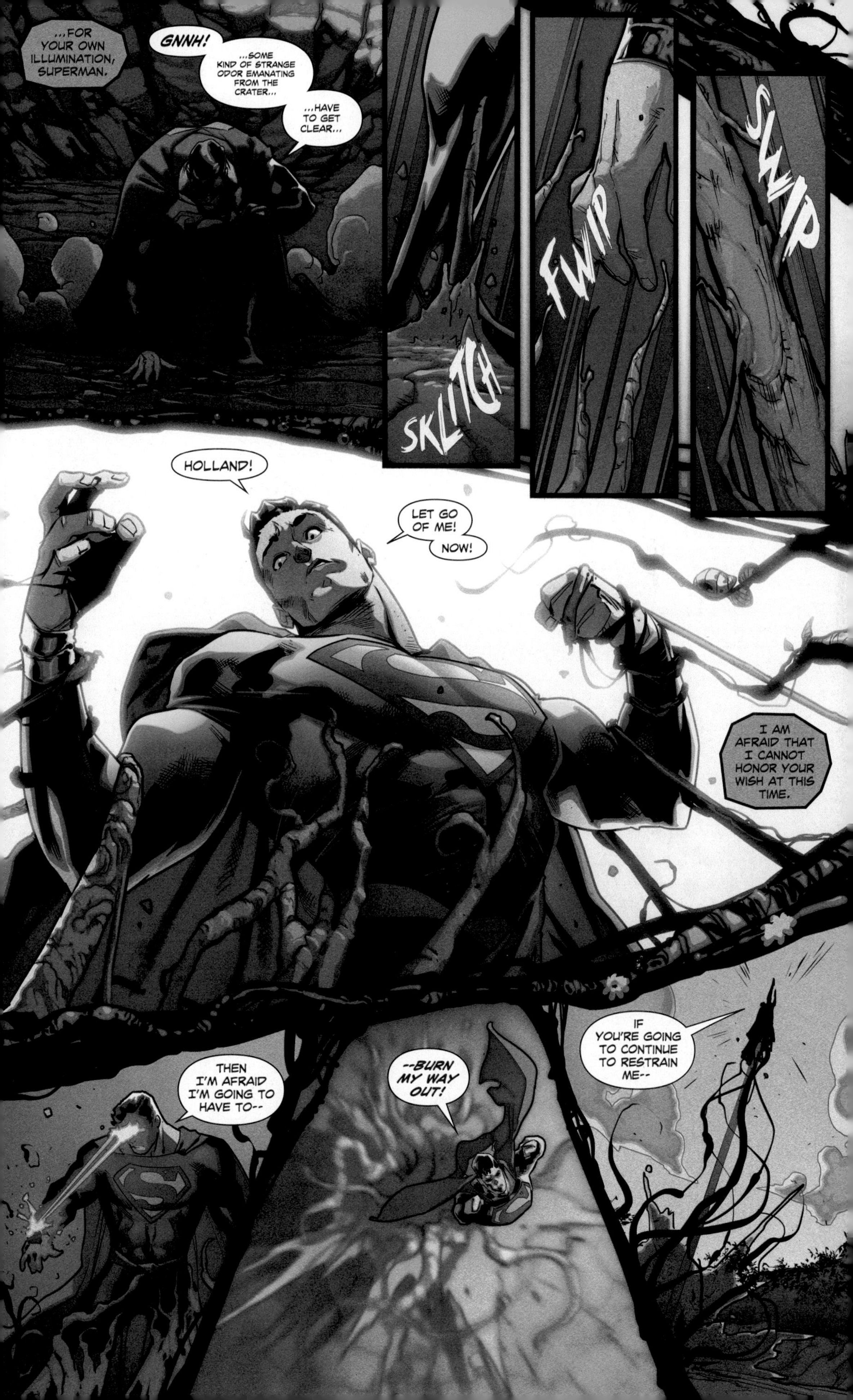
...FOR YOUR OWN ILLUMINATION, SUPERMAN.
GNNH!
...SOME KIND OF STRANGE ODOR EMANATING FROM THE CRATER...
...HAVE TO GET CLEAR...
SKLITCH
FWIP
SWIP
HOLLAND!
LET GO OF ME!
NOW!
I AM AFRAID THAT I CANNOT HONOR YOUR WISH AT THIS TIME.
IF YOU'RE GOING TO CONTINUE TO RESTRAIN ME--
THEN I'M AFRAID I'M GOING TO HAVE TO--
--BURN MY WAY OUT!

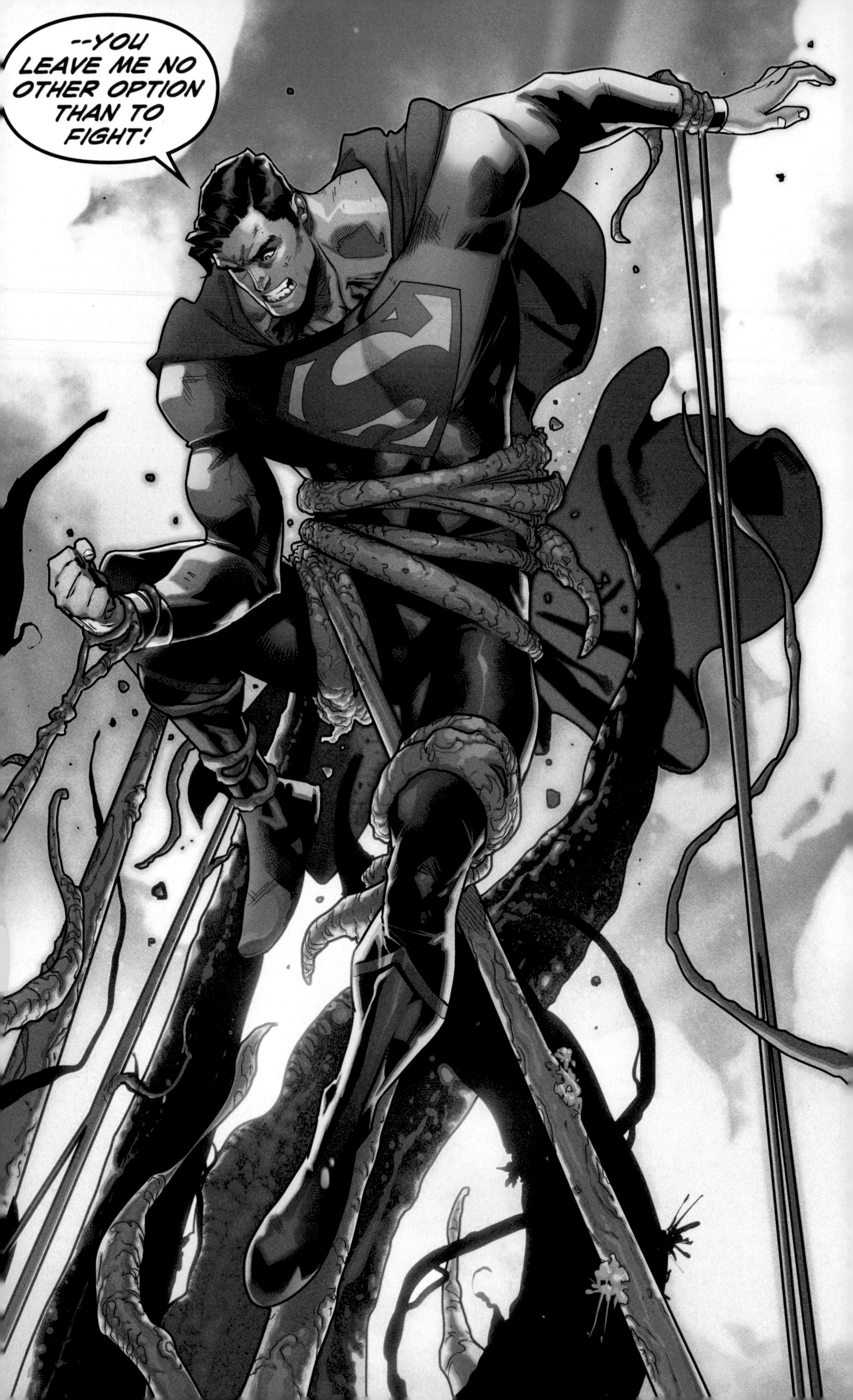
--YOU LEAVE ME NO OTHER OPTION THAN TO FIGHT!

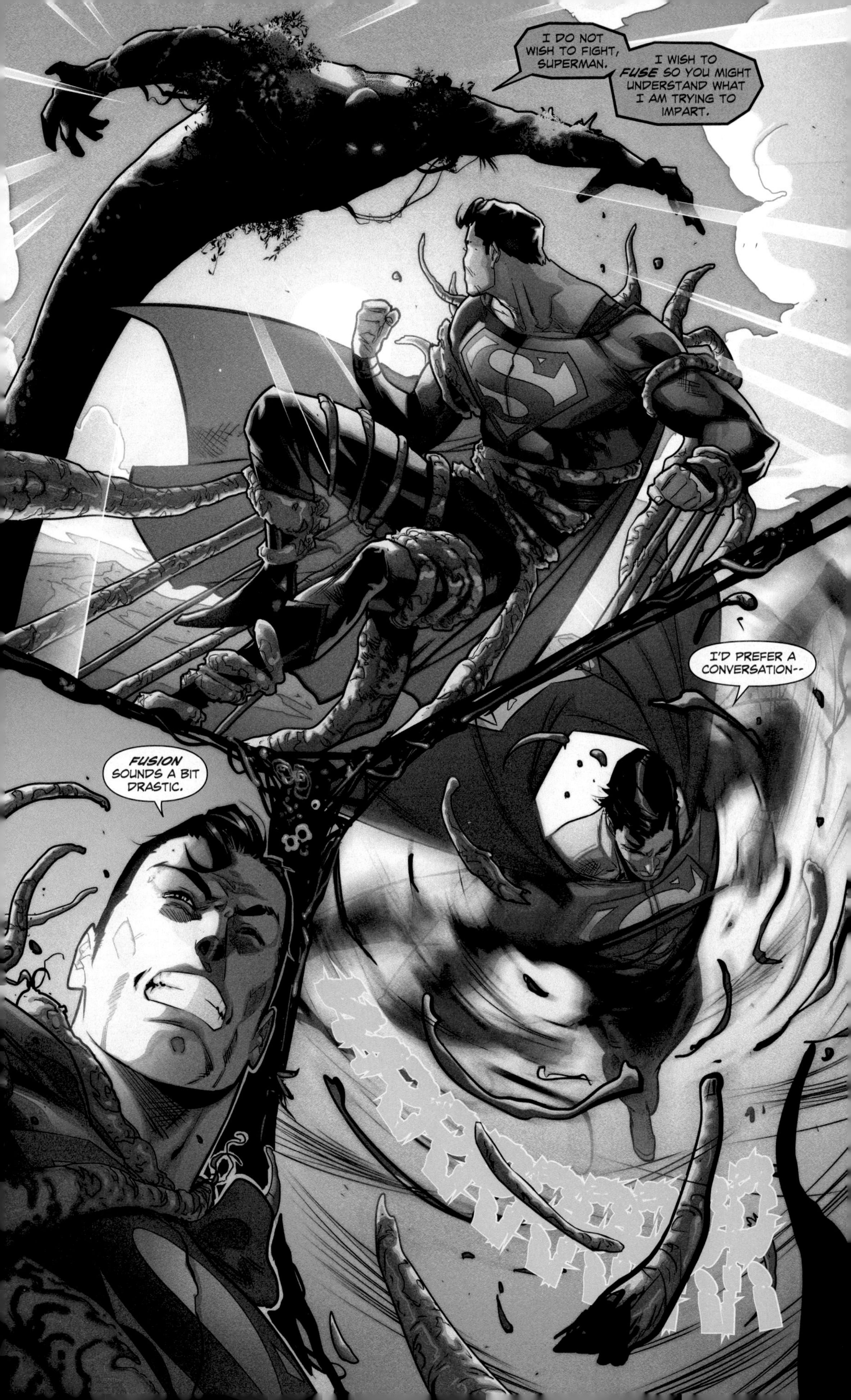
I DO NOT WISH TO FIGHT, SUPERMAN.
I WISH TO FUSE SO YOU MIGHT UNDERSTAND WHAT I AM TRYING TO IMPART.
I'D PREFER A CONVERSATION--
FUSION SOUNDS A BIT DRASTIC.

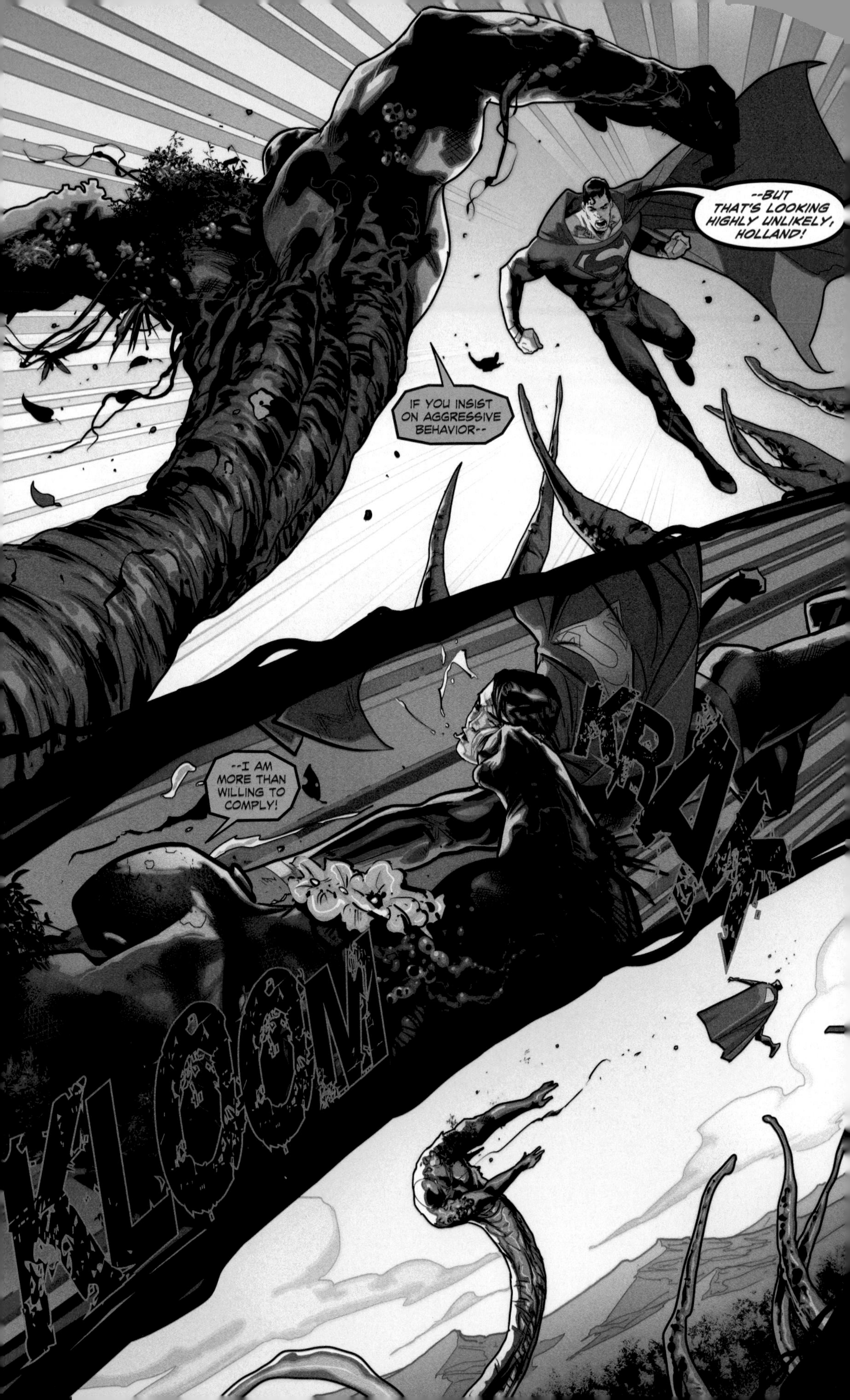
--BUT THAT'S LOOKING HIGHLY UNLIKELY, HOLLAND!
IF YOU INSIST ON AGGRESSIVE BEHAVIOR--
--I AM MORE THAN WILLING TO COMPLY!
KRAK
KLOOM

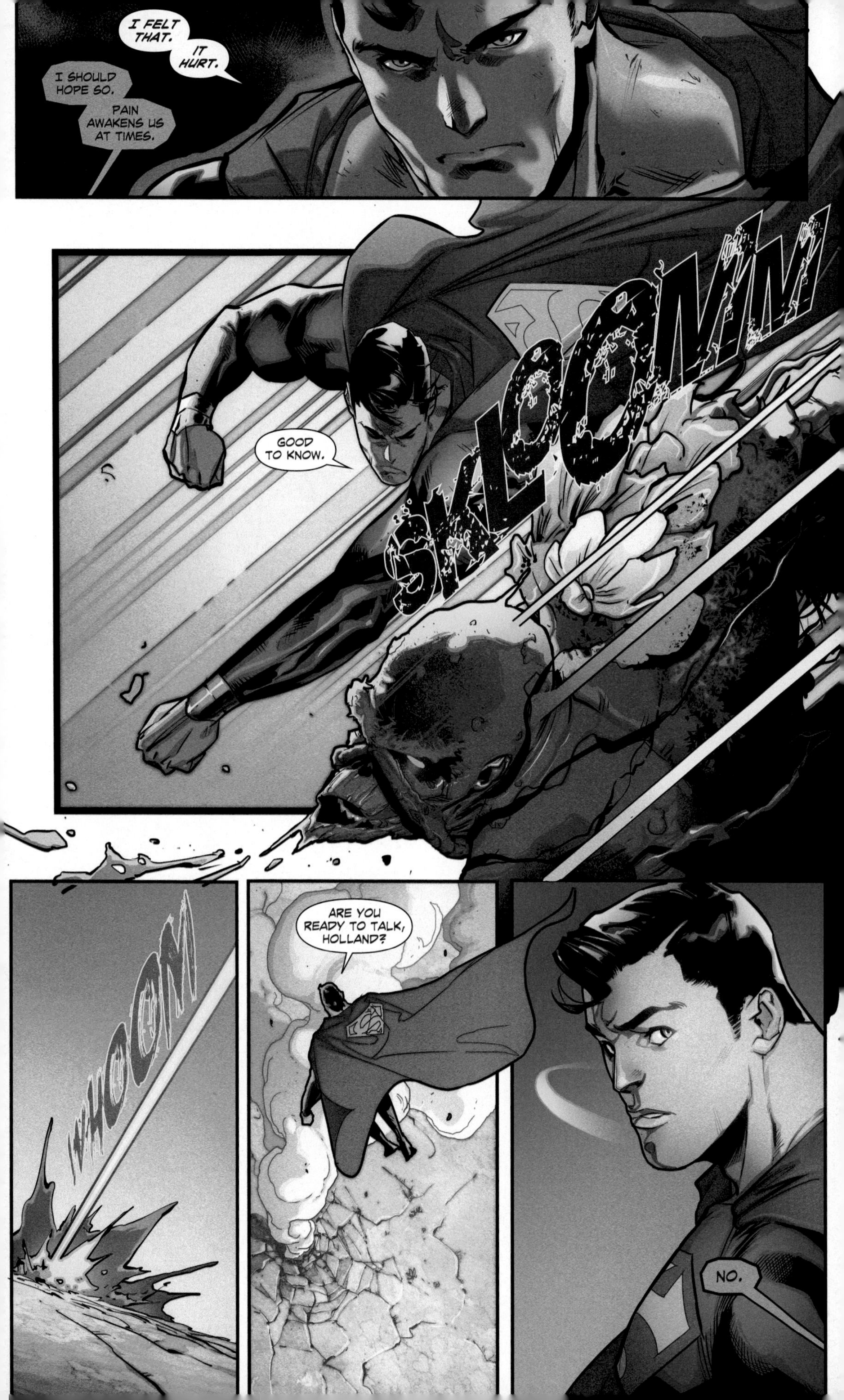
I FELT THAT.
IT HURT.
I SHOULD HOPE SO.
PAIN AWAKENS US AT TIMES.
GOOD TO KNOW.
SKLOOMM
WHOOM
ARE YOU READY TO TALK, HOLLAND?
NO.

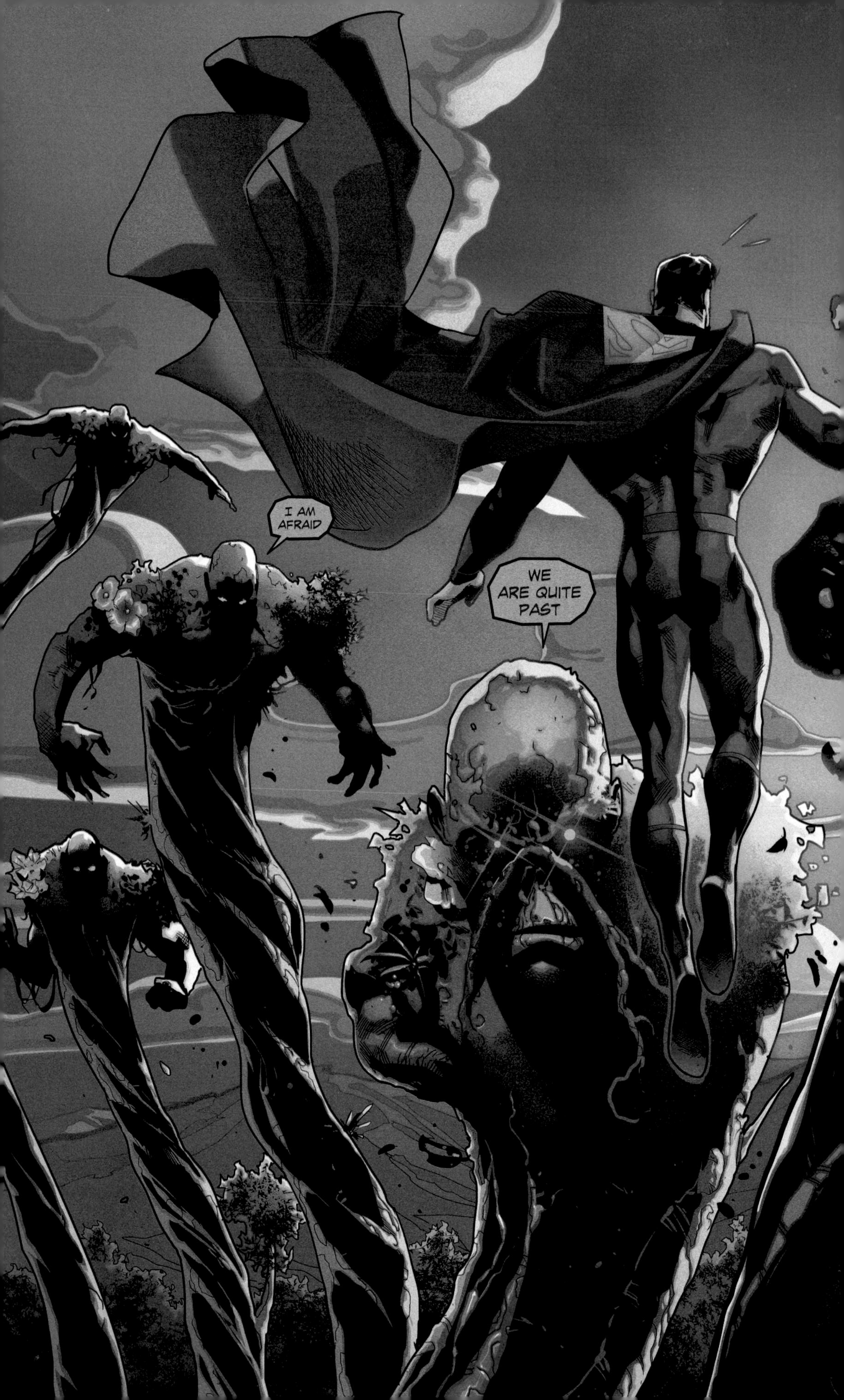
I AM AFRAID
WE ARE QUITE PAST

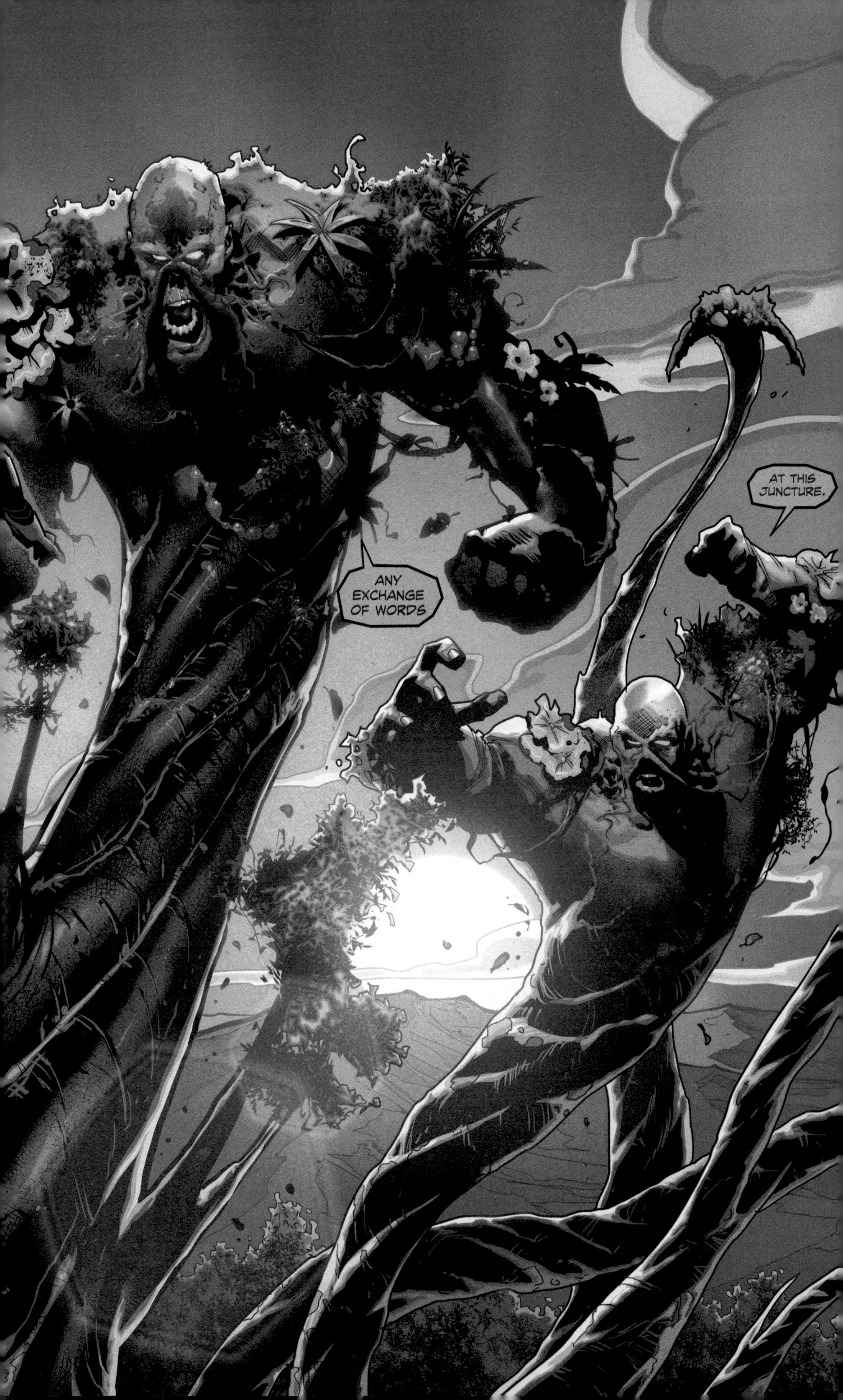
ANY EXCHANGE OF WORDS
AT THIS JUNCTURE.

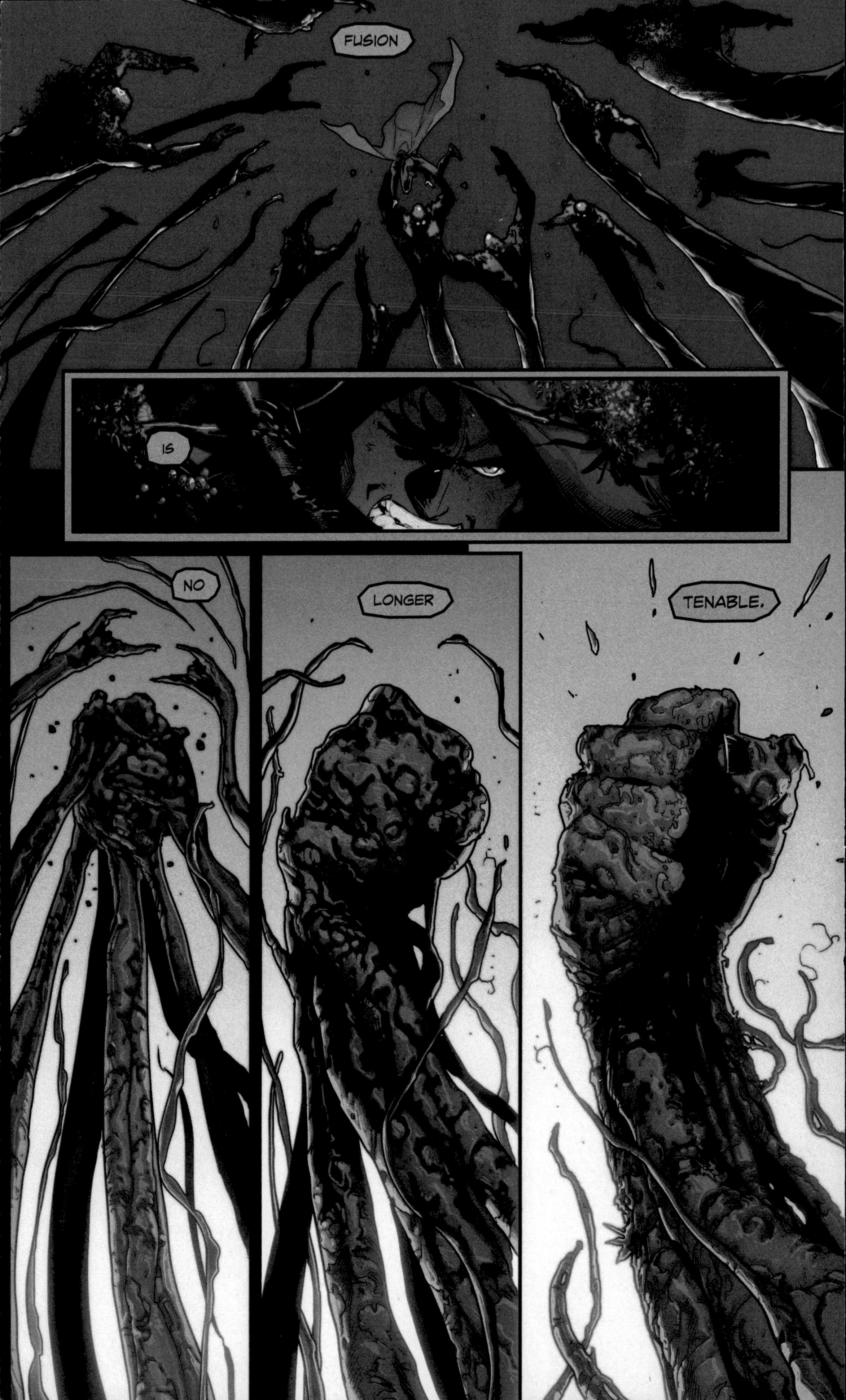
FUSION
IS
NO
LONGER
TENABLE.

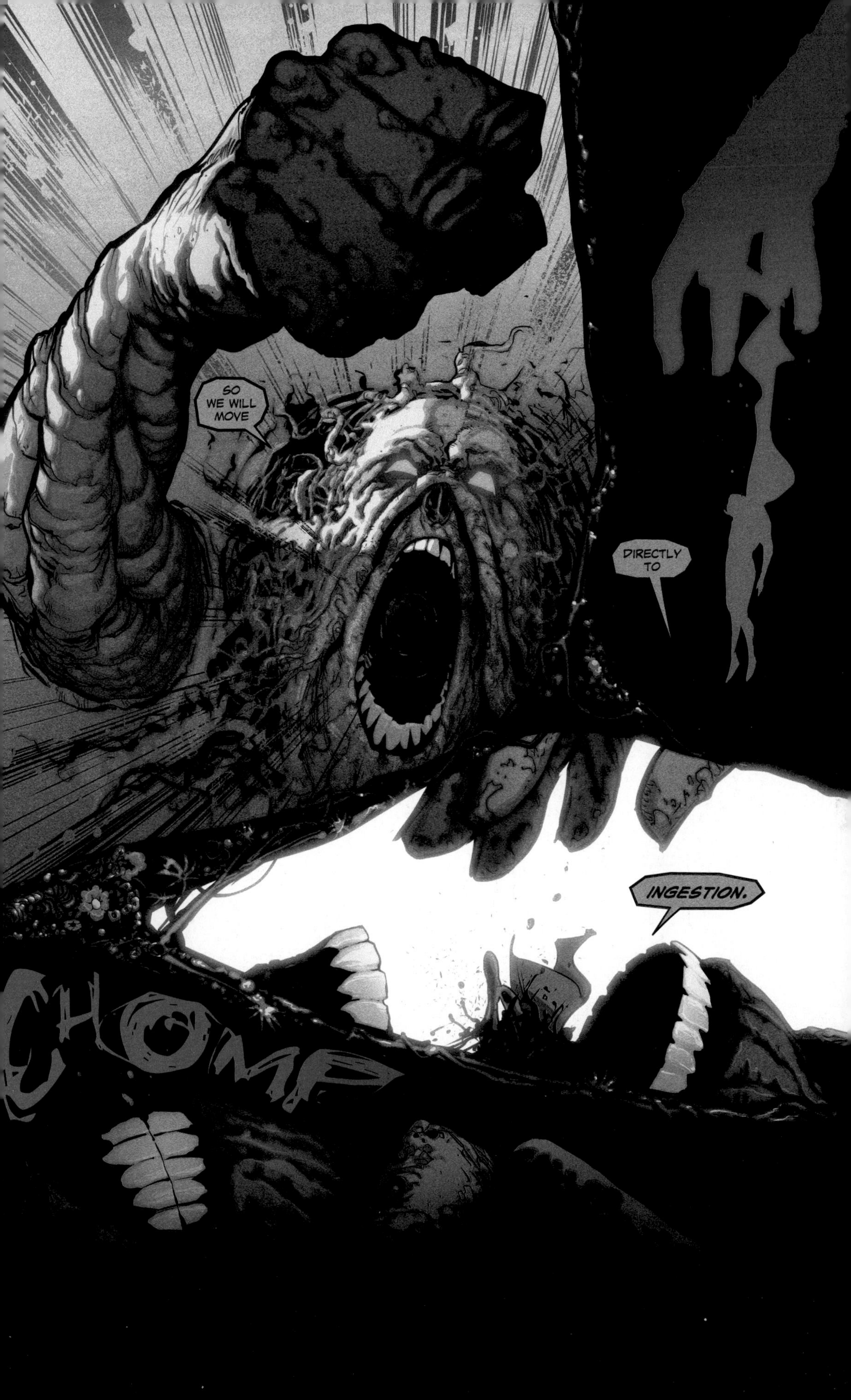
SO WE WILL MOVE
DIRECTLY TO
INGESTION.
CHOMP

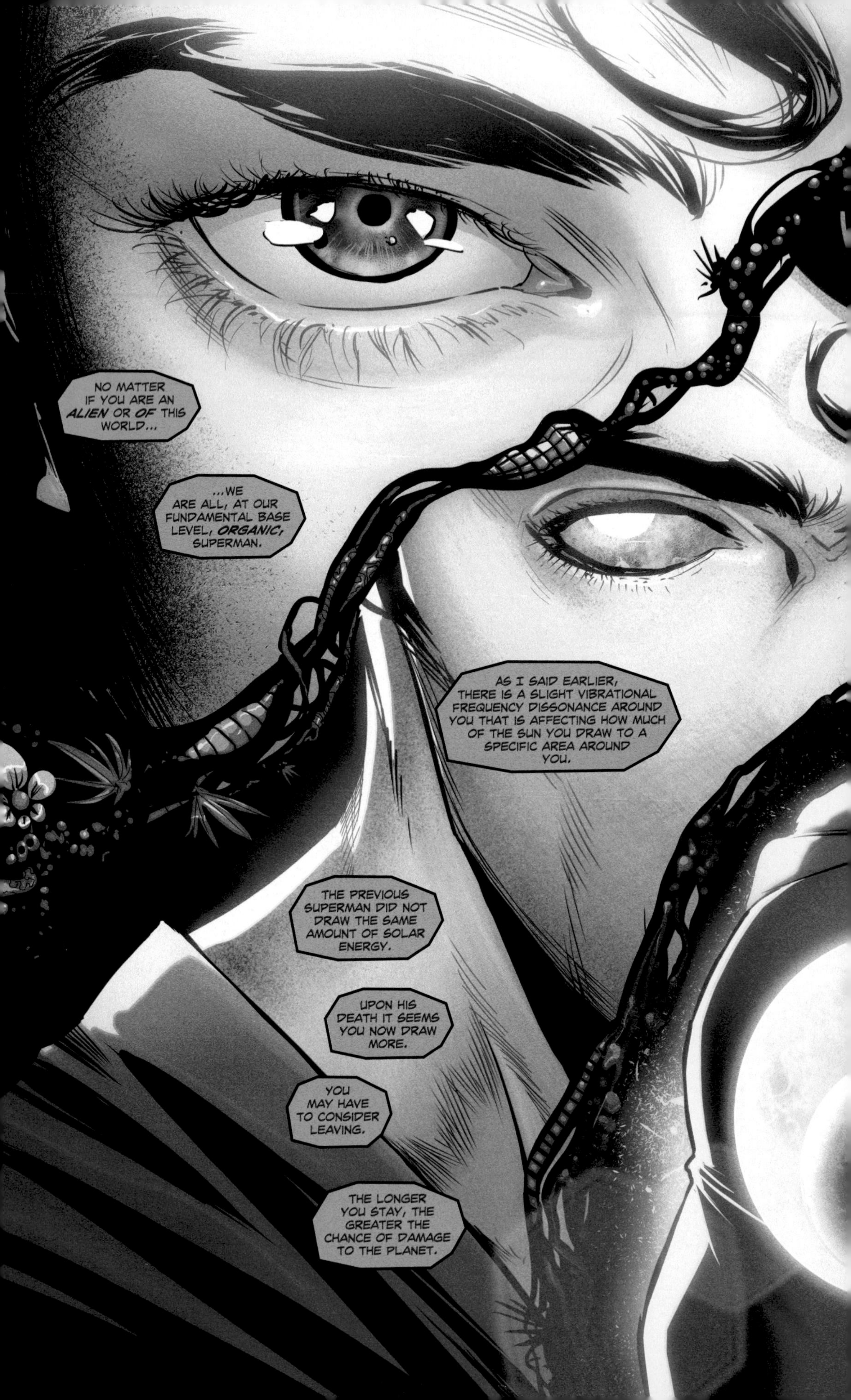
NO MATTER IF YOU ARE AN *ALIEN* OR *OF* THIS WORLD...
...WE ARE ALL, AT OUR FUNDAMENTAL BASE LEVEL, *ORGANIC,* SUPERMAN.
AS I SAID EARLIER, THERE IS A SLIGHT VIBRATIONAL FREQUENCY DISSONANCE AROUND YOU THAT IS AFFECTING HOW MUCH OF THE SUN YOU DRAW TO A SPECIFIC AREA AROUND YOU.
THE PREVIOUS SUPERMAN DID NOT DRAW THE SAME AMOUNT OF SOLAR ENERGY.
UPON HIS DEATH IT SEEMS YOU NOW DRAW MORE.
YOU MAY HAVE TO CONSIDER LEAVING.
THE LONGER YOU STAY, THE GREATER THE CHANCE OF DAMAGE TO THE PLANET.

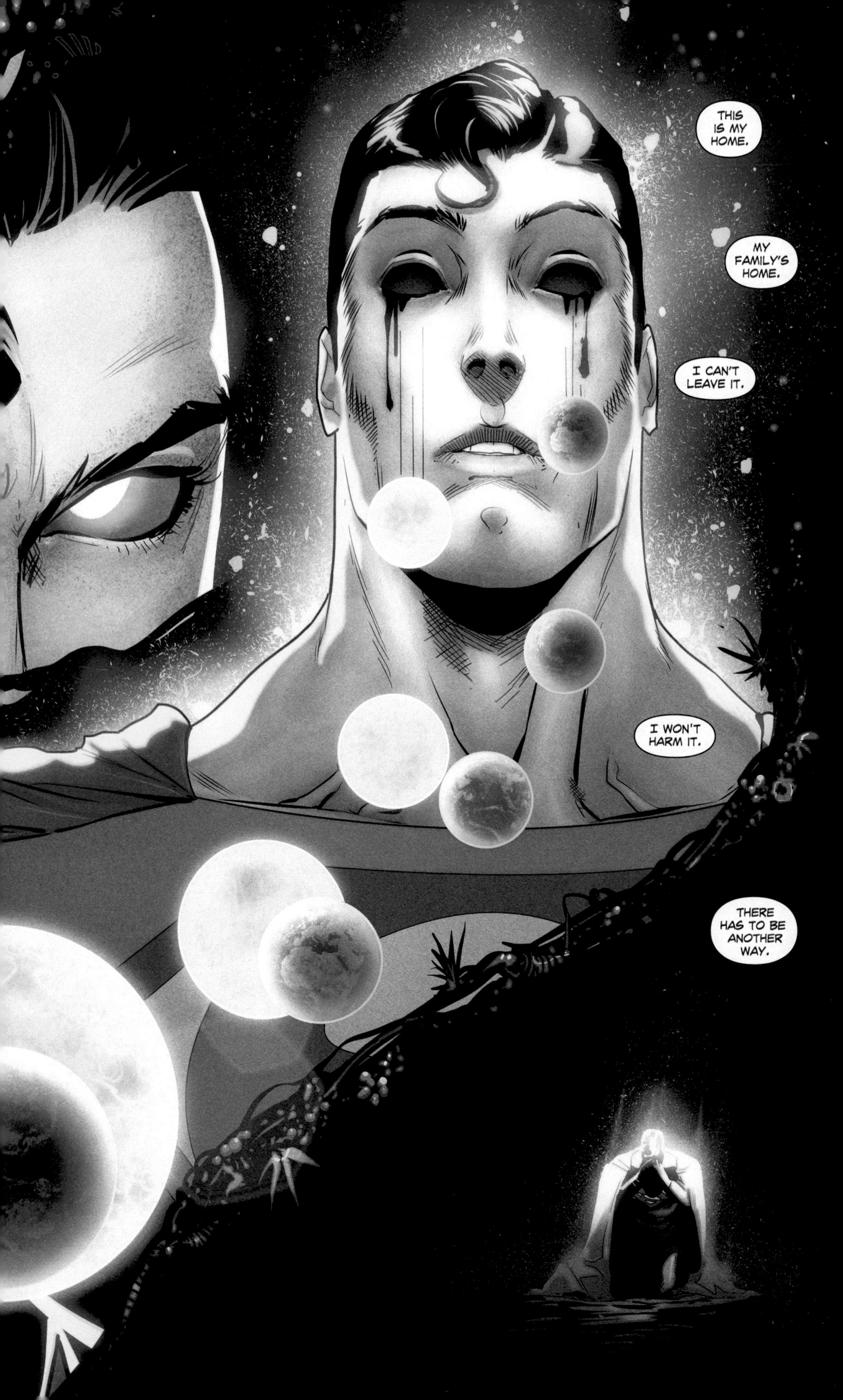
THIS IS MY HOME.
MY FAMILY'S HOME.
I CAN'T LEAVE IT.
I WON'T HARM IT.
THERE HAS TO BE ANOTHER WAY.

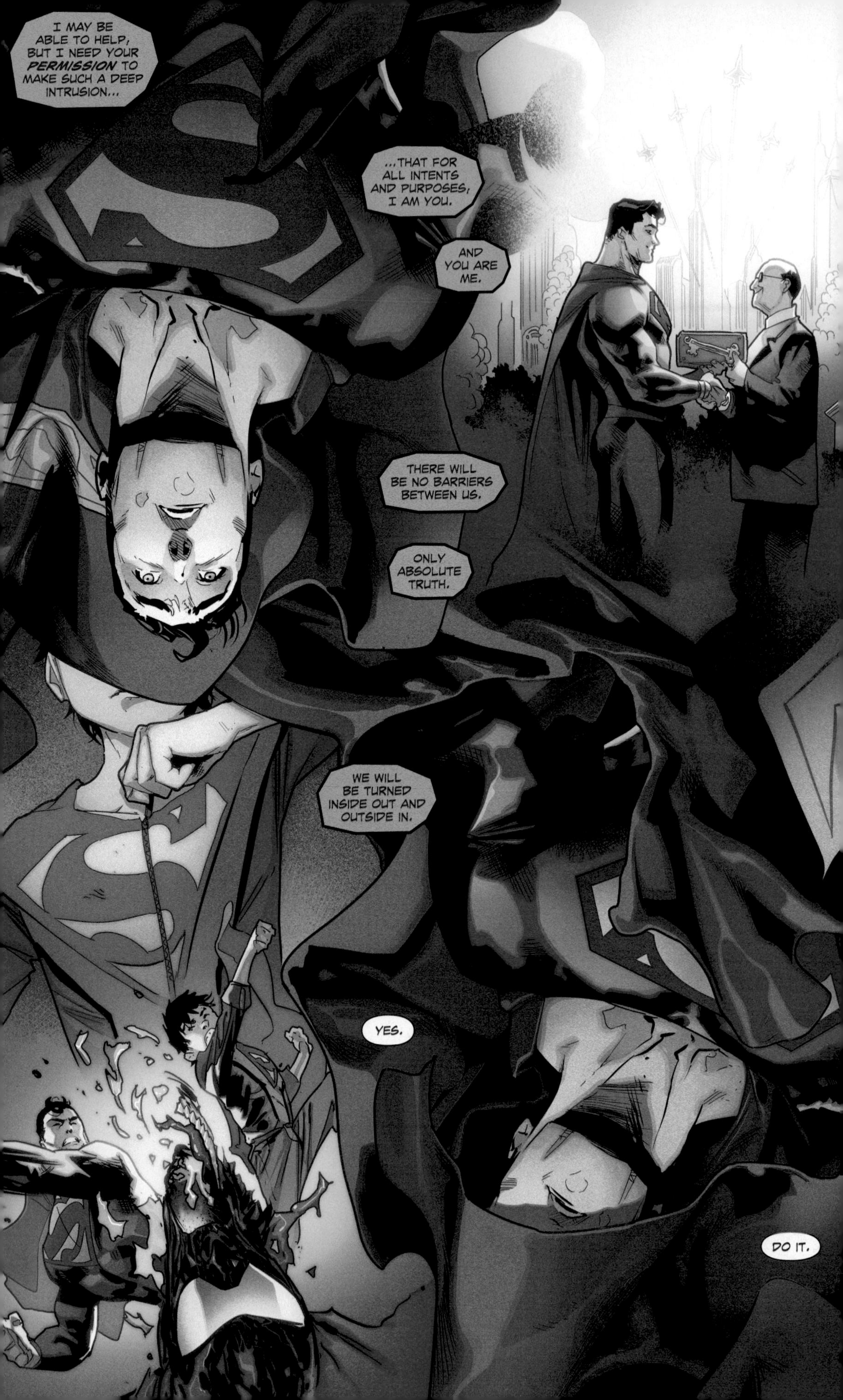
I MAY BE ABLE TO HELP, BUT I NEED YOUR PERMISSION TO MAKE SUCH A DEEP INTRUSION...
...THAT FOR ALL INTENTS AND PURPOSES, I AM YOU.
AND YOU ARE ME.
THERE WILL BE NO BARRIERS BETWEEN US.
ONLY ABSOLUTE TRUTH.
WE WILL BE TURNED INSIDE OUT AND OUTSIDE IN.
YES.
DO IT.

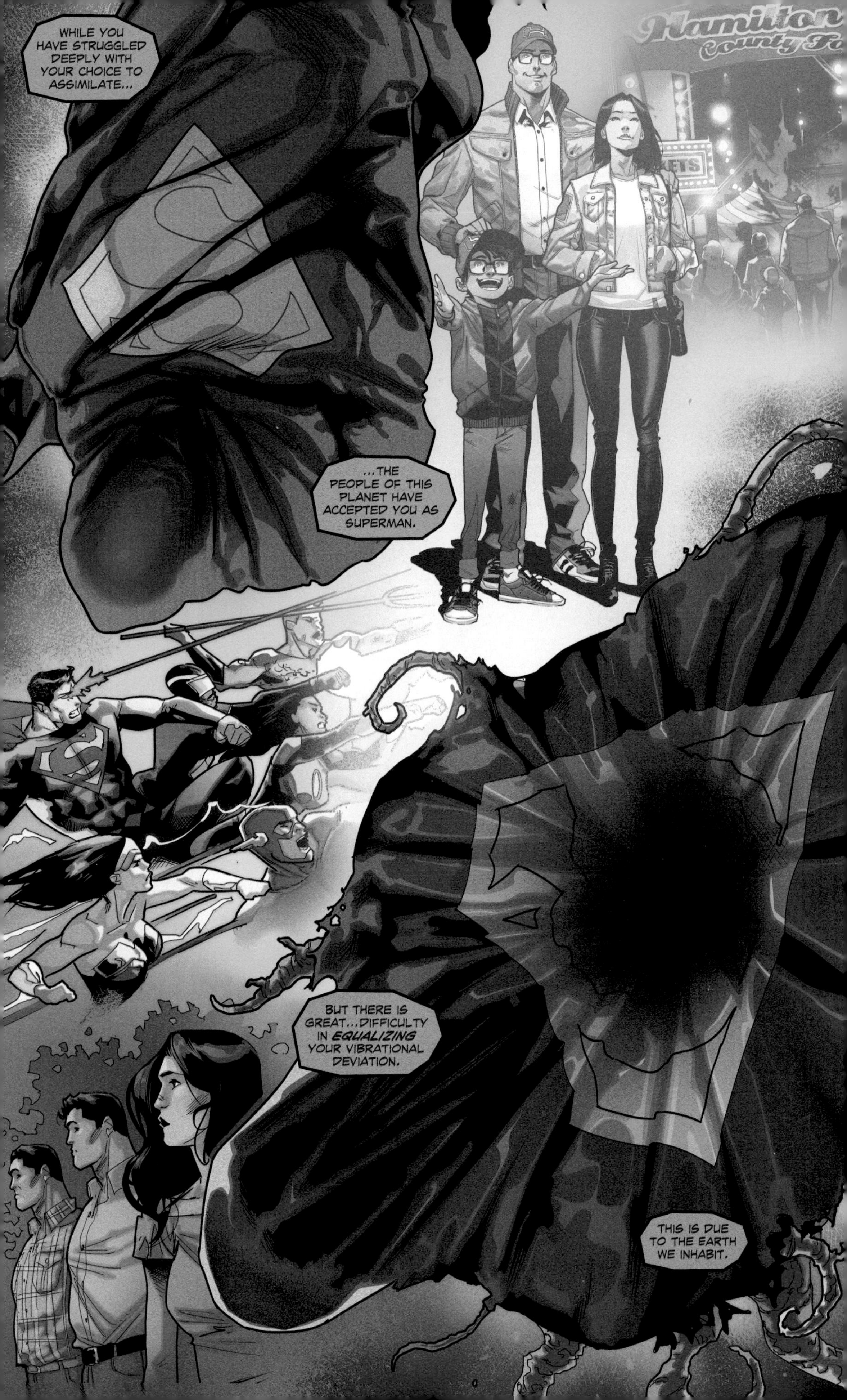
WHILE YOU HAVE STRUGGLED DEEPLY WITH YOUR CHOICE TO ASSIMILATE...
...THE PEOPLE OF THIS PLANET HAVE ACCEPTED YOU AS SUPERMAN.
Hamilton County Fa
BUT THERE IS GREAT...DIFFICULTY IN *EQUALIZING* YOUR VIBRATIONAL DEVIATION.
THIS IS DUE TO THE EARTH WE INHABIT.

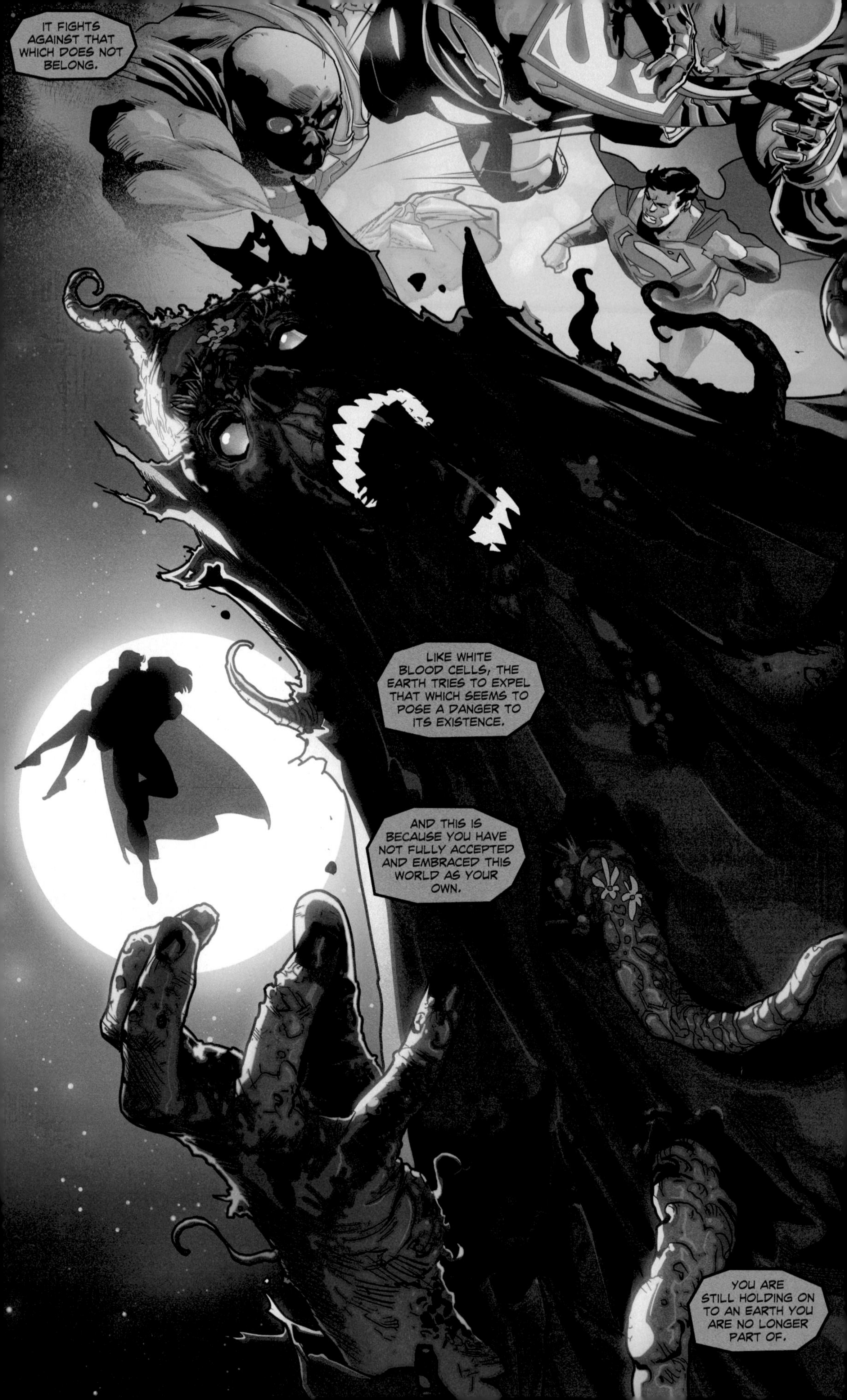
IT FIGHTS AGAINST THAT WHICH DOES NOT BELONG.
LIKE WHITE BLOOD CELLS, THE EARTH TRIES TO EXPEL THAT WHICH SEEMS TO POSE A DANGER TO ITS EXISTENCE.
AND THIS IS BECAUSE YOU HAVE NOT FULLY ACCEPTED AND EMBRACED THIS WORLD AS YOUR OWN.
YOU ARE STILL HOLDING ON TO AN EARTH YOU ARE NO LONGER PART OF.

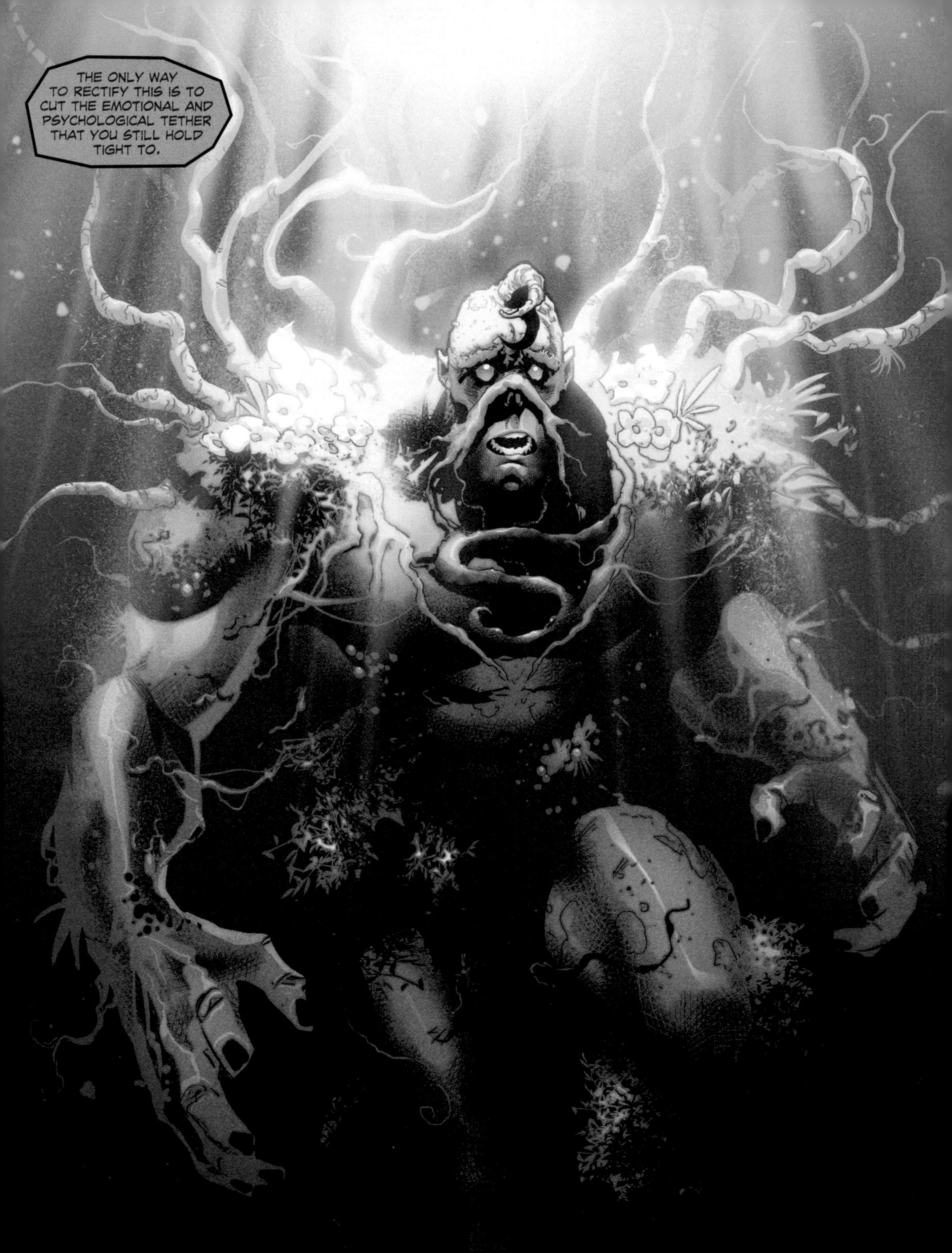
THE ONLY WAY TO RECTIFY THIS IS TO CUT THE EMOTIONAL AND PSYCHOLOGICAL TETHER THAT YOU STILL HOLD TIGHT TO.

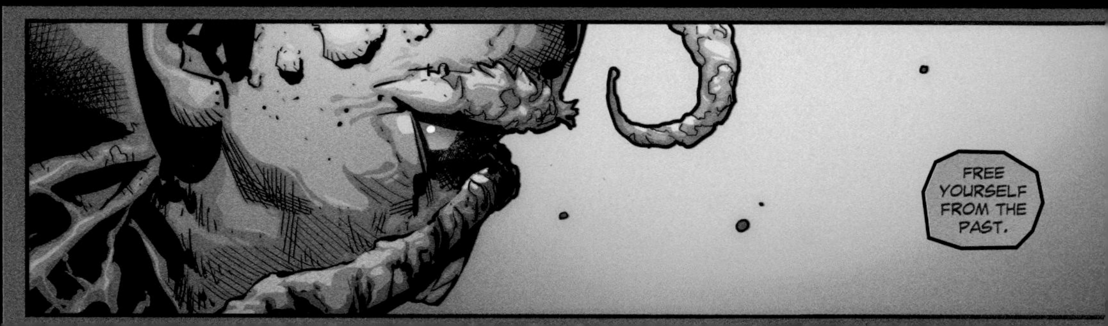
FREE YOURSELF FROM THE PAST.

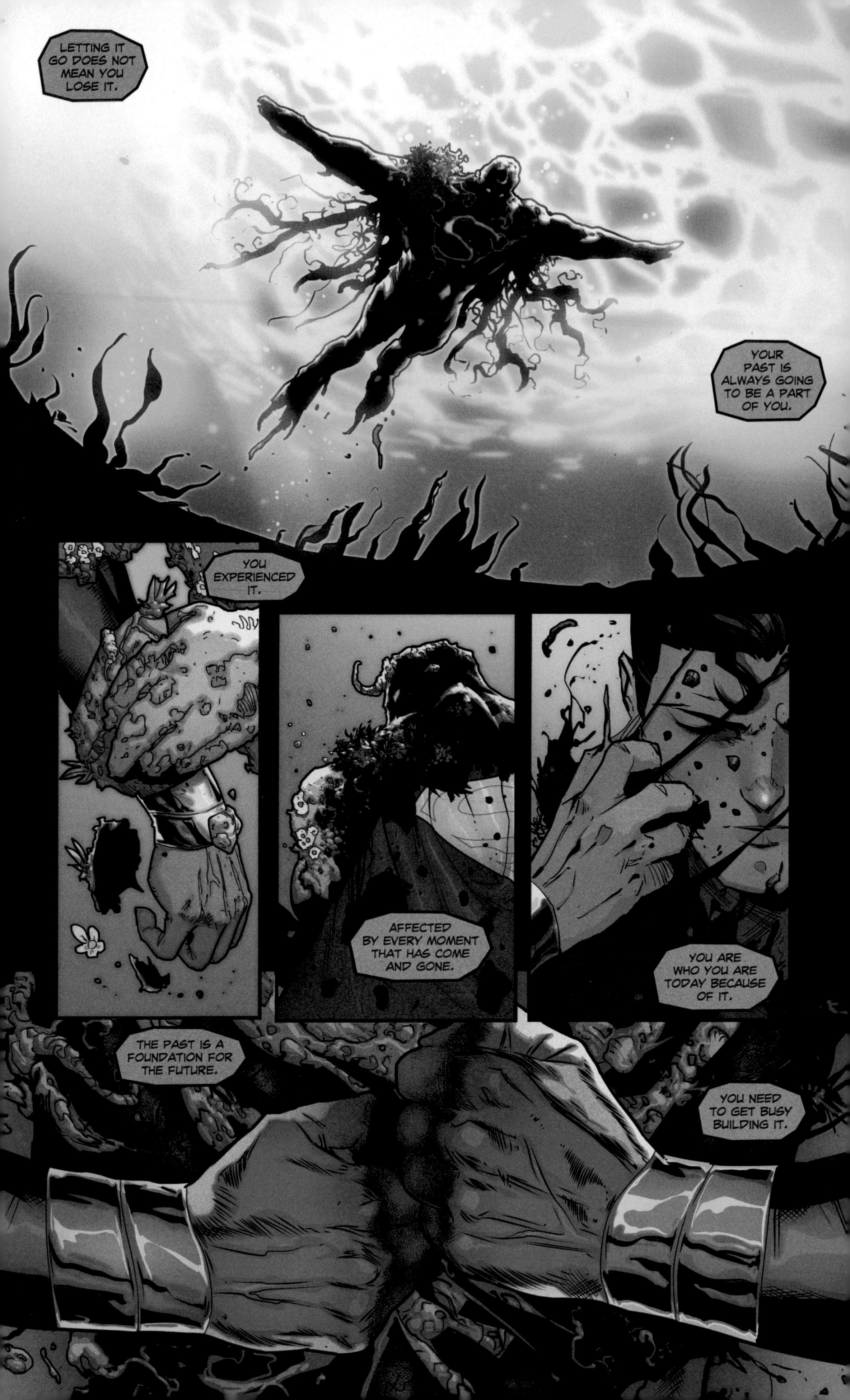
LETTING IT GO DOES NOT MEAN YOU LOSE IT.
YOUR PAST IS ALWAYS GOING TO BE A PART OF YOU.
YOU EXPERIENCED IT.
AFFECTED BY EVERY MOMENT THAT HAS COME AND GONE.
YOU ARE WHO YOU ARE TODAY BECAUSE OF IT.
THE PAST IS A FOUNDATION FOR THE FUTURE.
YOU NEED TO GET BUSY BUILDING IT.

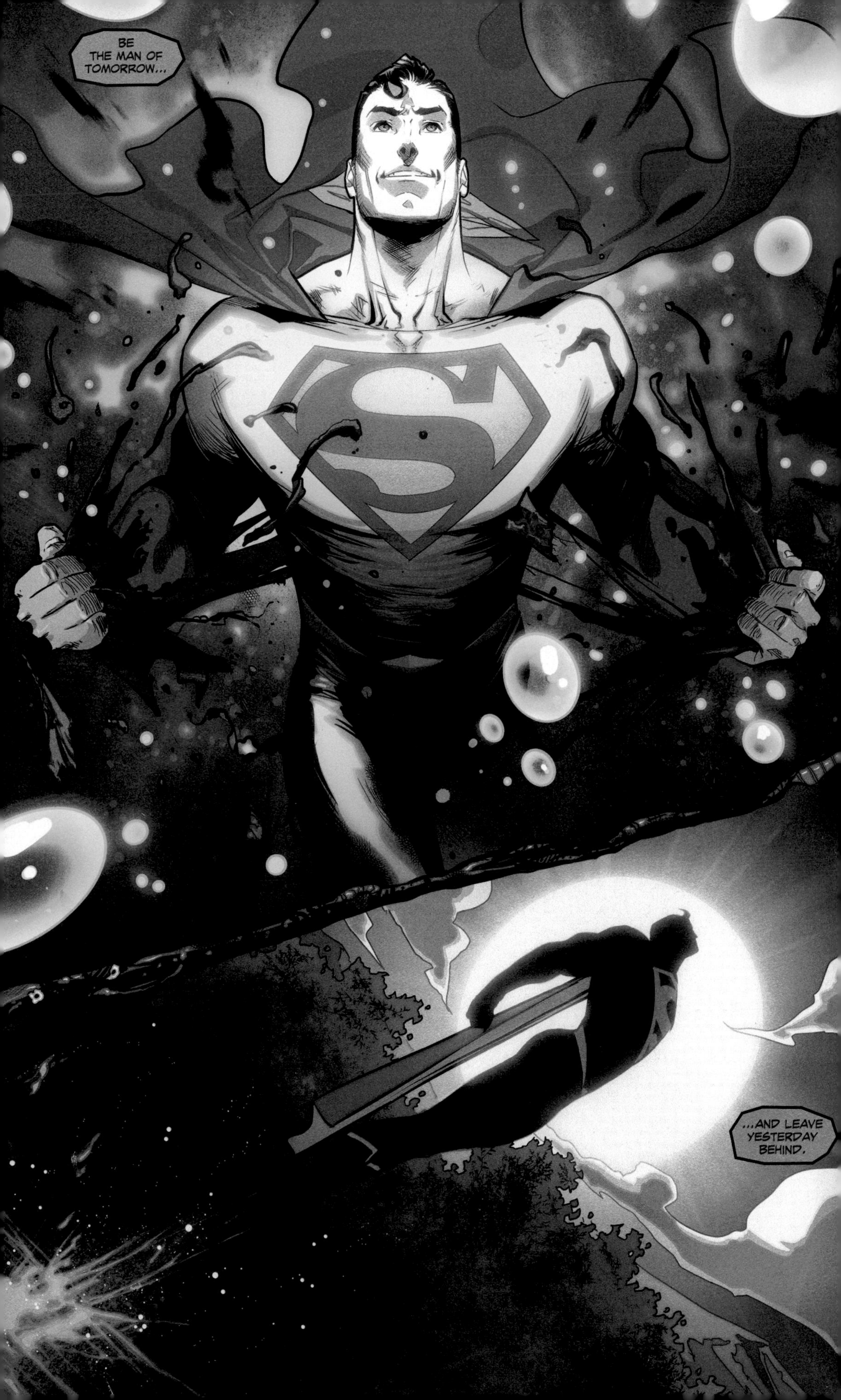
BE THE MAN OF TOMORROW...
...AND LEAVE YESTERDAY BEHIND.

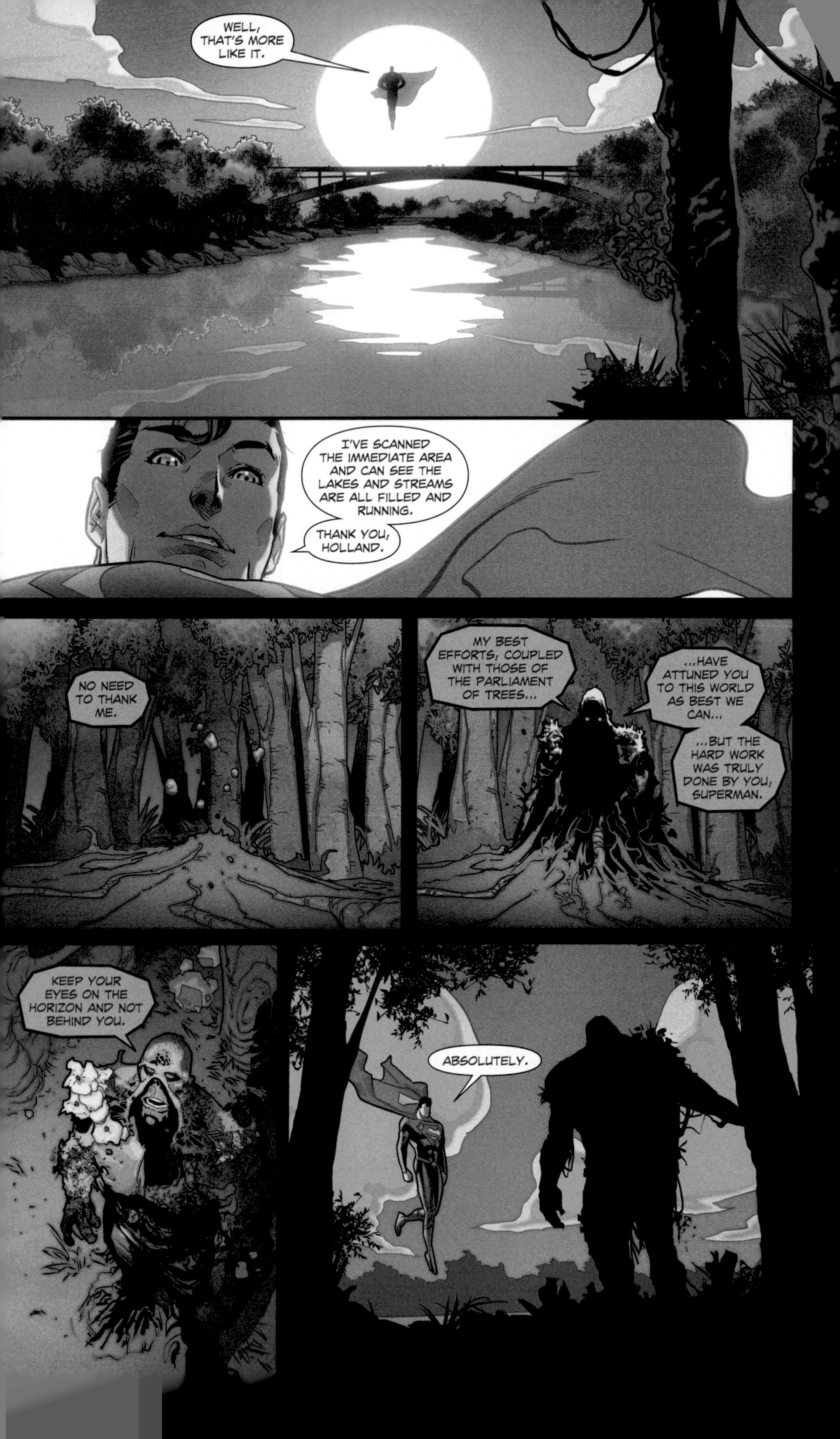
WELL, THAT'S MORE LIKE IT.
I'VE SCANNED THE IMMEDIATE AREA AND CAN SEE THE LAKES AND STREAMS ARE ALL FILLED AND RUNNING.
THANK YOU, HOLLAND.
NO NEED TO THANK ME.
MY BEST EFFORTS, COUPLED WITH THOSE OF THE PARLIAMENT OF TREES...
...HAVE ATTUNED YOU TO THIS WORLD AS BEST WE CAN...
...BUT THE HARD WORK WAS TRULY DONE BY YOU, SUPERMAN.
KEEP YOUR EYES ON THE HORIZON AND NOT BEHIND YOU.
ABSOLUTELY.

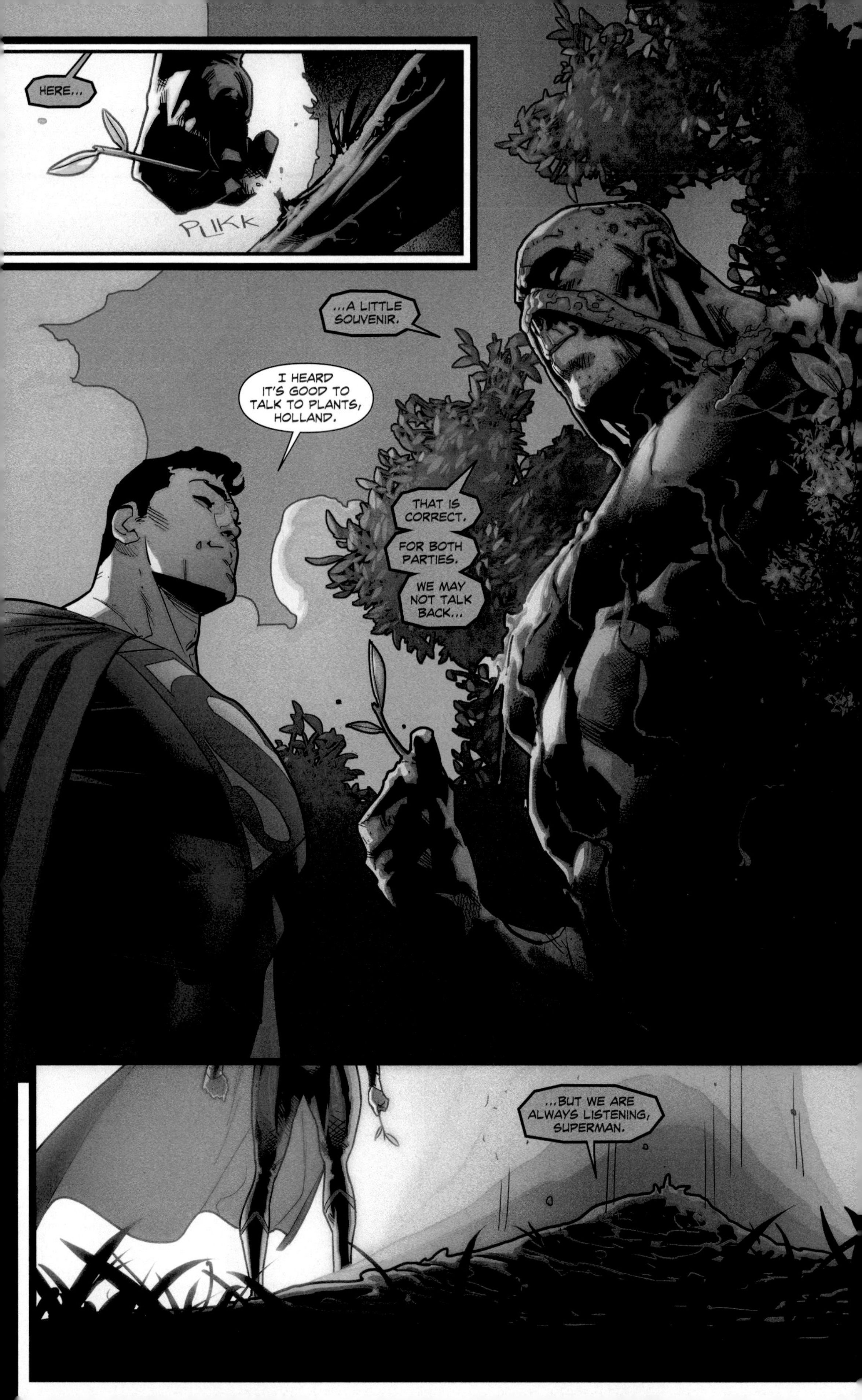
HERE...
PLIKK
...A LITTLE SOUVENIR.
I HEARD IT'S GOOD TO TALK TO PLANTS, HOLLAND.
THAT IS CORRECT.
FOR BOTH PARTIES.
WE MAY NOT TALK BACK...
...BUT WE ARE ALWAYS LISTENING, SUPERMAN.

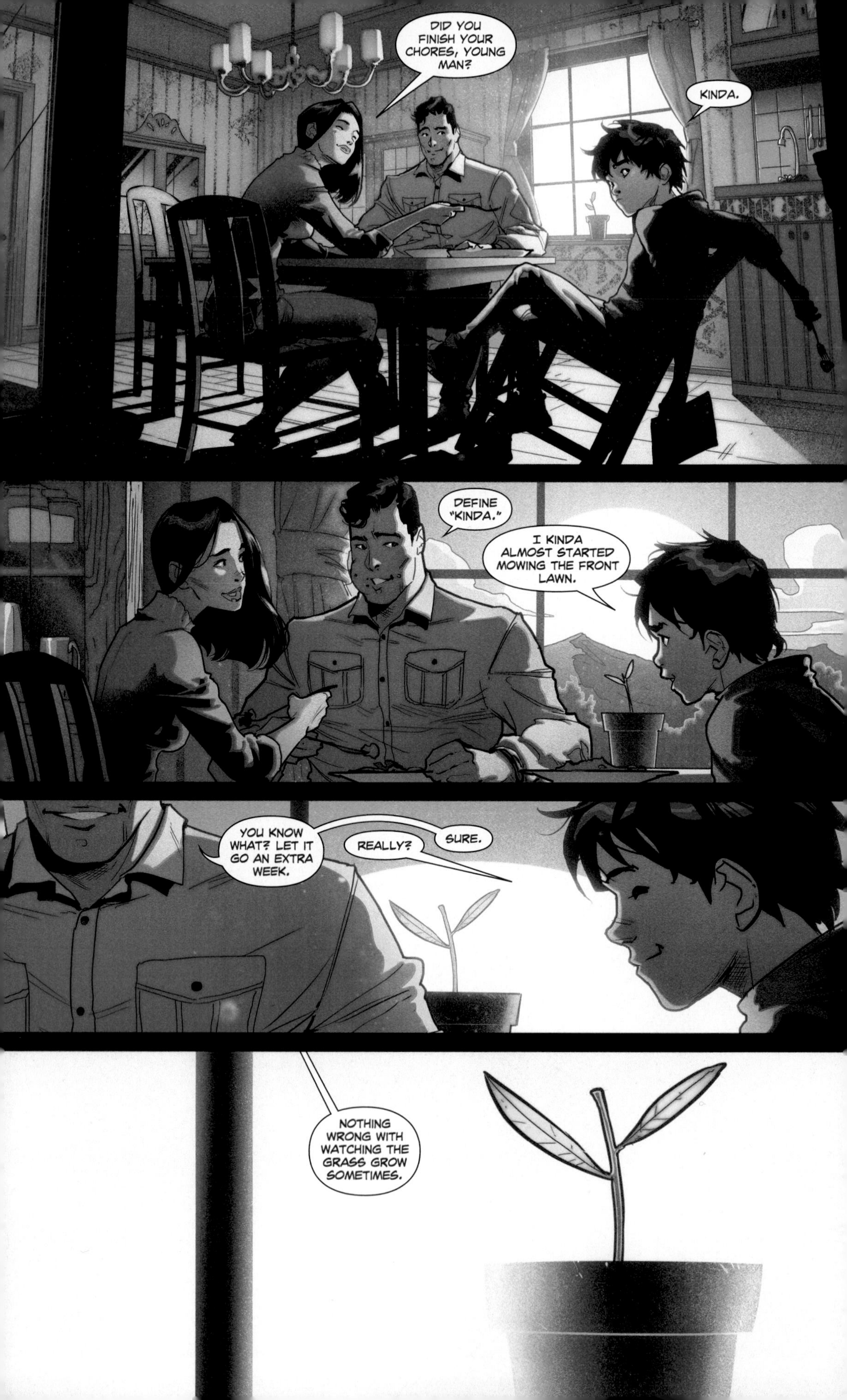
DID YOU FINISH YOUR CHORES, YOUNG MAN?
KINDA.
DEFINE "KINDA."
I KINDA ALMOST STARTED MOWING THE FRONT LAWN.
YOU KNOW WHAT? LET IT GO AN EXTRA WEEK.
REALLY?
SURE.
NOTHING WRONG WITH WATCHING THE GRASS GROW SOMETIMES.

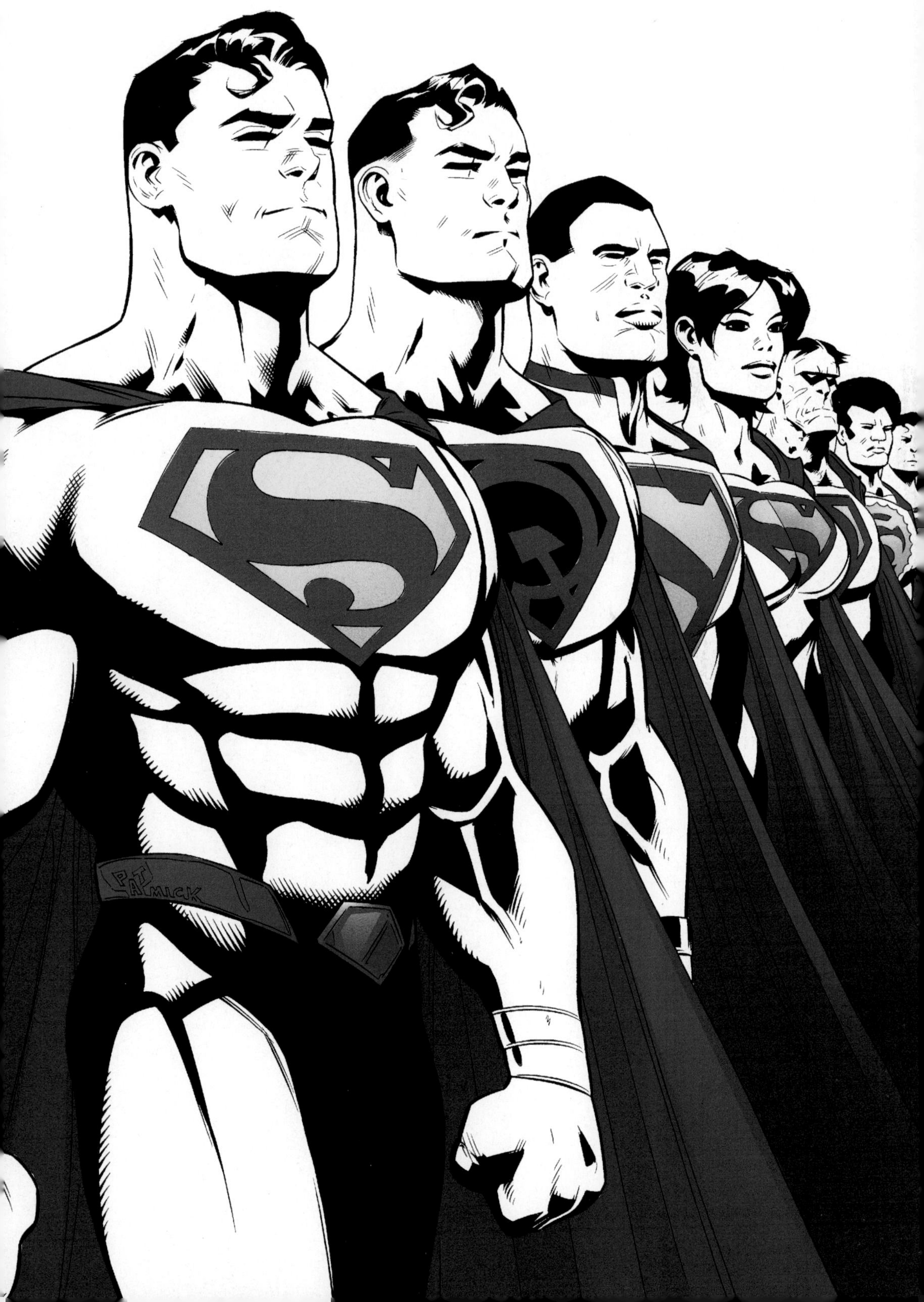
PAT MICK

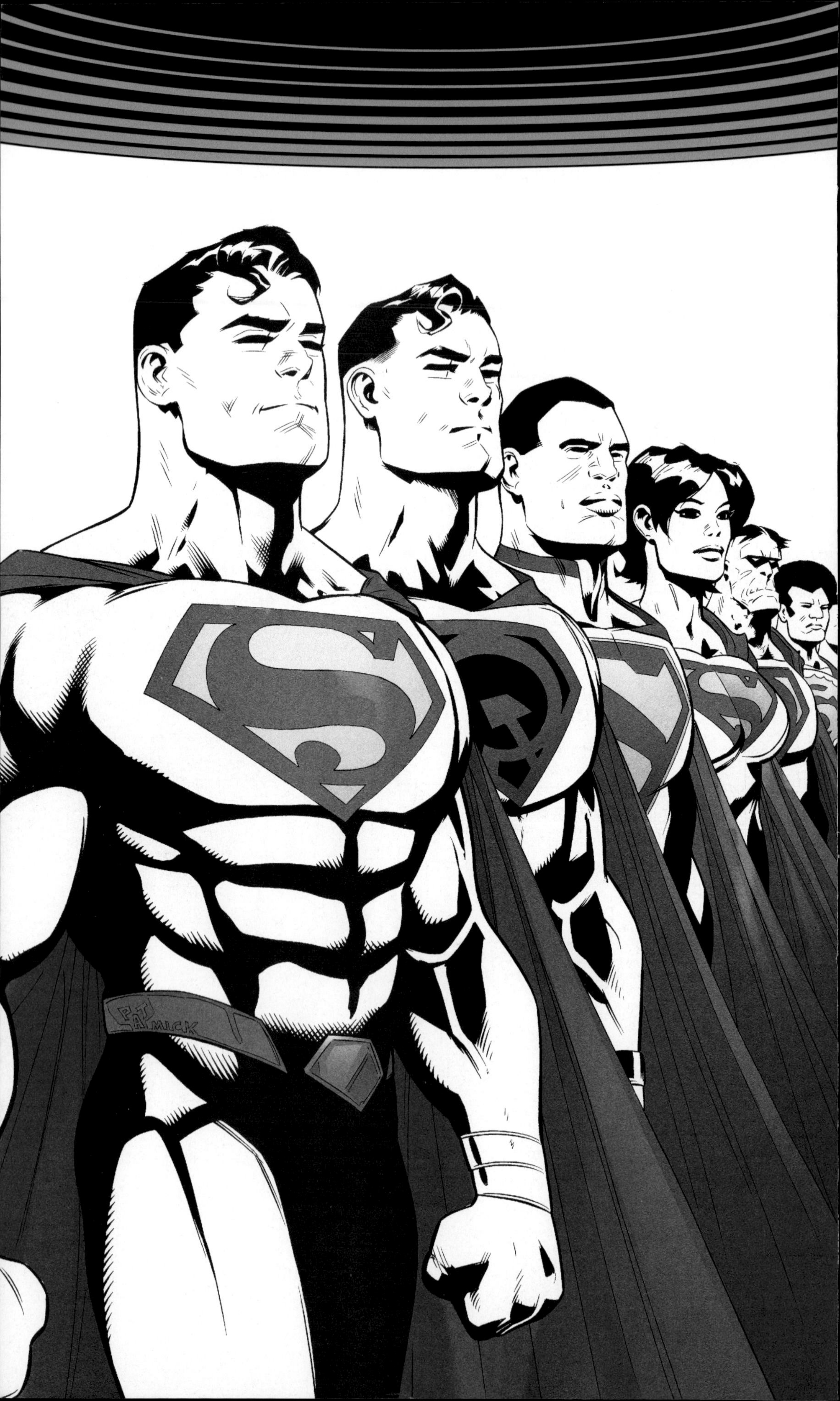

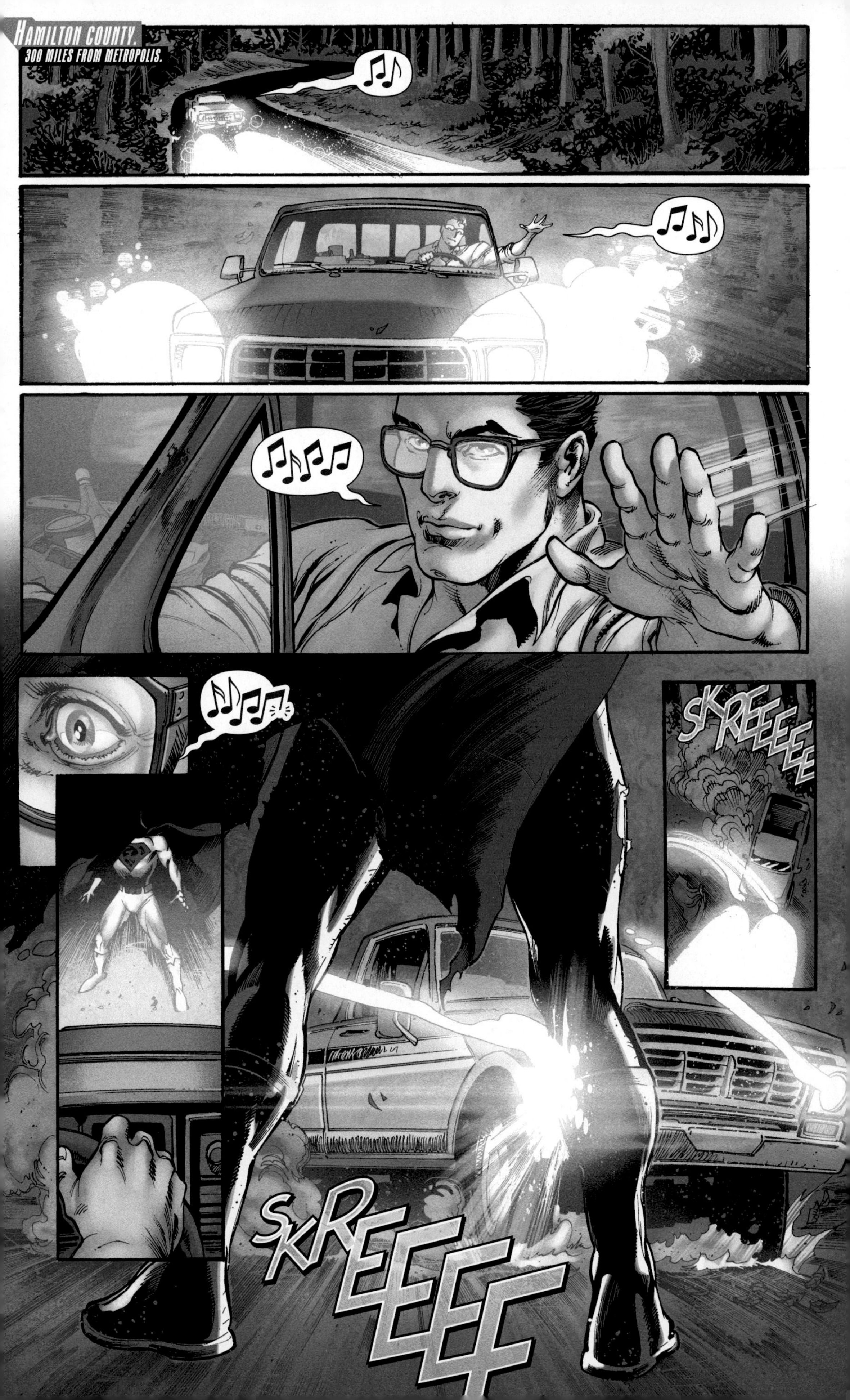

HAMILTON COUNTY.
300 MILES FROM METROPOLIS.
SKREEEEEE
SKREEEEEE

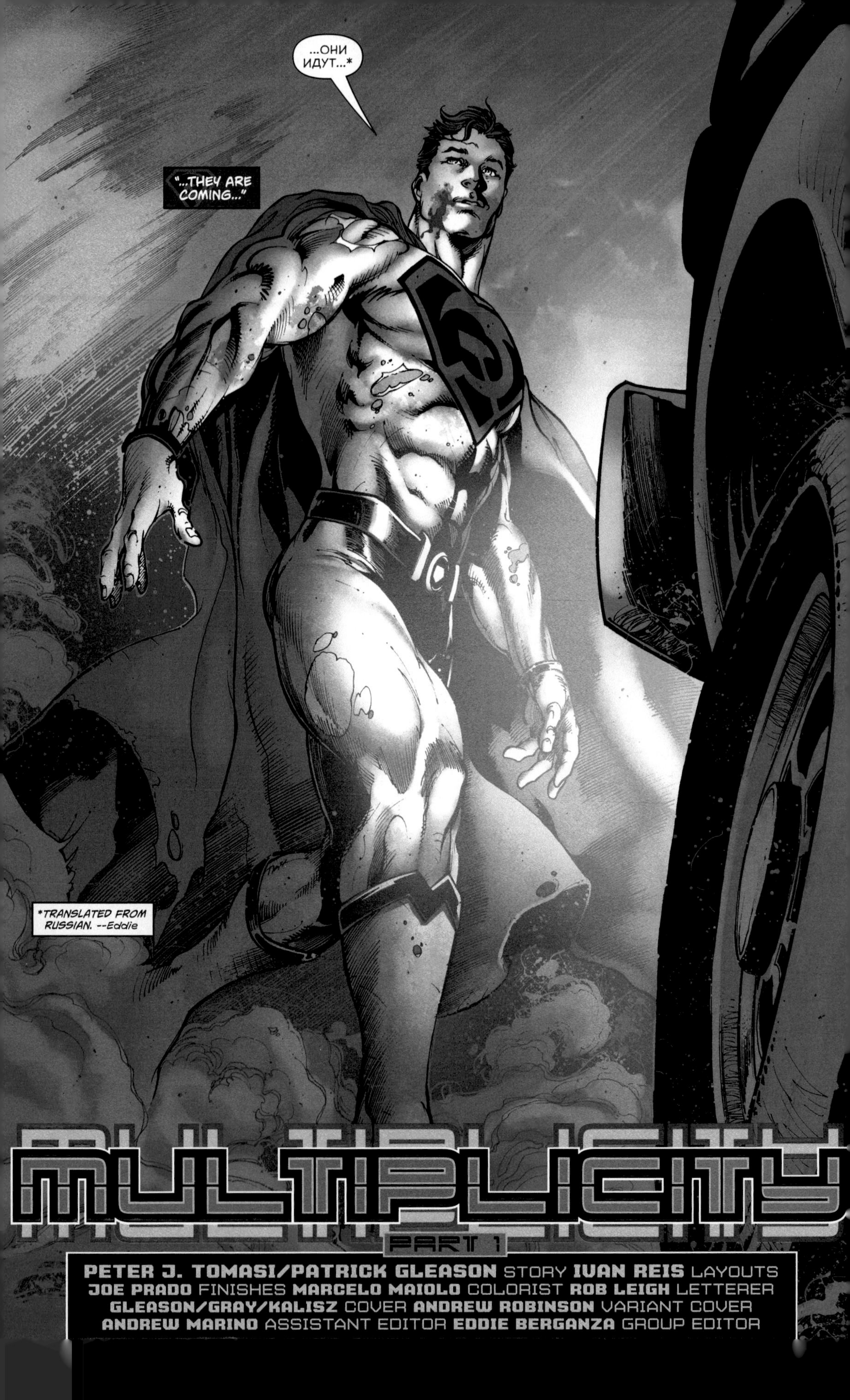
...ОНИ ИДУТ...*
"...THEY ARE COMING..."
*TRANSLATED FROM RUSSIAN. --Eddie
MULTIPLICITY
PART 1
PETER J. TOMASI/PATRICK GLEASON STORY IVAN REIS LAYOUTS
JOE PRADO FINISHES MARCELO MAIOLO COLORIST ROB LEIGH LETTERER
GLEASON/GRAY/KALISZ COVER ANDREW ROBINSON VARIANT COVER
ANDREW MARINO ASSISTANT EDITOR EDDIE BERGANZA GROUP EDITOR

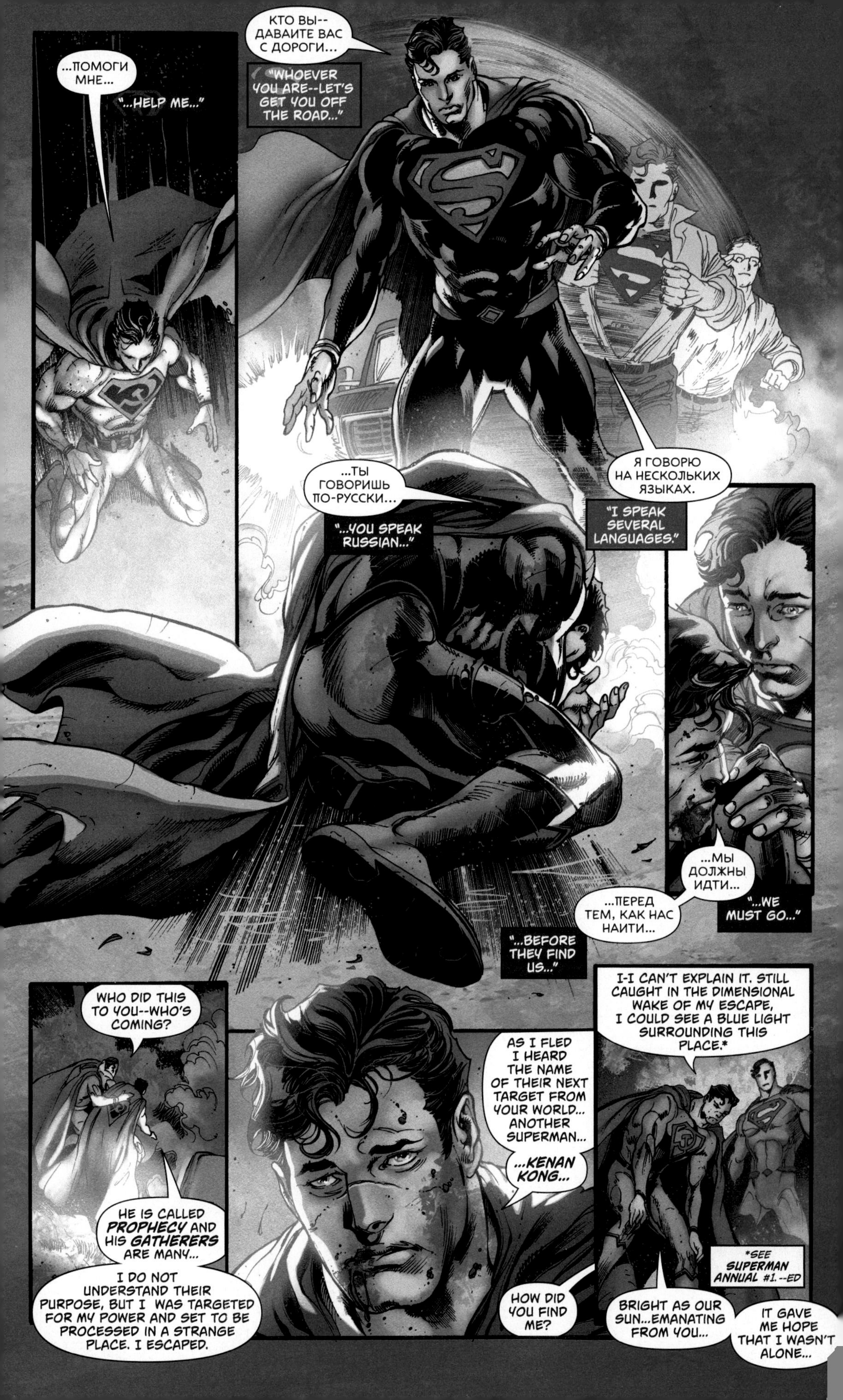
...ПОМОГИ МНЕ...
"...HELP ME..."
КТО ВЫ-- ДАВАИТЕ ВАС С ДОРОГИ...
"WHOEVER YOU ARE--LET'S GET YOU OFF THE ROAD..."
...ТЫ ГОВОРИШЬ ПО-РУССКИ...
"...YOU SPEAK RUSSIAN..."
Я ГОВОРЮ НА НЕСКОЛЬКИХ ЯЗЫКАХ.
"I SPEAK SEVERAL LANGUAGES."
...МЫ ДОЛЖНЫ ИДТИ...
"...WE MUST GO..."
...ПЕРЕД ТЕМ, КАК НАС НАИТИ...
"...BEFORE THEY FIND US..."
WHO DID THIS TO YOU--WHO'S COMING?
HE IS CALLED PROPHECY AND HIS GATHERERS ARE MANY...
I DO NOT UNDERSTAND THEIR PURPOSE, BUT I WAS TARGETED FOR MY POWER AND SET TO BE PROCESSED IN A STRANGE PLACE. I ESCAPED.
AS I FLED I HEARD THE NAME OF THEIR NEXT TARGET FROM YOUR WORLD... ANOTHER SUPERMAN...
...KENAN KONG...
HOW DID YOU FIND ME?
I-I CAN'T EXPLAIN IT. STILL CAUGHT IN THE DIMENSIONAL WAKE OF MY ESCAPE, I COULD SEE A BLUE LIGHT SURROUNDING THIS PLACE.*
*SEE SUPERMAN ANNUAL #1. --ED
BRIGHT AS OUR SUN...EMANATING FROM YOU...
IT GAVE ME HOPE THAT I WASN'T ALONE...

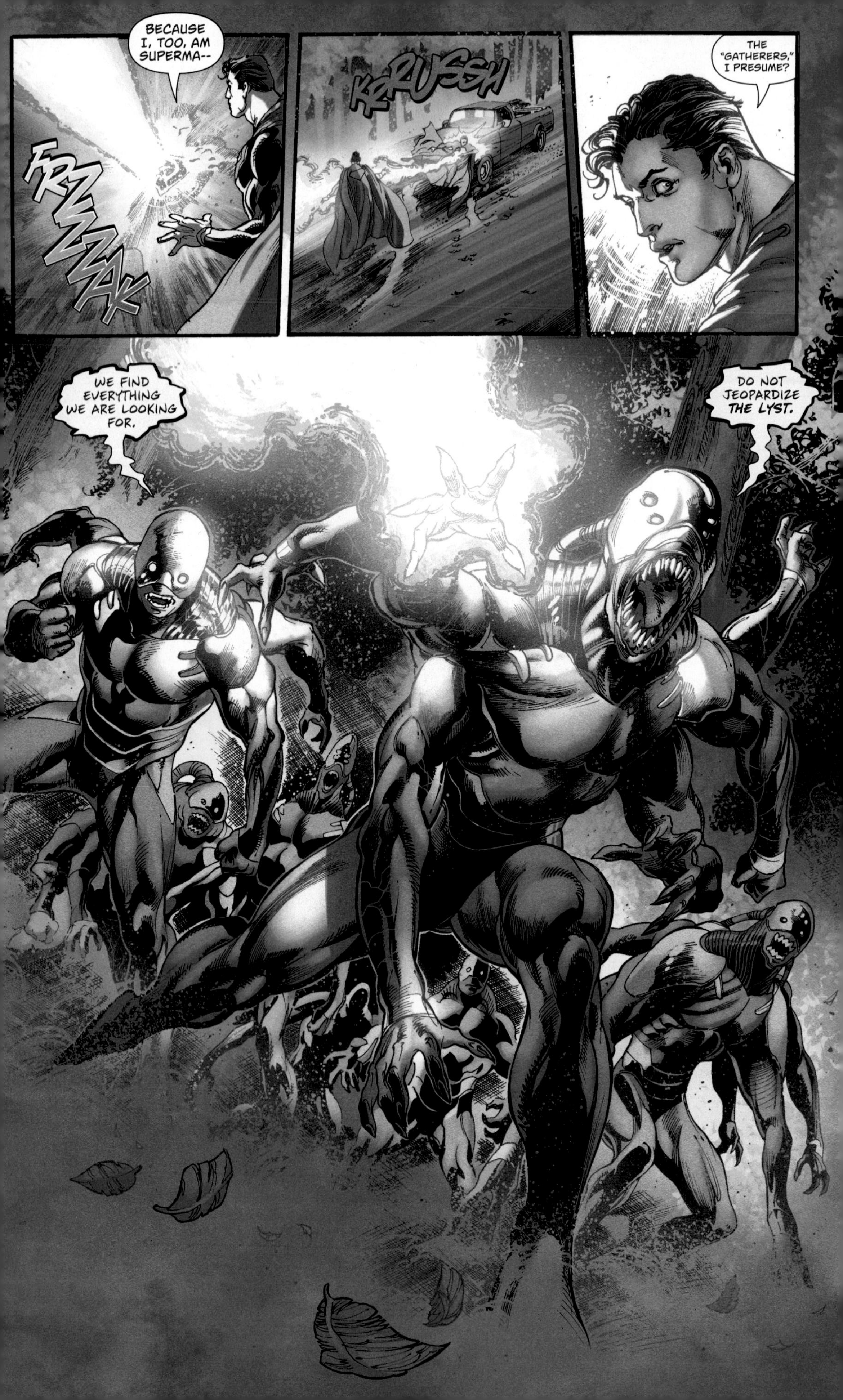
BECAUSE I, TOO, AM SUPERMA--
FRZZZZAK
KRUSSH
THE "GATHERERS," I PRESUME?
WE FIND EVERYTHING WE ARE LOOKING FOR.
DO NOT JEOPARDIZE THE LYST.

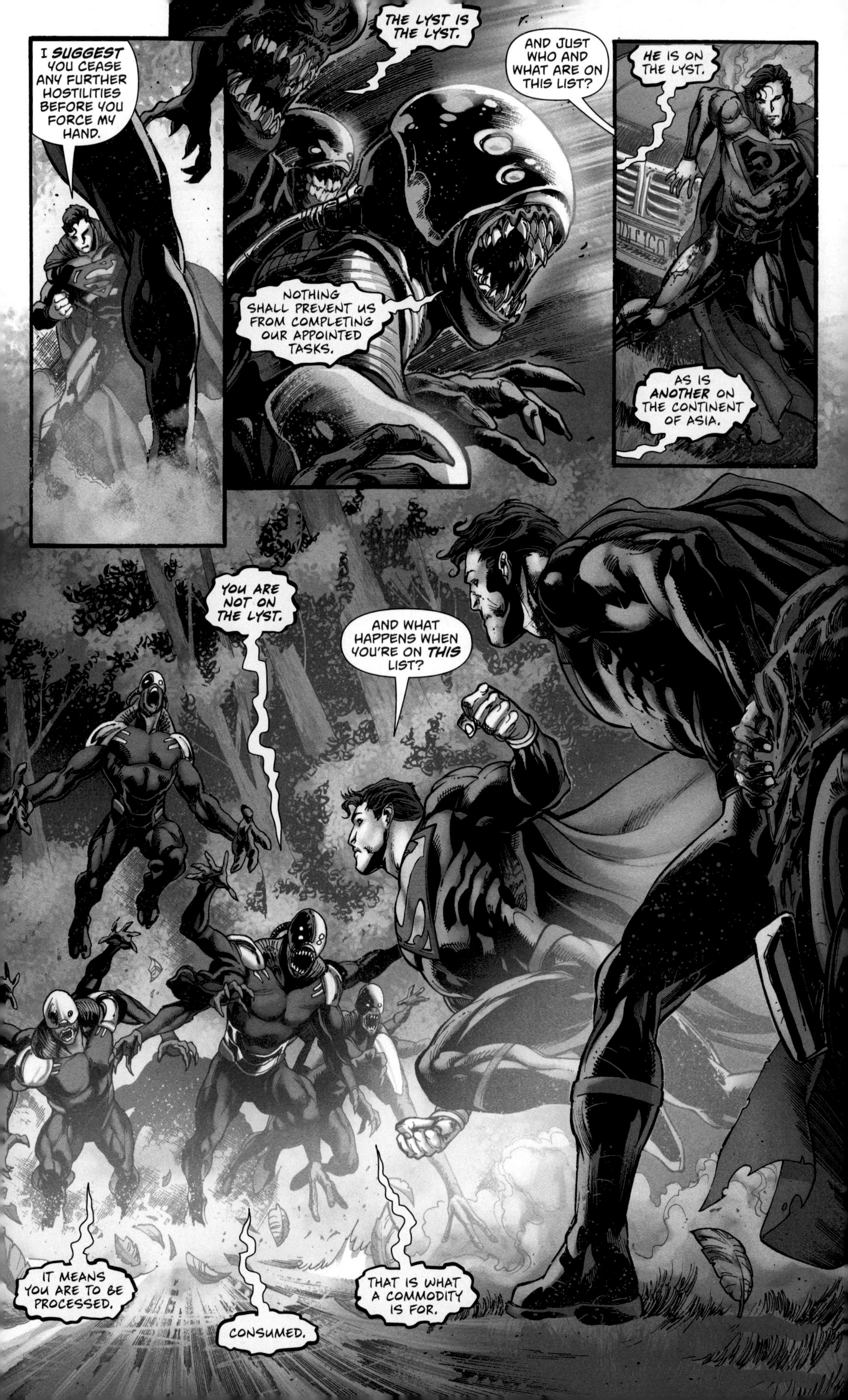
I SUGGEST YOU CEASE ANY FURTHER HOSTILITIES BEFORE YOU FORCE MY HAND.
THE LYST IS THE LYST.
NOTHING SHALL PREVENT US FROM COMPLETING OUR APPOINTED TASKS.
AND JUST WHO AND WHAT ARE ON THIS LIST?
HE IS ON THE LYST.
AS IS ANOTHER ON THE CONTINENT OF ASIA.
YOU ARE NOT ON THE LYST.
AND WHAT HAPPENS WHEN YOU'RE ON THIS LIST?
IT MEANS YOU ARE TO BE PROCESSED.
CONSUMED.
THAT IS WHAT A COMMODITY IS FOR.

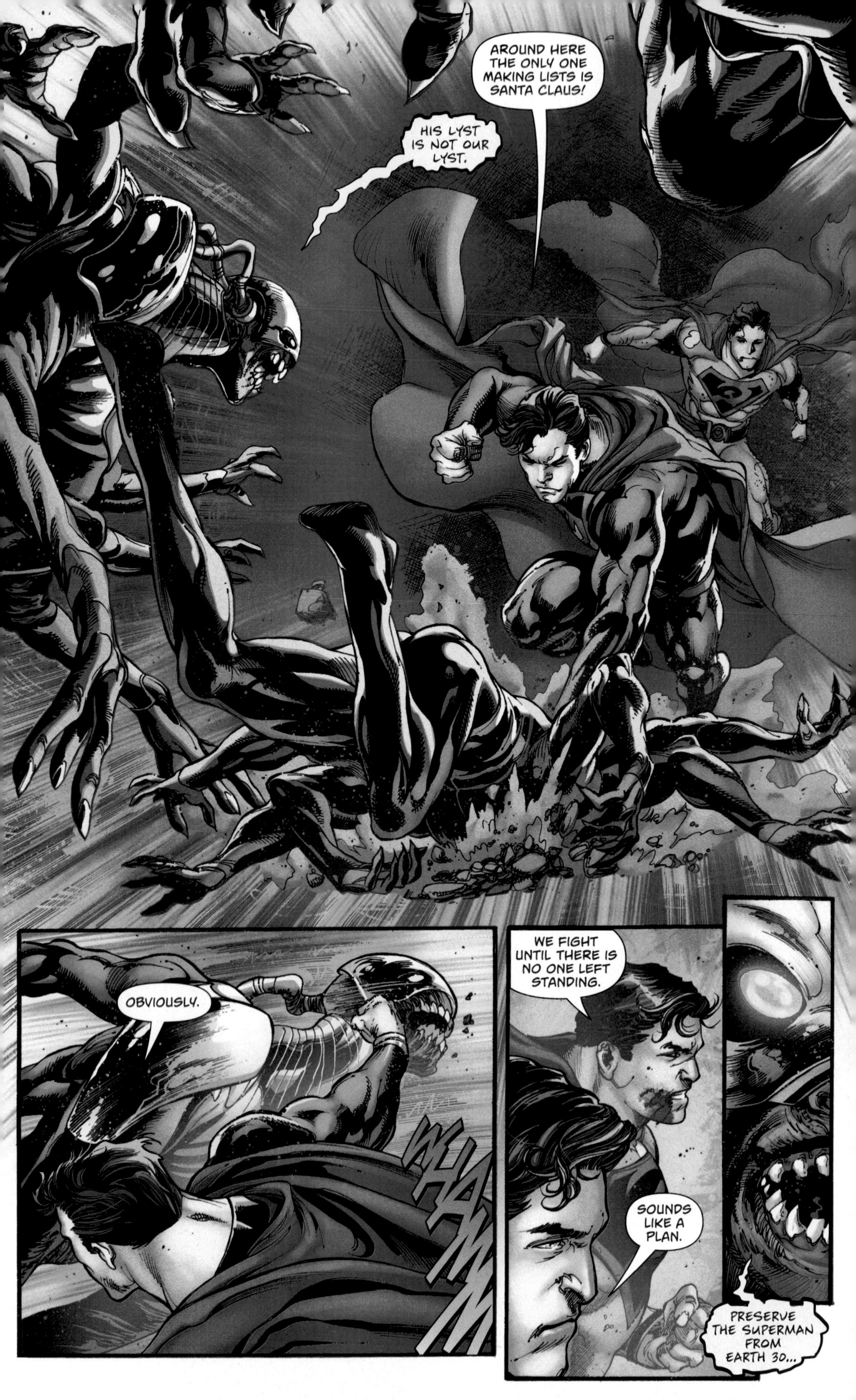
AROUND HERE THE ONLY ONE MAKING LISTS IS SANTA CLAUS!
HIS LYST IS NOT OUR LYST.
OBVIOUSLY.
WHAM
WE FIGHT UNTIL THERE IS NO ONE LEFT STANDING.
SOUNDS LIKE A PLAN.
PRESERVE THE SUPERMAN FROM EARTH 30...

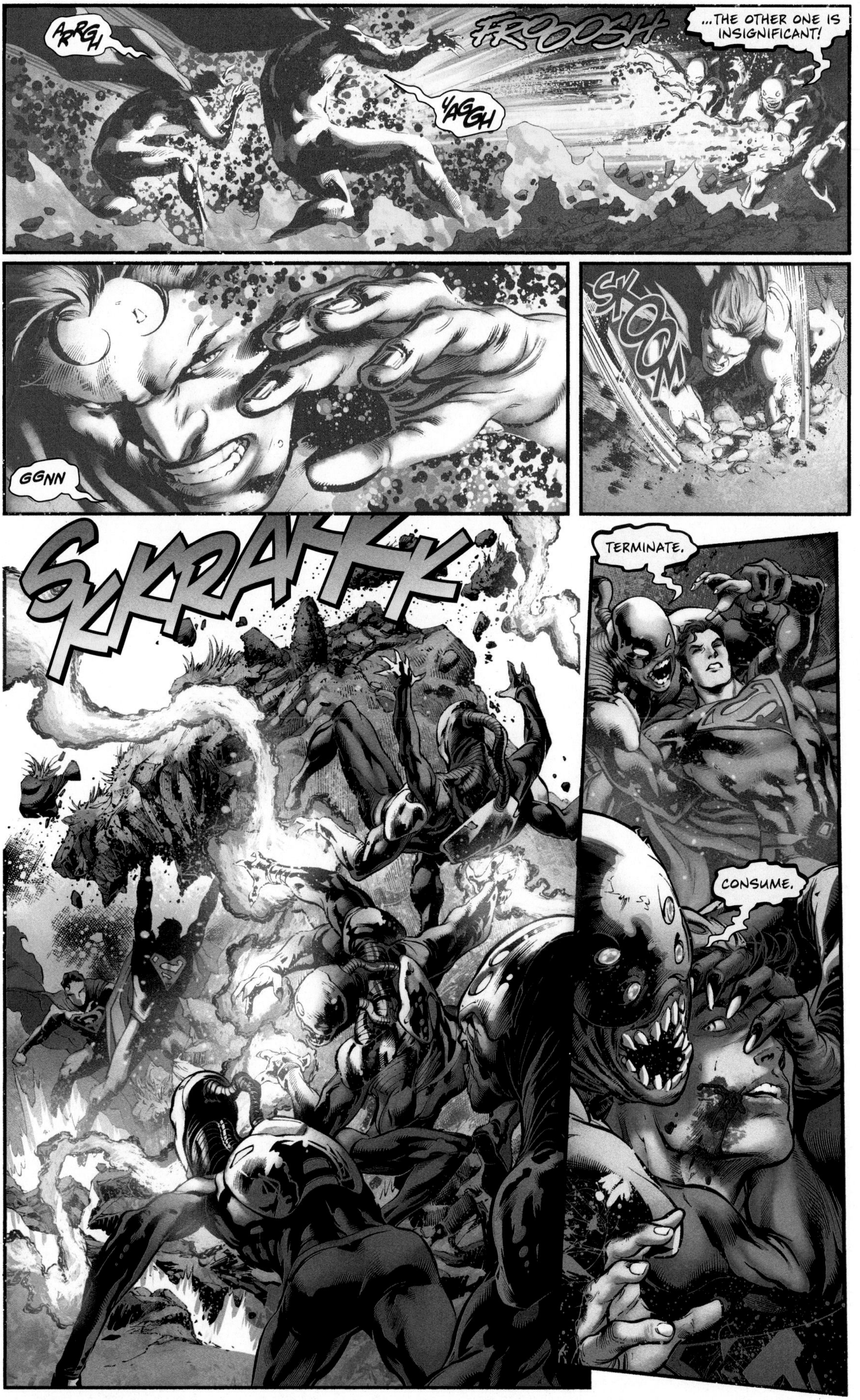
ARRGH
FROOOSH
...THE OTHER ONE IS INSIGNIFICANT!
YAGGH
GGNN
SKOOM
SKRAKK
TERMINATE.
CONSUME.

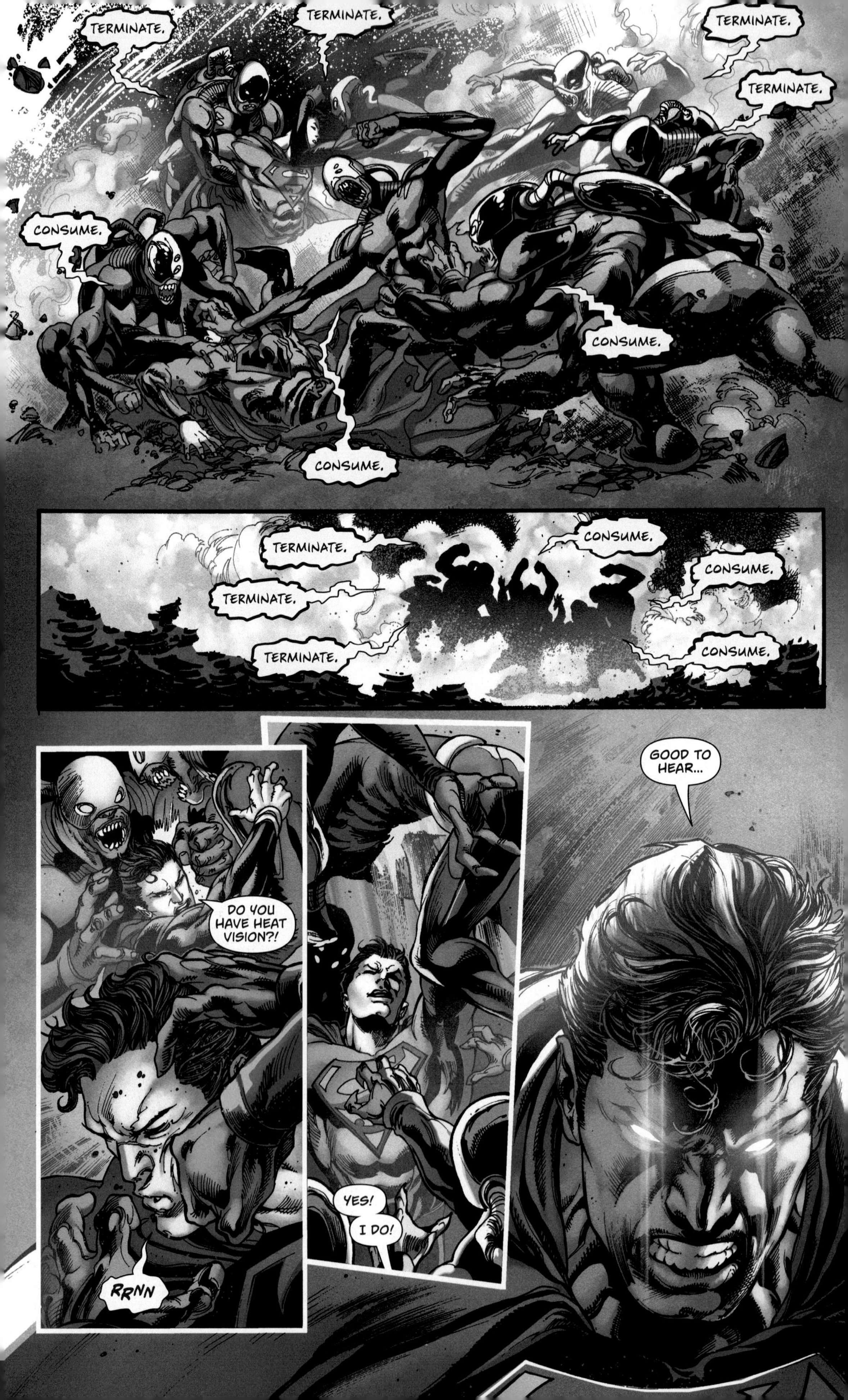
TERMINATE.
TERMINATE.
TERMINATE.
TERMINATE.
CONSUME.
CONSUME.
CONSUME.
TERMINATE.
CONSUME.
TERMINATE.
CONSUME.
TERMINATE.
CONSUME.
DO YOU HAVE HEAT VISION?!
RRNN
YES!
I DO!
GOOD TO HEAR...

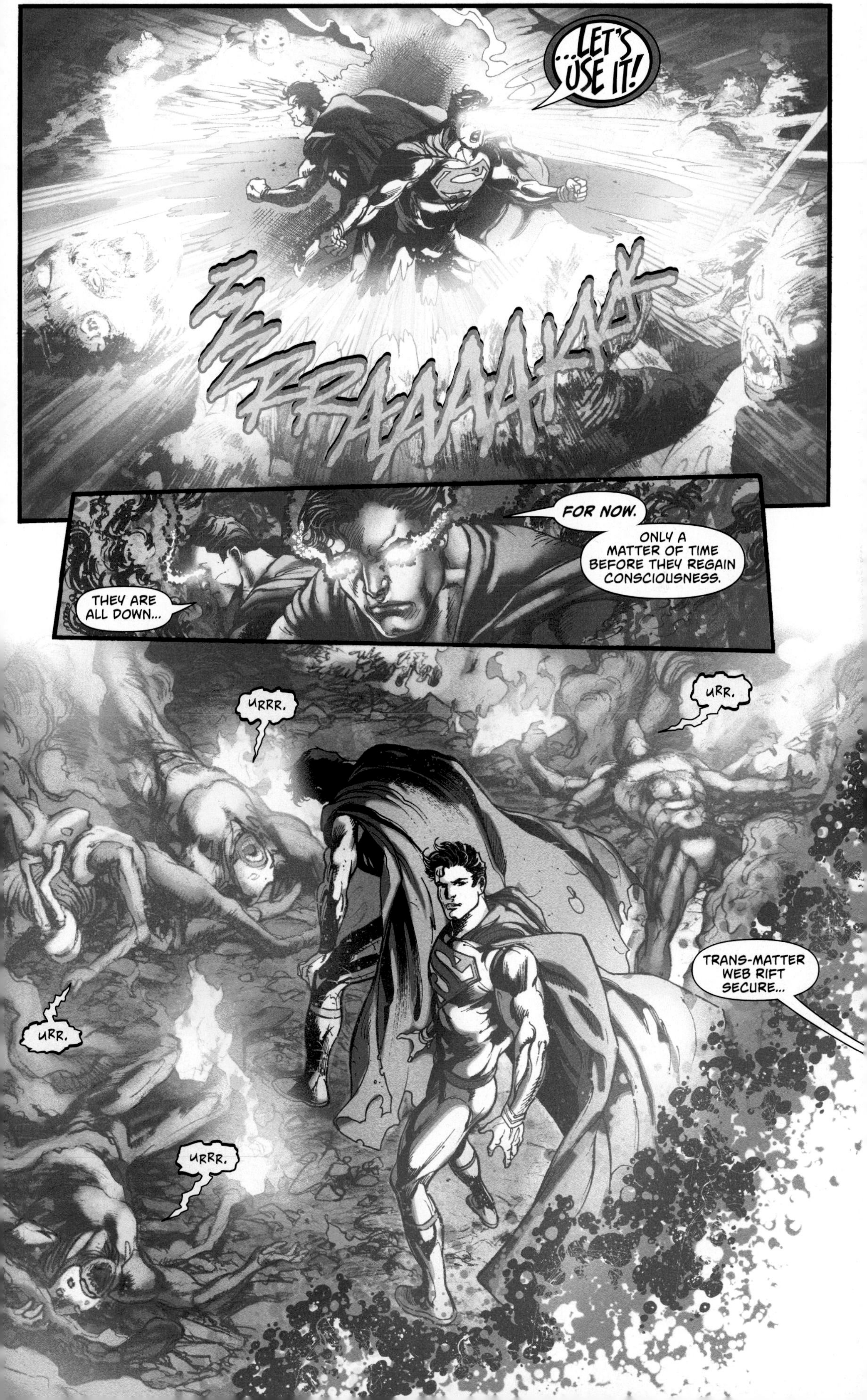
...LET'S USE IT!
ZZRRAAAAKK
THEY ARE ALL DOWN...
FOR NOW.
ONLY A MATTER OF TIME BEFORE THEY REGAIN CONSCIOUSNESS.
URRR.
URR.
URR.
URRR.
TRANS-MATTER WEB RIFT SECURE...

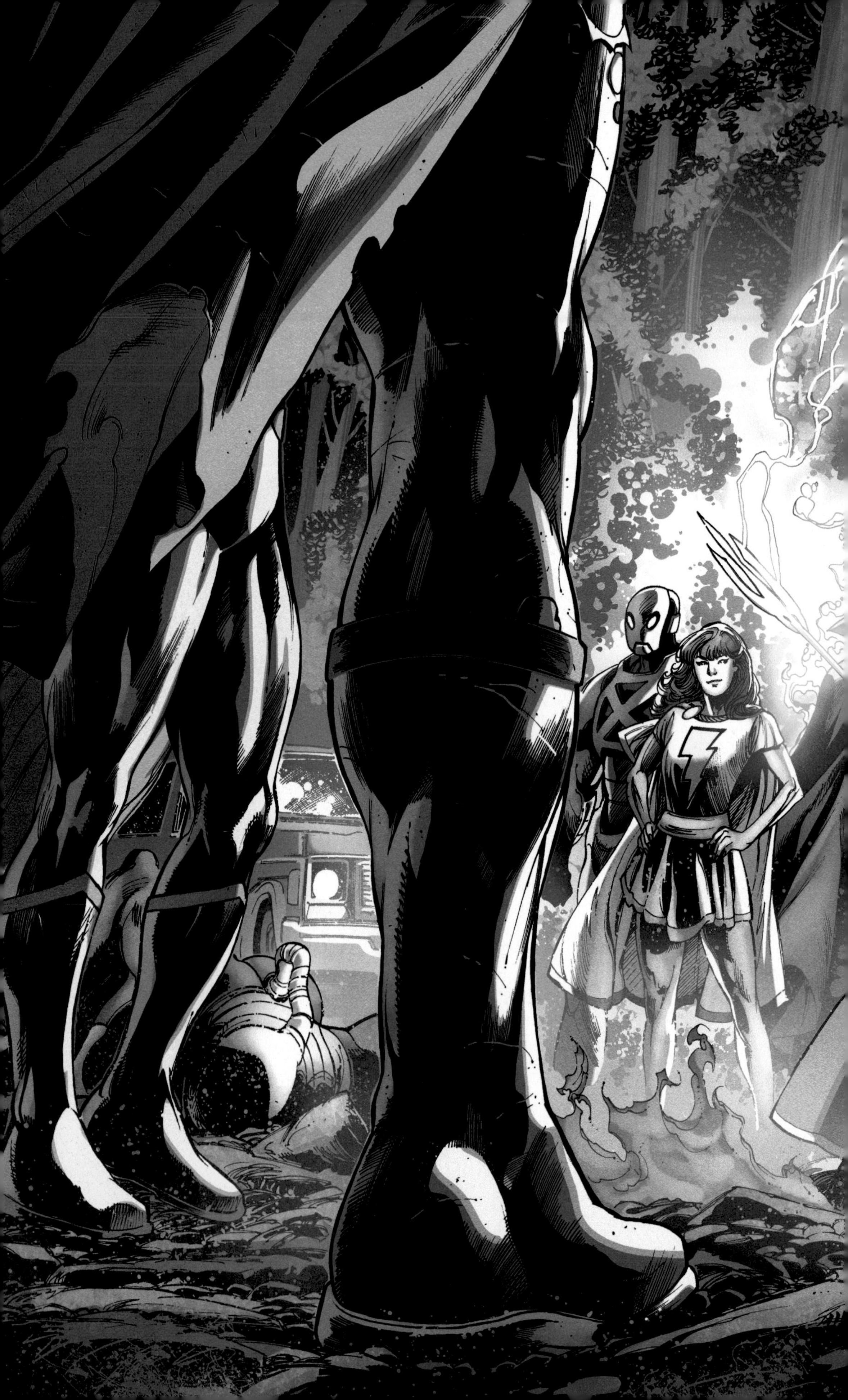

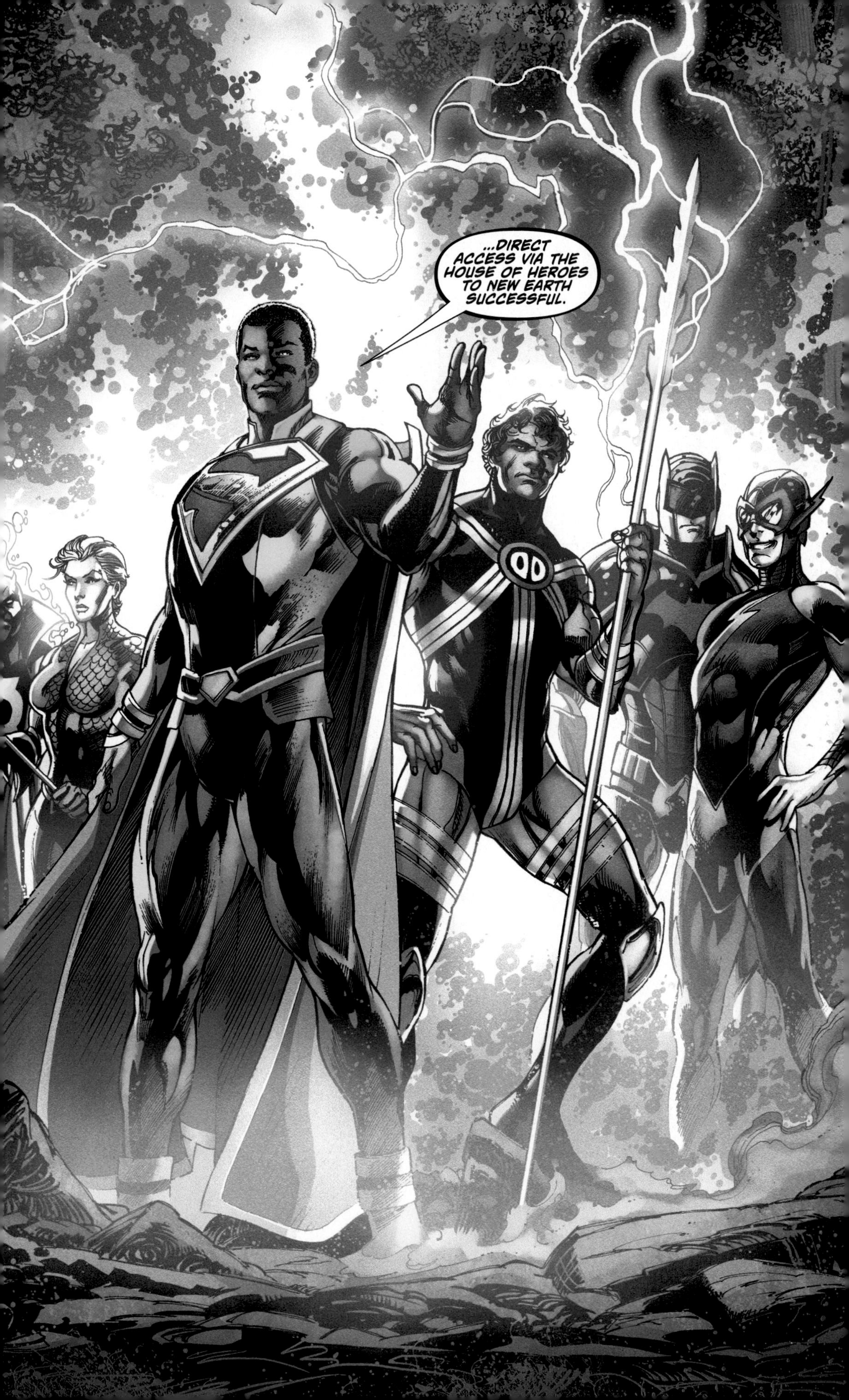
...DIRECT ACCESS VIA THE HOUSE OF HEROES TO NEW EARTH SUCCESSFUL.

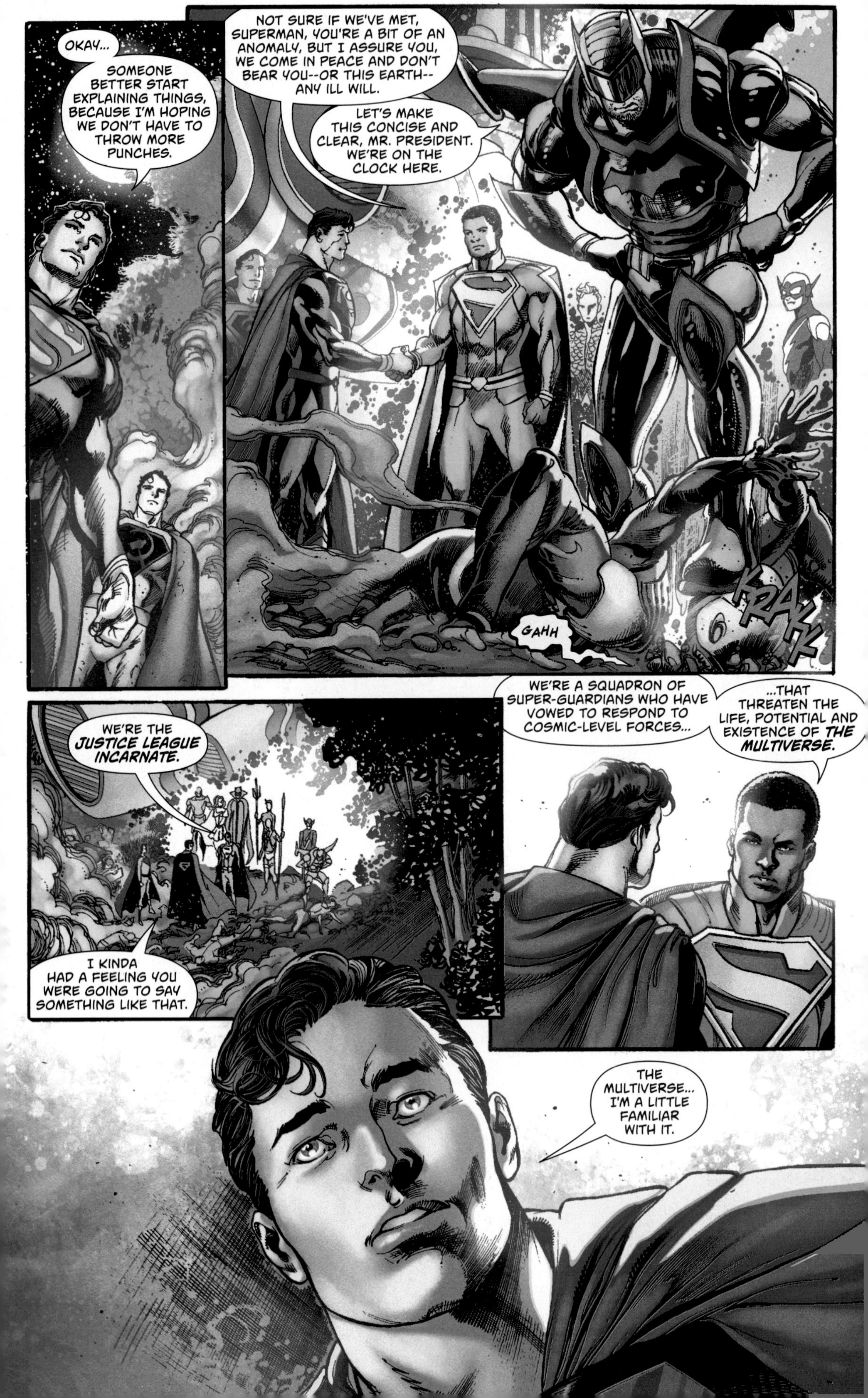
OKAY...
SOMEONE BETTER START EXPLAINING THINGS, BECAUSE I'M HOPING WE DON'T HAVE TO THROW MORE PUNCHES.
NOT SURE IF WE'VE MET, SUPERMAN, YOU'RE A BIT OF AN ANOMALY, BUT I ASSURE YOU, WE COME IN PEACE AND DON'T BEAR YOU--OR THIS EARTH--ANY ILL WILL.
LET'S MAKE THIS CONCISE AND CLEAR, MR. PRESIDENT. WE'RE ON THE CLOCK HERE.
GAHH
KRAKK
WE'RE THE JUSTICE LEAGUE INCARNATE.
I KINDA HAD A FEELING YOU WERE GOING TO SAY SOMETHING LIKE THAT.
WE'RE A SQUADRON OF SUPER-GUARDIANS WHO HAVE VOWED TO RESPOND TO COSMIC-LEVEL FORCES...
...THAT THREATEN THE LIFE, POTENTIAL AND EXISTENCE OF THE MULTIVERSE.
THE MULTIVERSE... I'M A LITTLE FAMILIAR WITH IT.

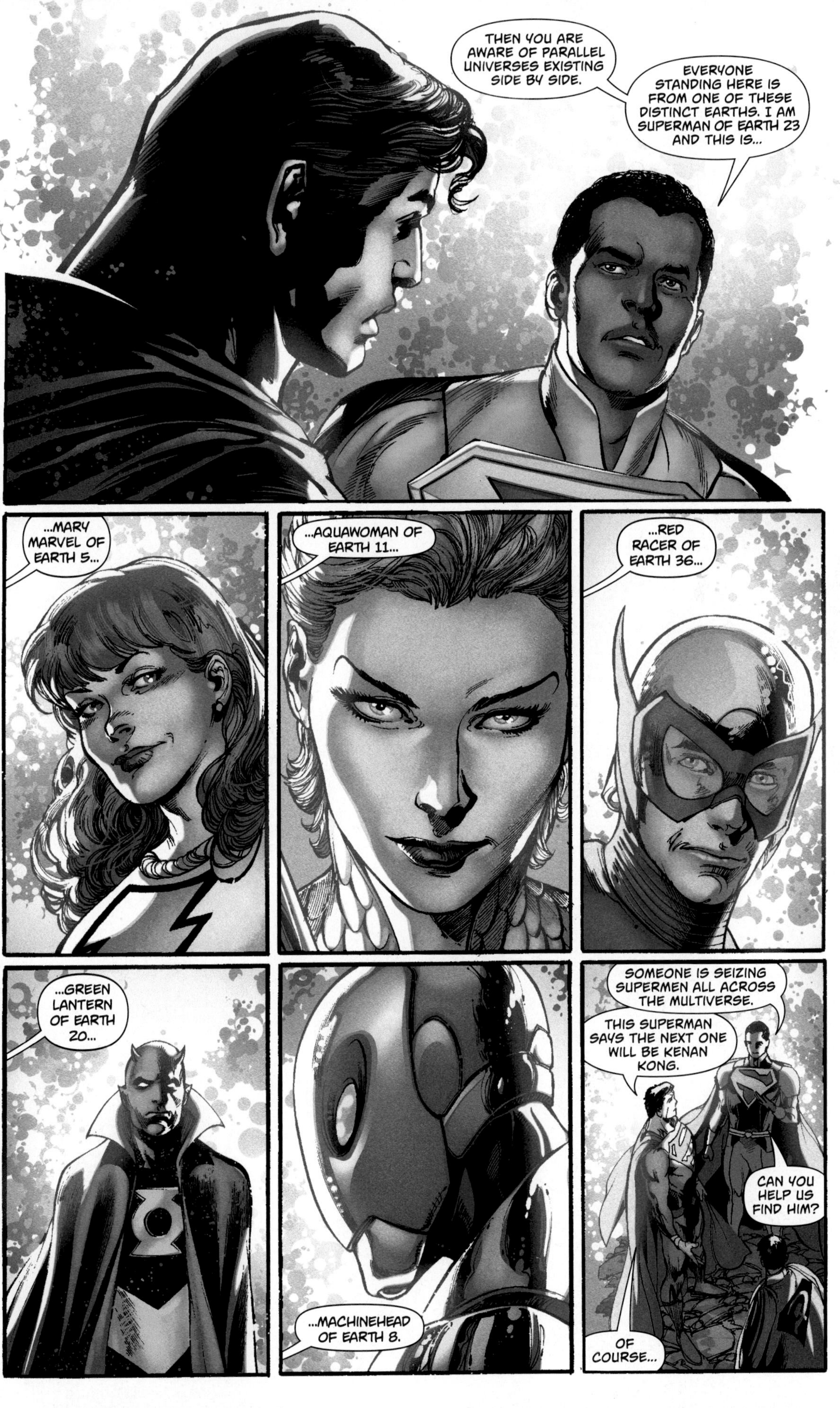
THEN YOU ARE AWARE OF PARALLEL UNIVERSES EXISTING SIDE BY SIDE.
EVERYONE STANDING HERE IS FROM ONE OF THESE DISTINCT EARTHS. I AM SUPERMAN OF EARTH 23 AND THIS IS...
...MARY MARVEL OF EARTH 5...
...AQUAWOMAN OF EARTH 11...
...RED RACER OF EARTH 36...
...GREEN LANTERN OF EARTH 20...
...MACHINEHEAD OF EARTH 8.
SOMEONE IS SEIZING SUPERMEN ALL ACROSS THE MULTIVERSE.
THIS SUPERMAN SAYS THE NEXT ONE WILL BE KENAN KONG.
CAN YOU HELP US FIND HIM?
OF COURSE...

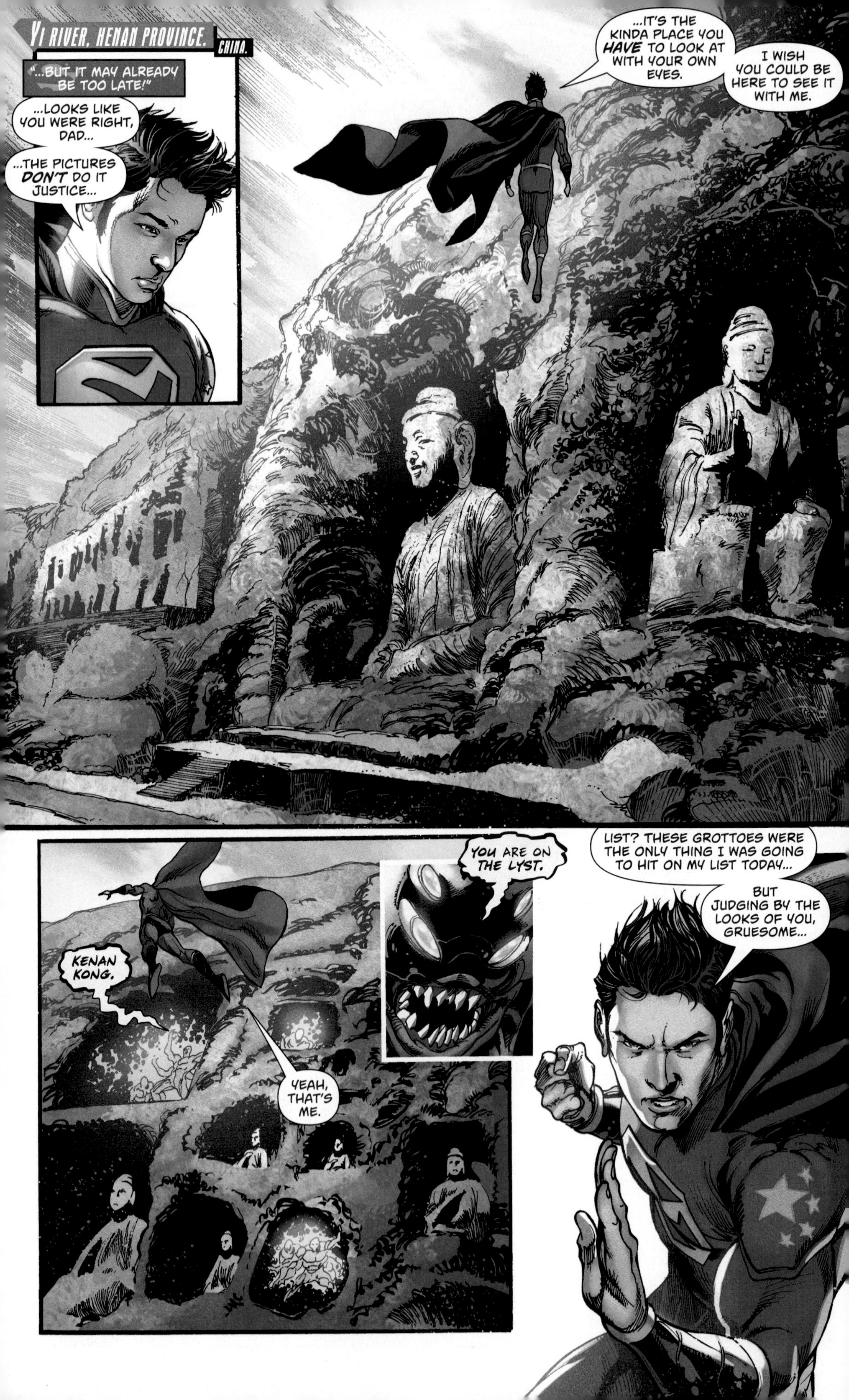
YI RIVER, HENAN PROVINCE.
CHINA.
"...BUT IT MAY ALREADY BE TOO LATE!"
...LOOKS LIKE YOU WERE RIGHT, DAD...
...THE PICTURES DON'T DO IT JUSTICE...
...IT'S THE KINDA PLACE YOU HAVE TO LOOK AT WITH YOUR OWN EYES.
I WISH YOU COULD BE HERE TO SEE IT WITH ME.
KENAN KONG.
YEAH, THAT'S ME.
YOU ARE ON THE LYST.
LIST? THESE GROTTOES WERE THE ONLY THING I WAS GOING TO HIT ON MY LIST TODAY...
BUT JUDGING BY THE LOOKS OF YOU, GRUESOME...

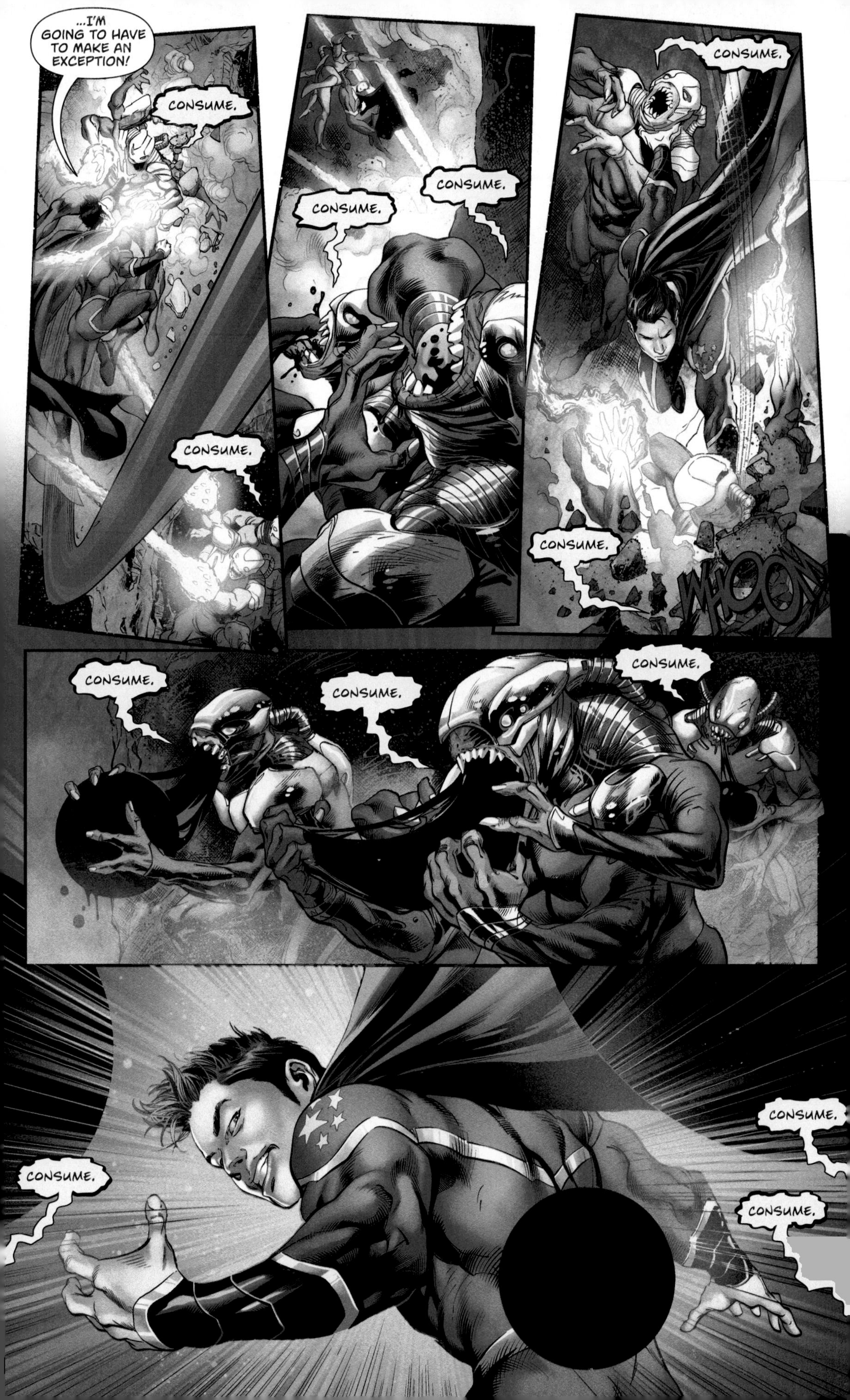

...I'M GOING TO HAVE TO MAKE AN EXCEPTION!
CONSUME.
CONSUME.
CONSUME.
CONSUME.
CONSUME.
CONSUME.
WHOOM
CONSUME.
CONSUME.
CONSUME.
CONSUME.
CONSUME.
CONSUME.

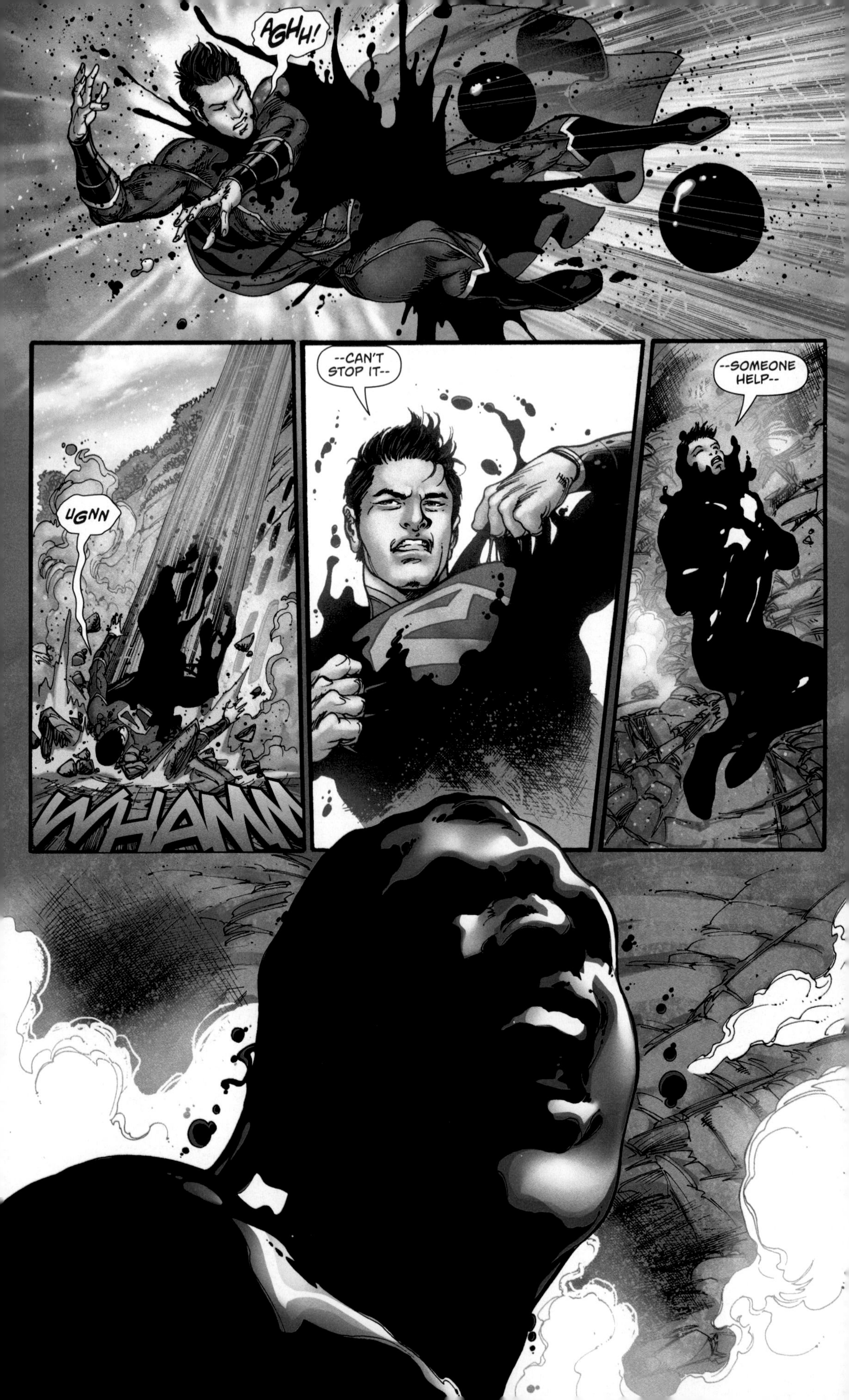
AGHH!
UGNN
WHAMM
--CAN'T STOP IT--
--SOMEONE HELP--

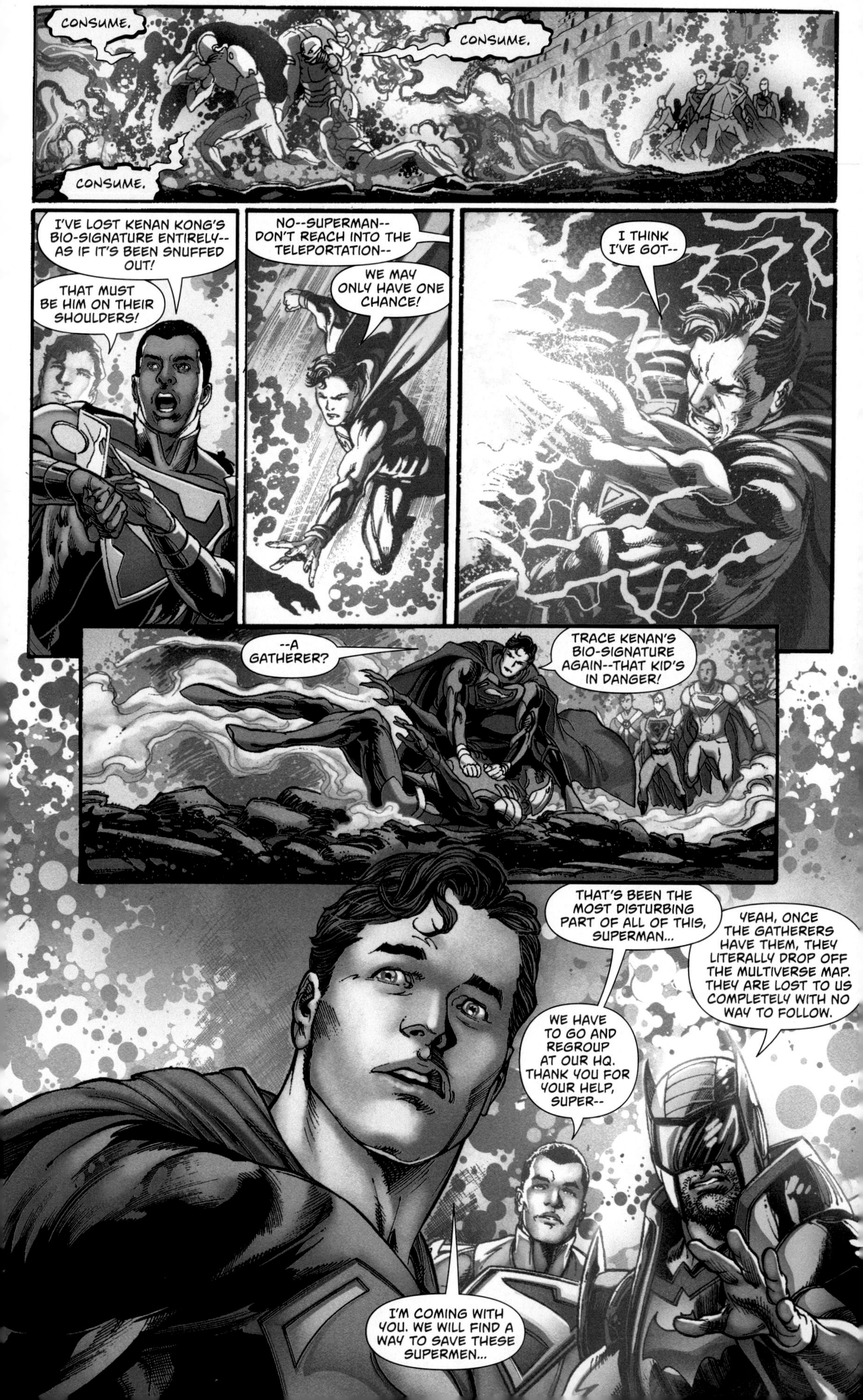

CONSUME.
CONSUME.
CONSUME.
I'VE LOST KENAN KONG'S BIO-SIGNATURE ENTIRELY--AS IF IT'S BEEN SNUFFED OUT!
THAT MUST BE HIM ON THEIR SHOULDERS!
NO--SUPERMAN--DON'T REACH INTO THE TELEPORTATION--
WE MAY ONLY HAVE ONE CHANCE!
I THINK I'VE GOT--
--A GATHERER?
TRACE KENAN'S BIO-SIGNATURE AGAIN--THAT KID'S IN DANGER!
THAT'S BEEN THE MOST DISTURBING PART OF ALL OF THIS, SUPERMAN...
YEAH, ONCE THE GATHERERS HAVE THEM, THEY LITERALLY DROP OFF THE MULTIVERSE MAP. THEY ARE LOST TO US COMPLETELY WITH NO WAY TO FOLLOW.
WE HAVE TO GO AND REGROUP AT OUR HQ. THANK YOU FOR YOUR HELP, SUPER--
I'M COMING WITH YOU. WE WILL FIND A WAY TO SAVE THESE SUPERMEN...

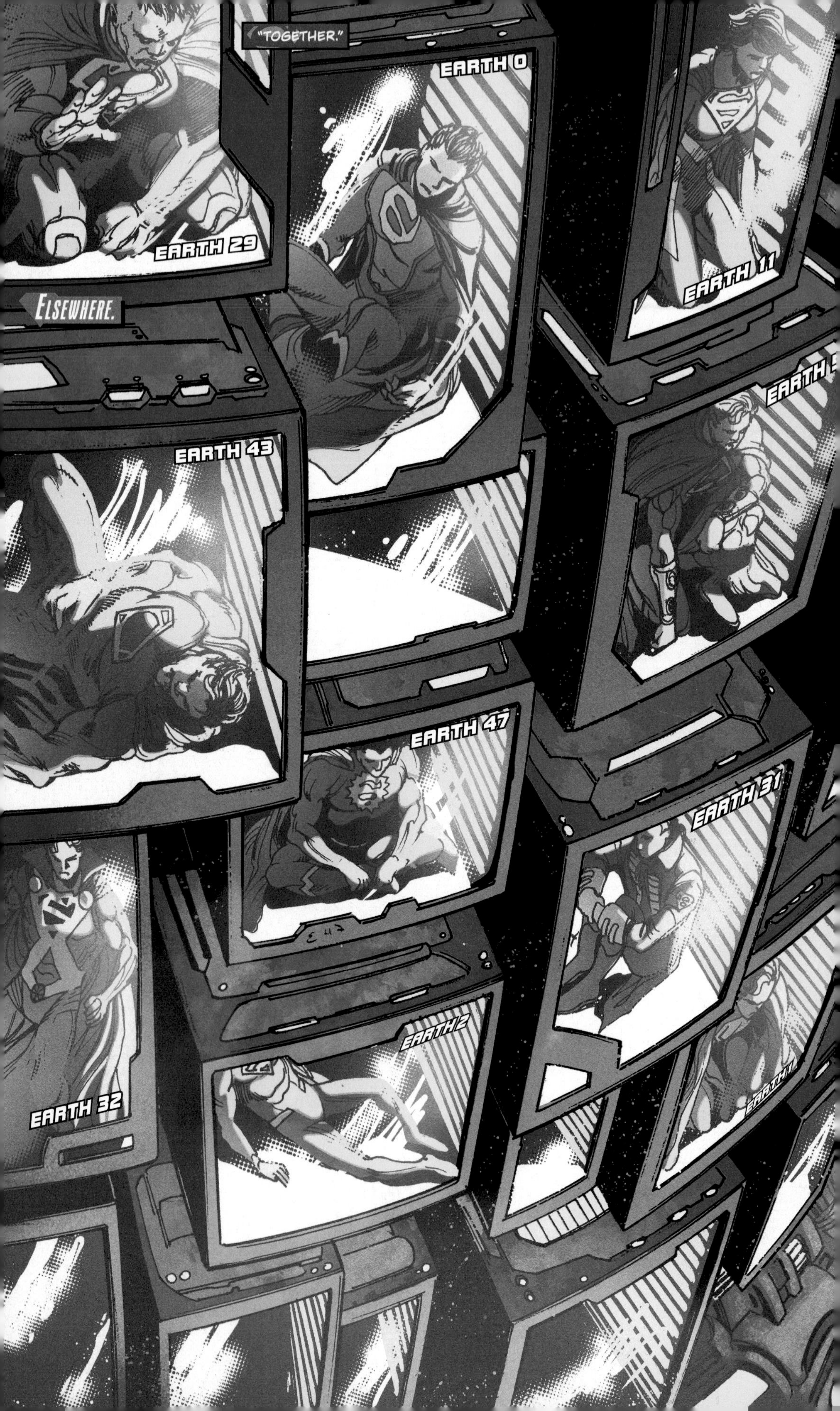

"TOGETHER."
EARTH 29
EARTH 0
EARTH 11
ELSEWHERE.
EARTH
EARTH 43
EARTH 47
EARTH 31
EARTH 32
EARTH 2
EARTH

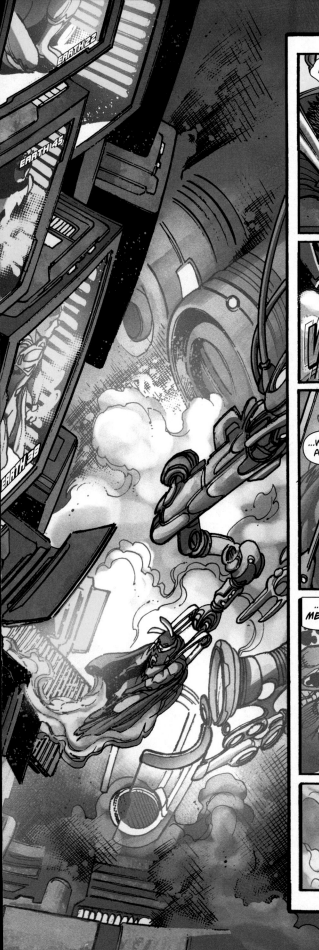

EARTH 22

EARTH 45

EARTH 38

UNN

KKAKK

...WHAT'S HAPPENING...

VMMMMMMMMA

...WHERE AM I?

BAM BAM

WHAT ARE YOU DOING...

...TO MEEEEEEEEE!

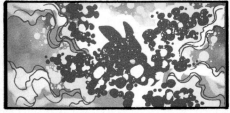

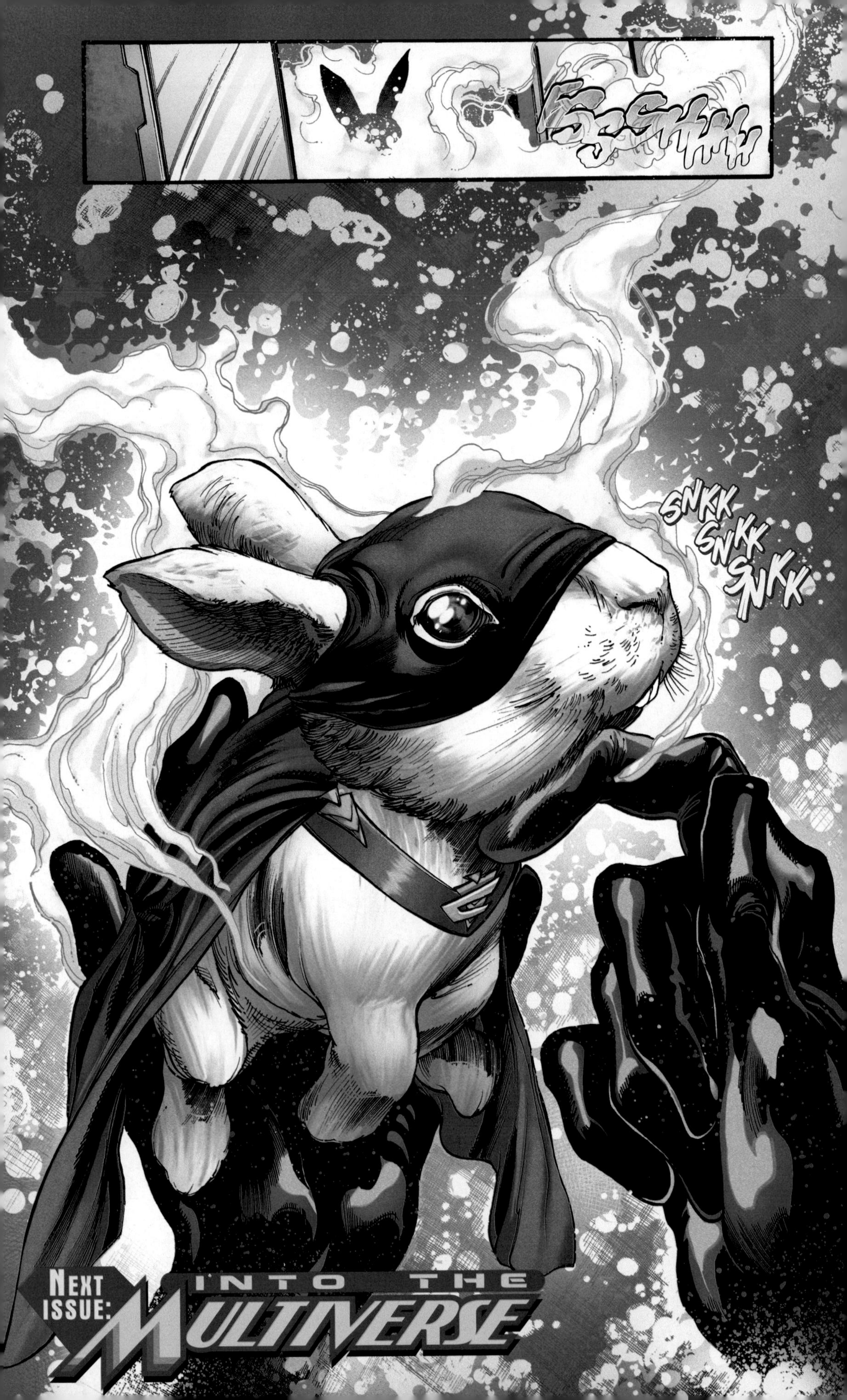

FSSSHHH
SNKK
SNKK
SNKK
NEXT ISSUE: INTO THE MULTIVERSE

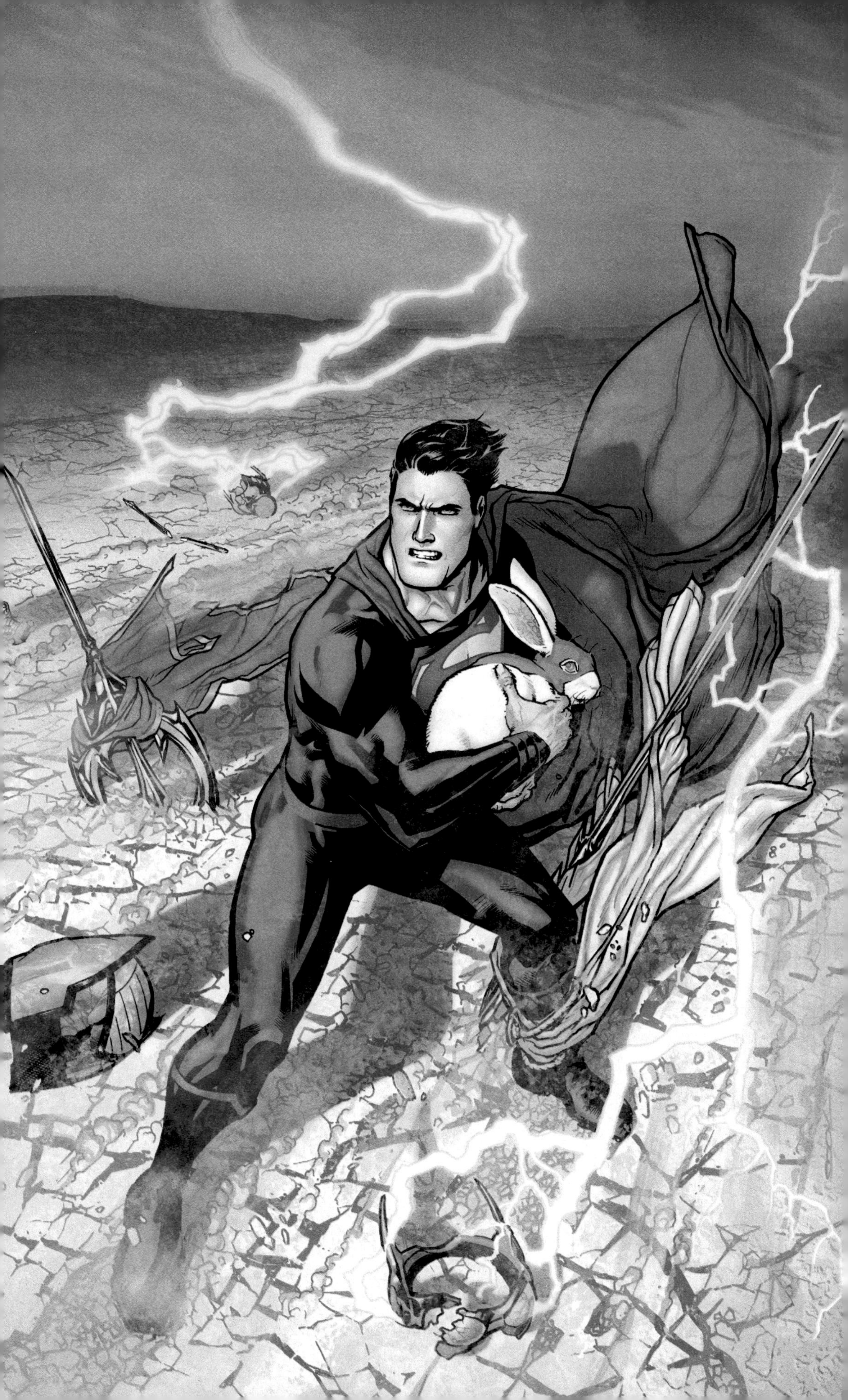

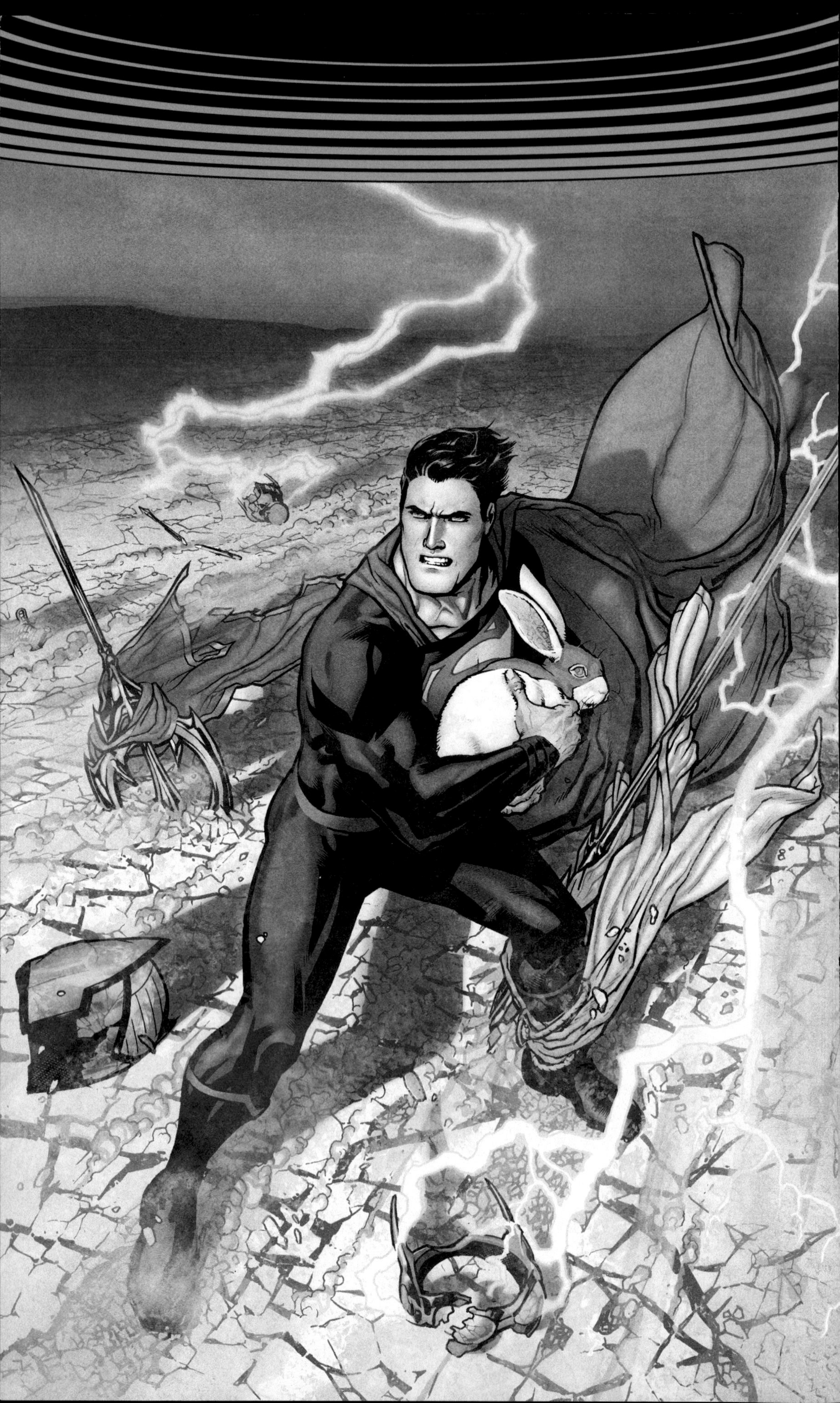

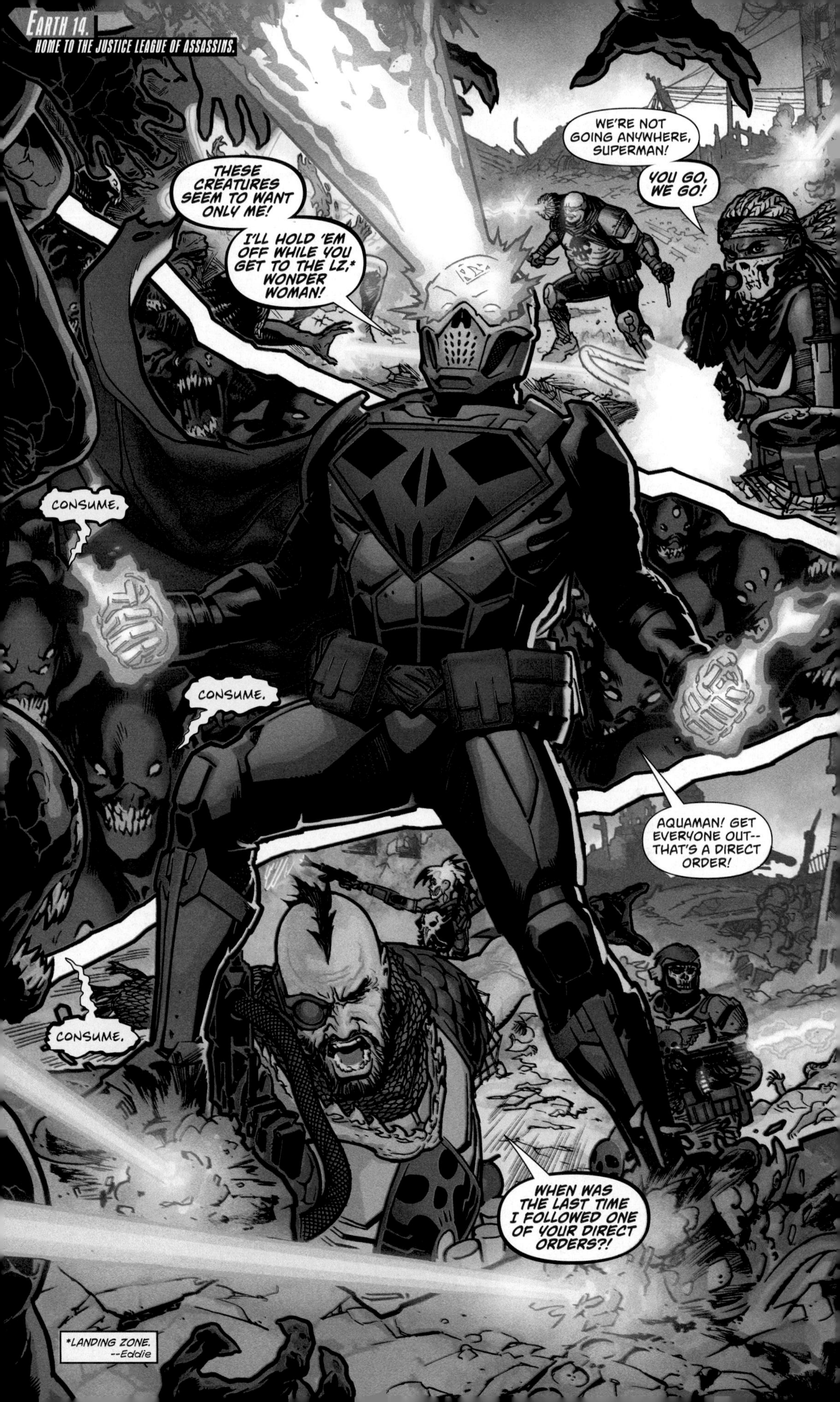
EARTH 14.
HOME TO THE JUSTICE LEAGUE OF ASSASSINS.
THESE CREATURES SEEM TO WANT ONLY ME!
I'LL HOLD 'EM OFF WHILE YOU GET TO THE LZ,* WONDER WOMAN!
WE'RE NOT GOING ANYWHERE, SUPERMAN!
YOU GO, WE GO!
CONSUME.
CONSUME.
AQUAMAN! GET EVERYONE OUT-- THAT'S A DIRECT ORDER!
CONSUME.
WHEN WAS THE LAST TIME I FOLLOWED ONE OF YOUR DIRECT ORDERS?!
*LANDING ZONE. --Eddie

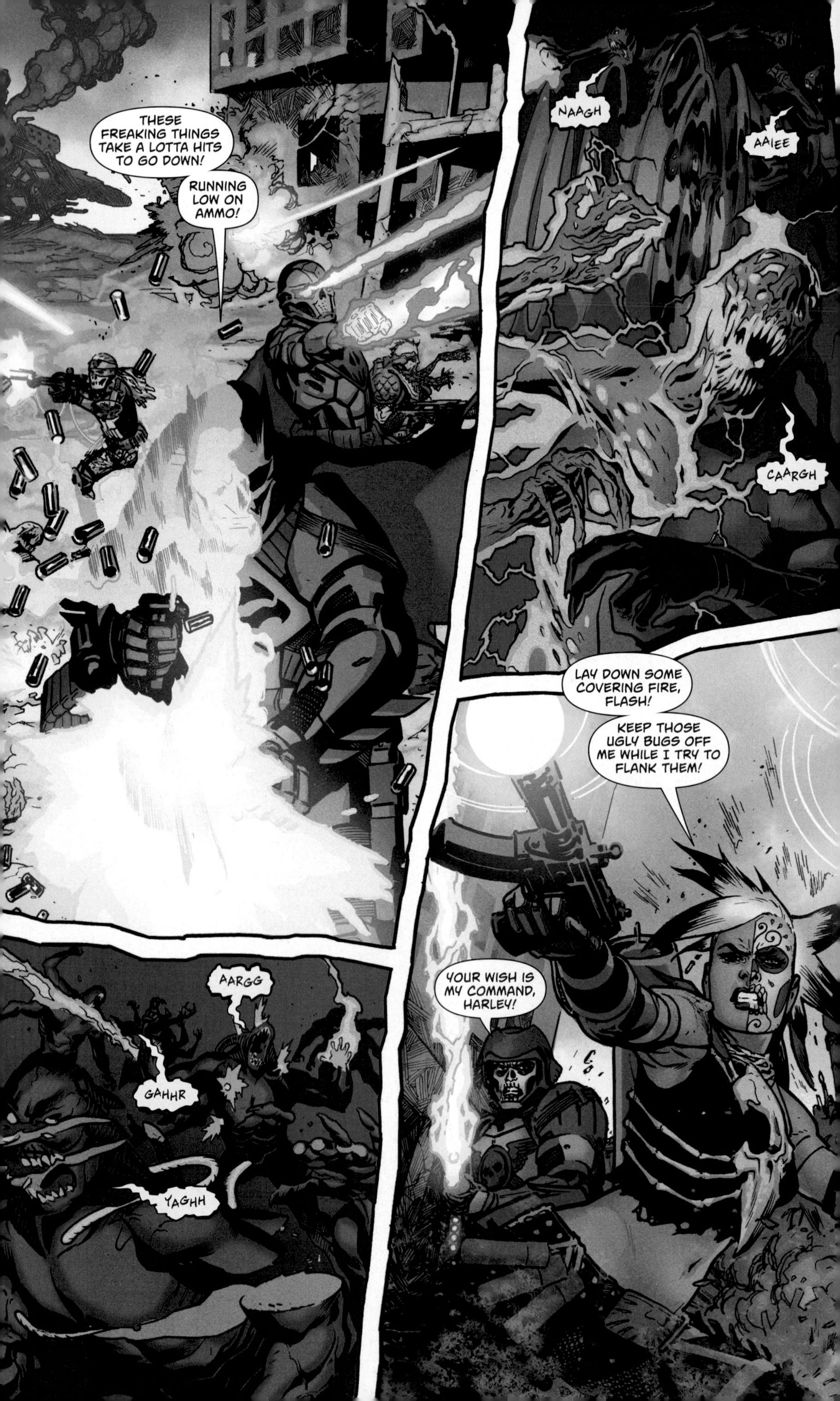

THESE FREAKING THINGS TAKE A LOTTA HITS TO GO DOWN!
RUNNING LOW ON AMMO!
NAAGH
AAIEE
CAARGH
AARGG
GAHHR
YAGHH
LAY DOWN SOME COVERING FIRE, FLASH!
KEEP THOSE UGLY BUGS OFF ME WHILE I TRY TO FLANK THEM!
YOUR WISH IS MY COMMAND, HARLEY!

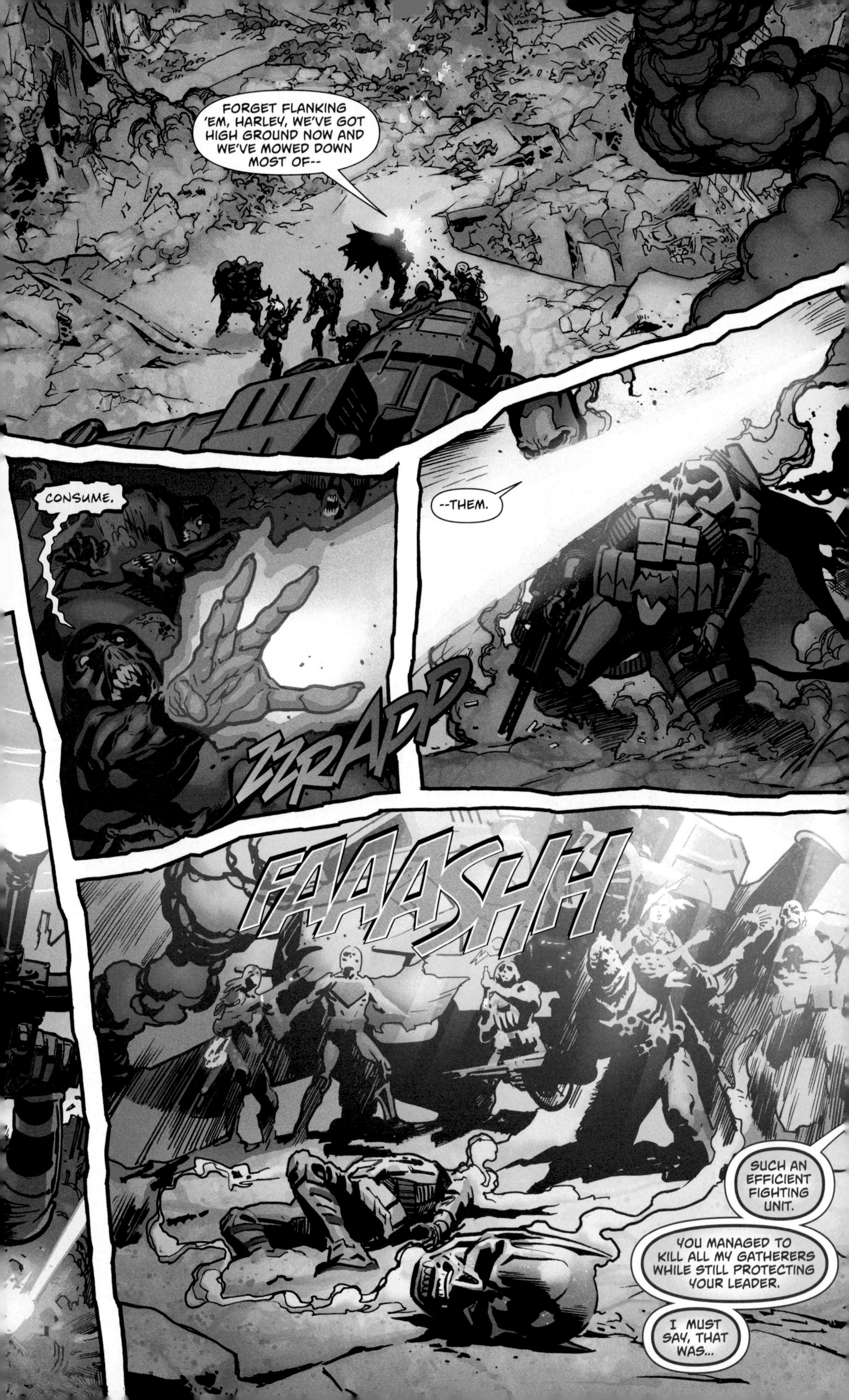
FORGET FLANKING 'EM, HARLEY, WE'VE GOT HIGH GROUND NOW AND WE'VE MOWED DOWN MOST OF--
CONSUME.
ZZRAPP
--THEM.
FAAASHH
SUCH AN EFFICIENT FIGHTING UNIT.
YOU MANAGED TO KILL ALL MY GATHERERS WHILE STILL PROTECTING YOUR LEADER.
I MUST SAY, THAT WAS...

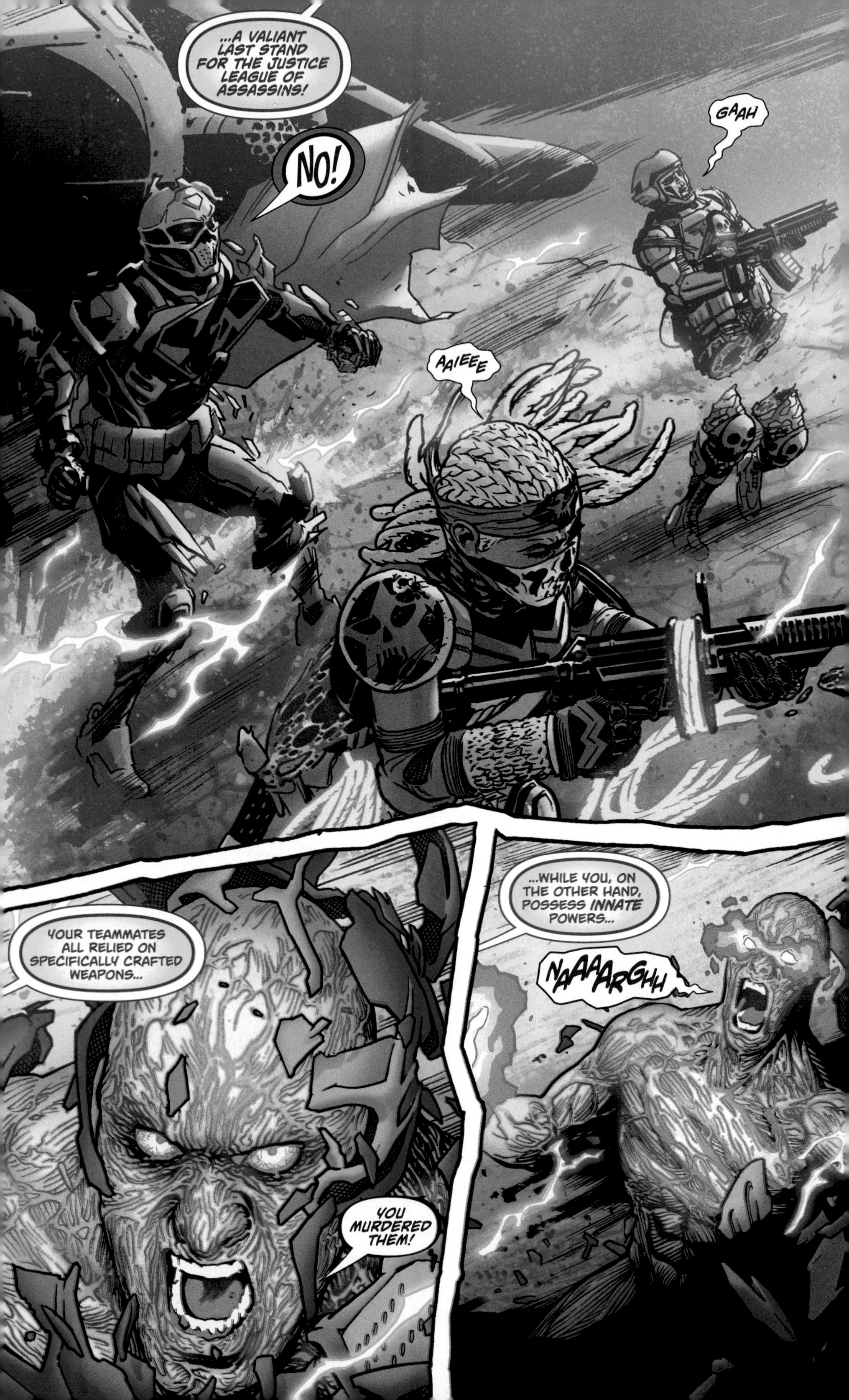
...A VALIANT LAST STAND FOR THE JUSTICE LEAGUE OF ASSASSINS!
NO!
GAAH
AAIEEE
YOUR TEAMMATES ALL RELIED ON SPECIFICALLY CRAFTED WEAPONS...
YOU MURDERED THEM!
...WHILE YOU, ON THE OTHER HAND, POSSESS *INNATE* POWERS...
NAAAARGHH

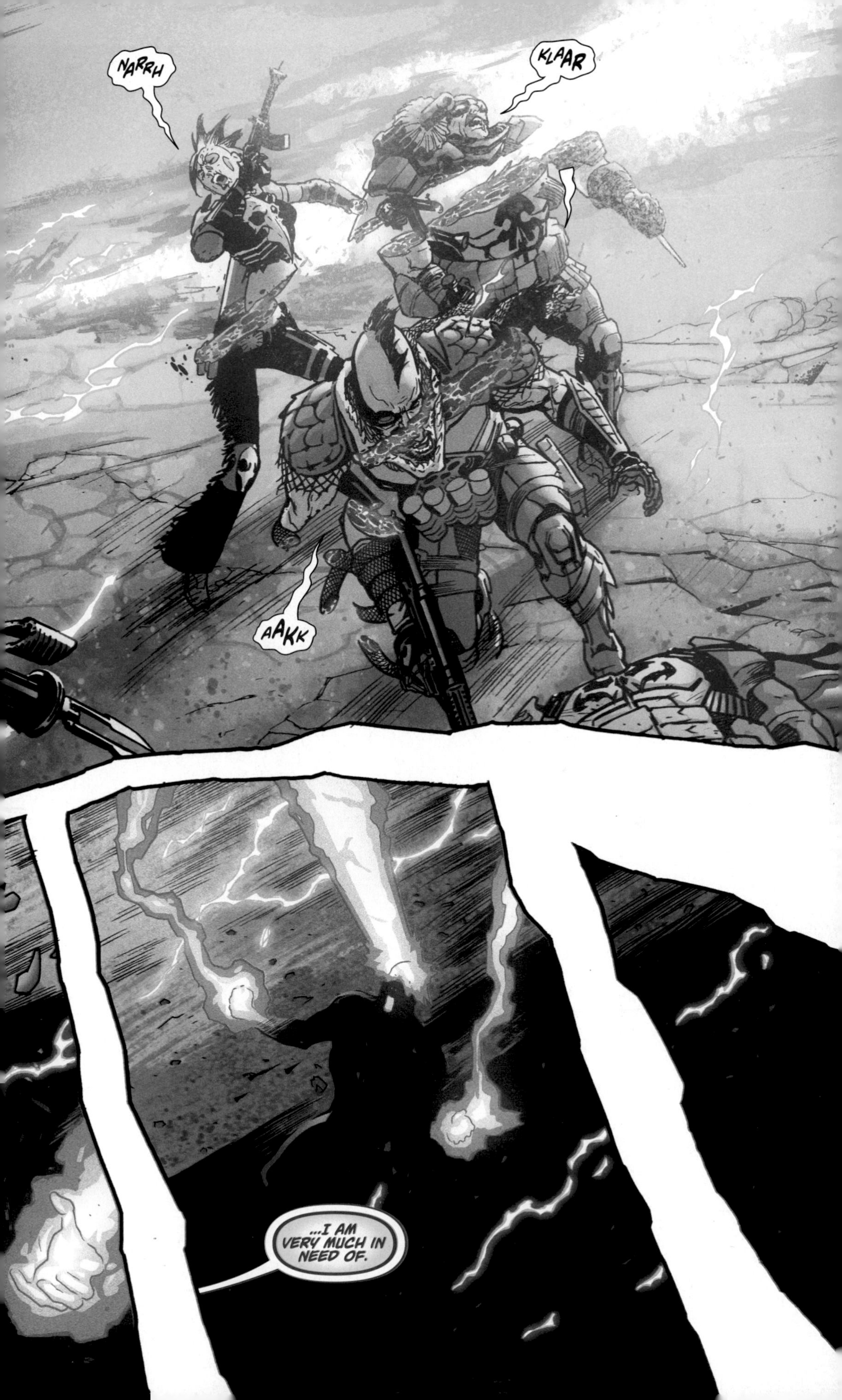
NARRH
KLAAR
AAKK
...I AM VERY MUCH IN NEED OF.

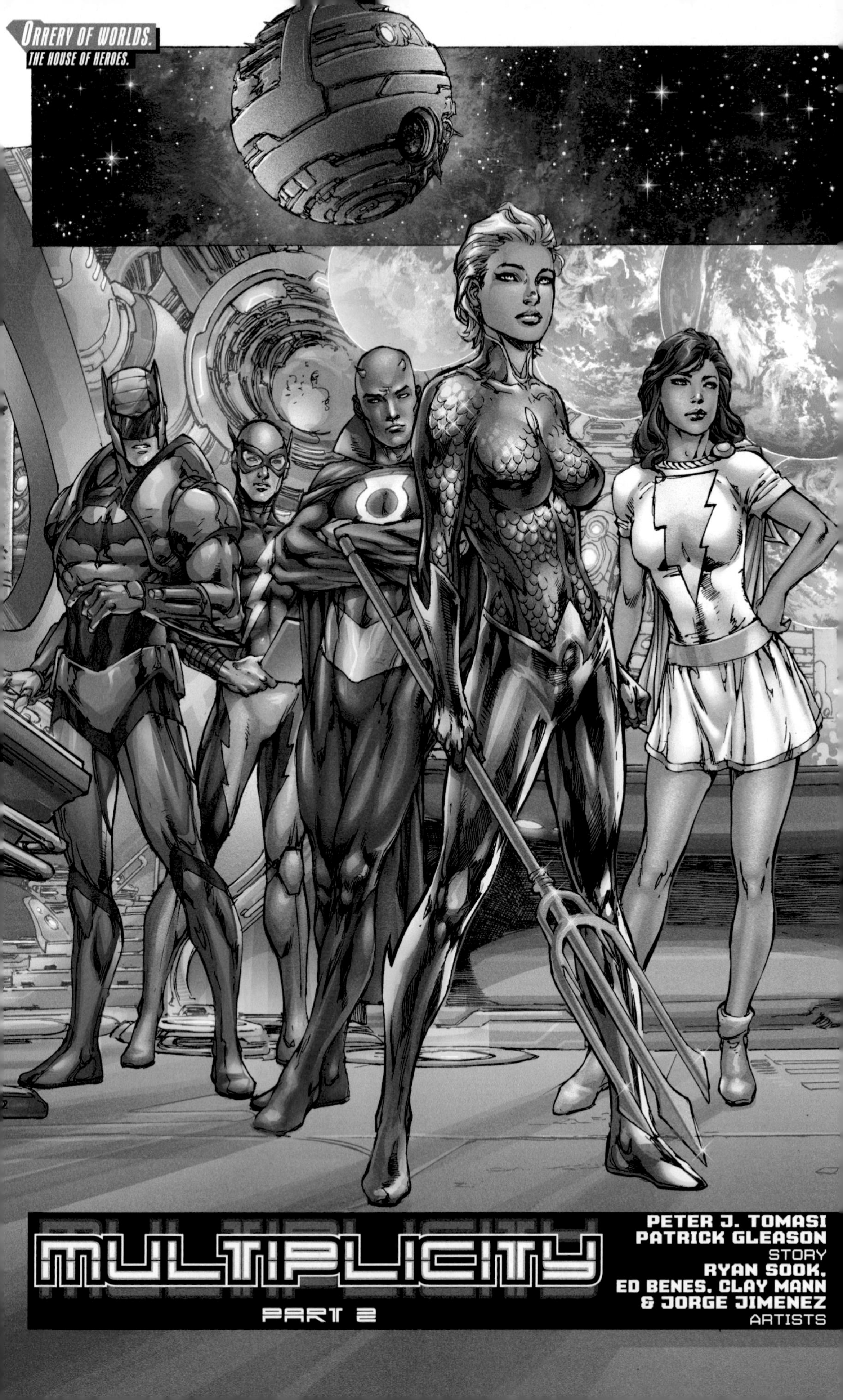
ORRERY OF WORLDS.
THE HOUSE OF HEROES.
MULTIPLICITY
PART 2
PETER J. TOMASI
PATRICK GLEASON
STORY
RYAN SOOK,
ED BENES, CLAY MANN
& JORGE JIMENEZ
ARTISTS

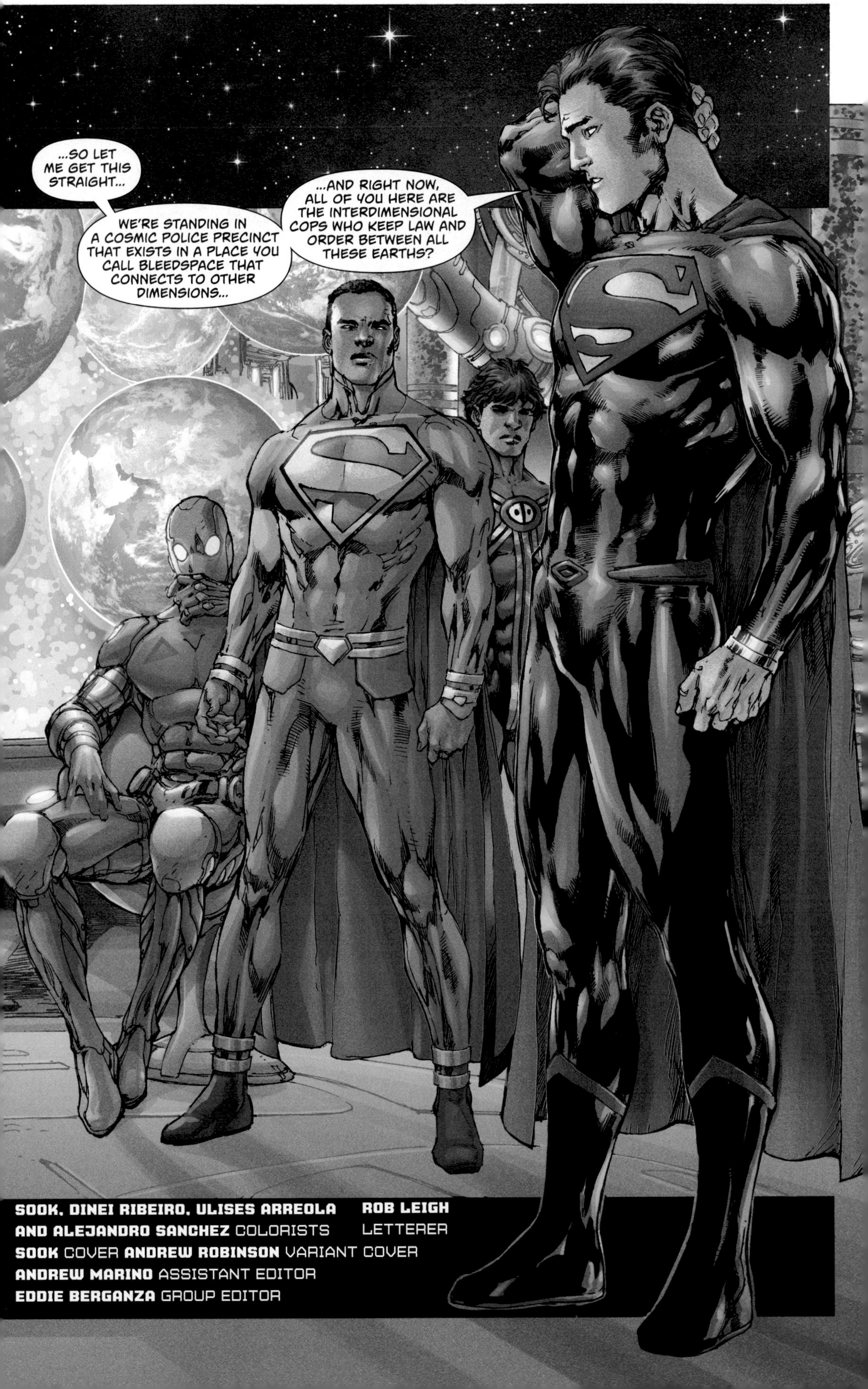
...SO LET ME GET THIS STRAIGHT...
WE'RE STANDING IN A COSMIC POLICE PRECINCT THAT EXISTS IN A PLACE YOU CALL BLEEDSPACE THAT CONNECTS TO OTHER DIMENSIONS...
...AND RIGHT NOW, ALL OF YOU HERE ARE THE INTERDIMENSIONAL COPS WHO KEEP LAW AND ORDER BETWEEN ALL THESE EARTHS?
SOOK, DINEI RIBEIRO, ULISES ARREOLA AND ALEJANDRO SANCHEZ COLORISTS
ROB LEIGH LETTERER
SOOK COVER **ANDREW ROBINSON** VARIANT COVER
ANDREW MARINO ASSISTANT EDITOR
EDDIE BERGANZA GROUP EDITOR

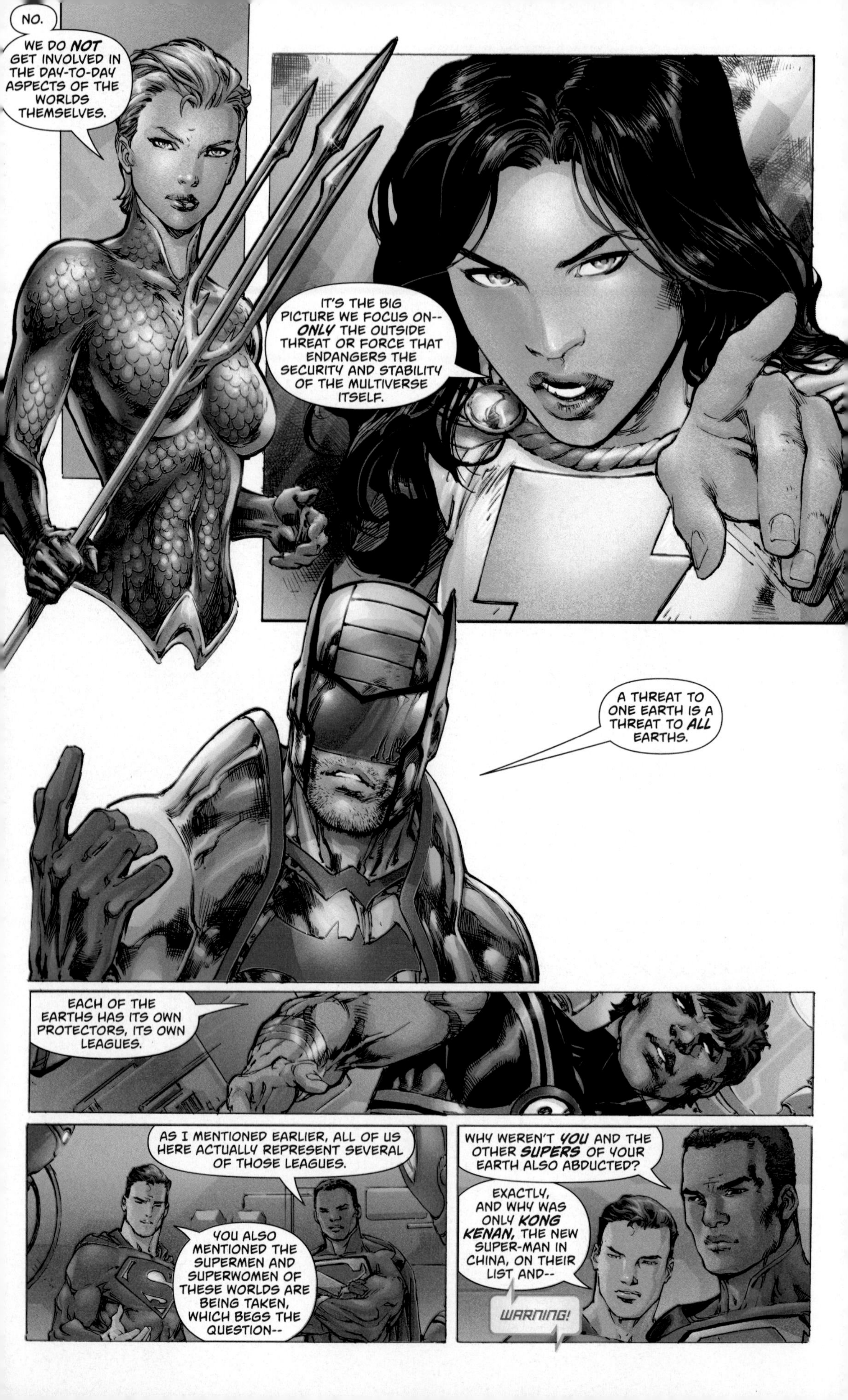
NO.
WE DO NOT GET INVOLVED IN THE DAY-TO-DAY ASPECTS OF THE WORLDS THEMSELVES.
IT'S THE BIG PICTURE WE FOCUS ON--ONLY THE OUTSIDE THREAT OR FORCE THAT ENDANGERS THE SECURITY AND STABILITY OF THE MULTIVERSE ITSELF.
A THREAT TO ONE EARTH IS A THREAT TO ALL EARTHS.
EACH OF THE EARTHS HAS ITS OWN PROTECTORS, ITS OWN LEAGUES.
AS I MENTIONED EARLIER, ALL OF US HERE ACTUALLY REPRESENT SEVERAL OF THOSE LEAGUES.
YOU ALSO MENTIONED THE SUPERMEN AND SUPERWOMEN OF THESE WORLDS ARE BEING TAKEN, WHICH BEGS THE QUESTION--
WHY WEREN'T YOU AND THE OTHER SUPERS OF YOUR EARTH ALSO ABDUCTED?
EXACTLY, AND WHY WAS ONLY KONG KENAN, THE NEW SUPER-MAN IN CHINA, ON THEIR LIST AND--
WARNING!

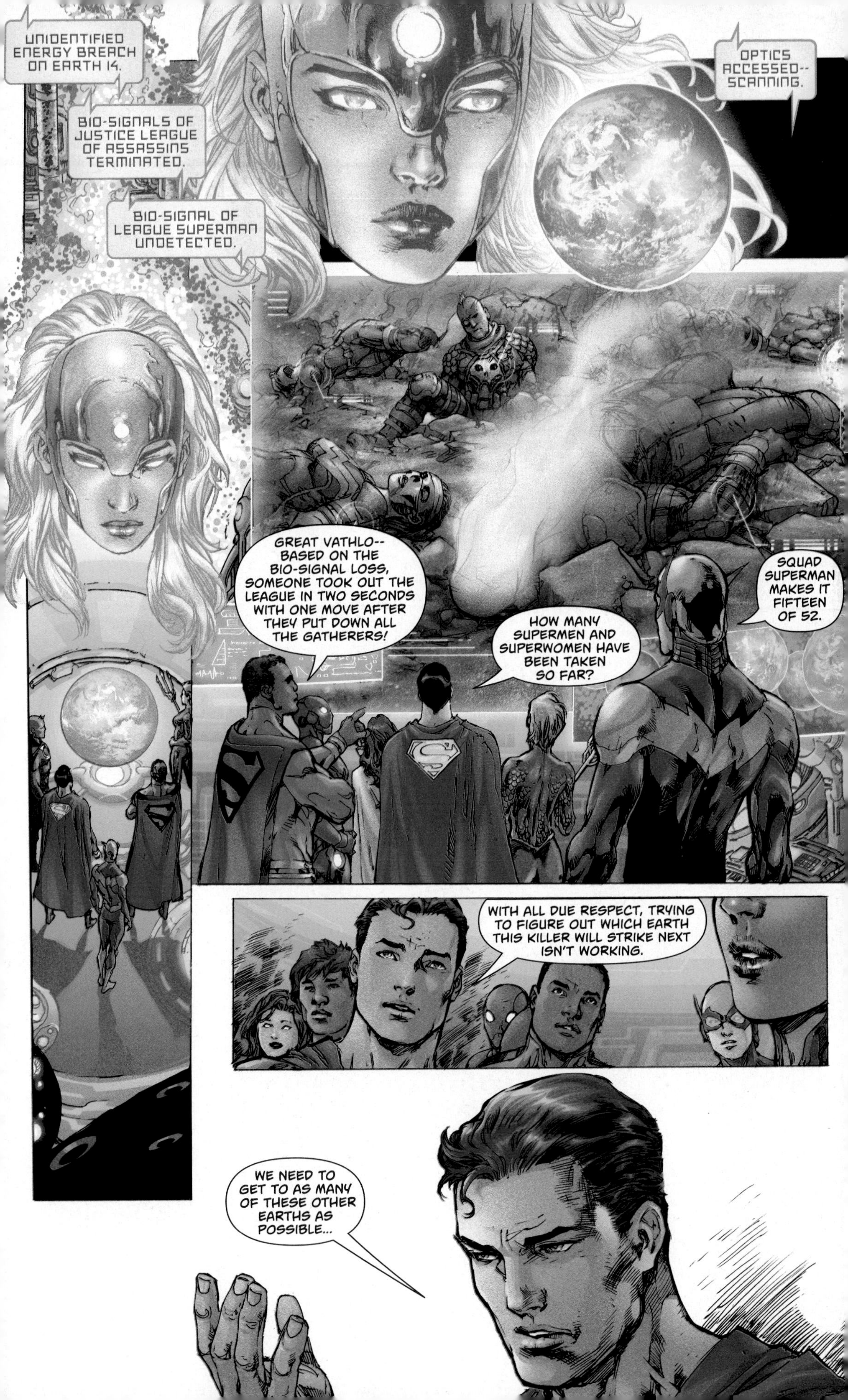
UNIDENTIFIED ENERGY BREACH ON EARTH 14.
BIO-SIGNALS OF JUSTICE LEAGUE OF ASSASSINS TERMINATED.
BIO-SIGNAL OF LEAGUE SUPERMAN UNDETECTED.
OPTICS ACCESSED-- SCANNING.
GREAT VATHLO-- BASED ON THE BIO-SIGNAL LOSS, SOMEONE TOOK OUT THE LEAGUE IN TWO SECONDS WITH ONE MOVE AFTER THEY PUT DOWN ALL THE GATHERERS!
HOW MANY SUPERMEN AND SUPERWOMEN HAVE BEEN TAKEN SO FAR?
SQUAD SUPERMAN MAKES IT FIFTEEN OF 52.
WITH ALL DUE RESPECT, TRYING TO FIGURE OUT WHICH EARTH THIS KILLER WILL STRIKE NEXT ISN'T WORKING.
WE NEED TO GET TO AS MANY OF THESE OTHER EARTHS AS POSSIBLE...

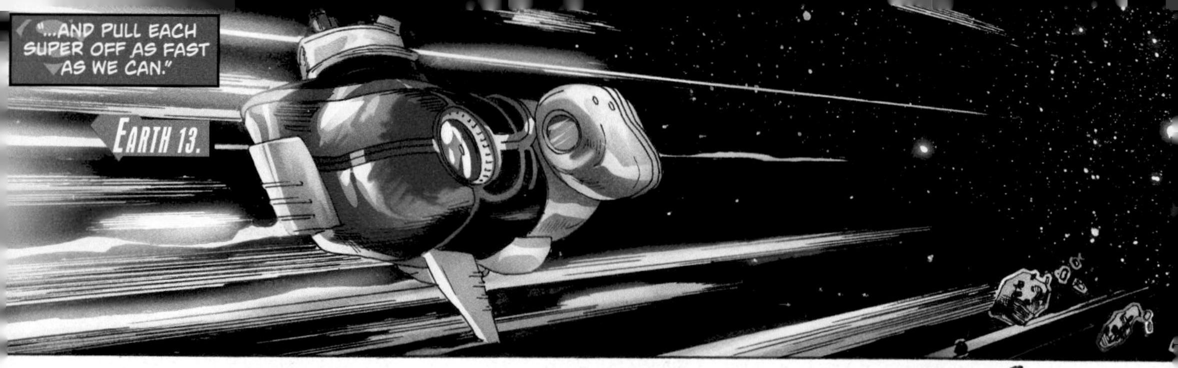
"...AND PULL EACH SUPER OFF AS FAST AS WE CAN."
EARTH 13.

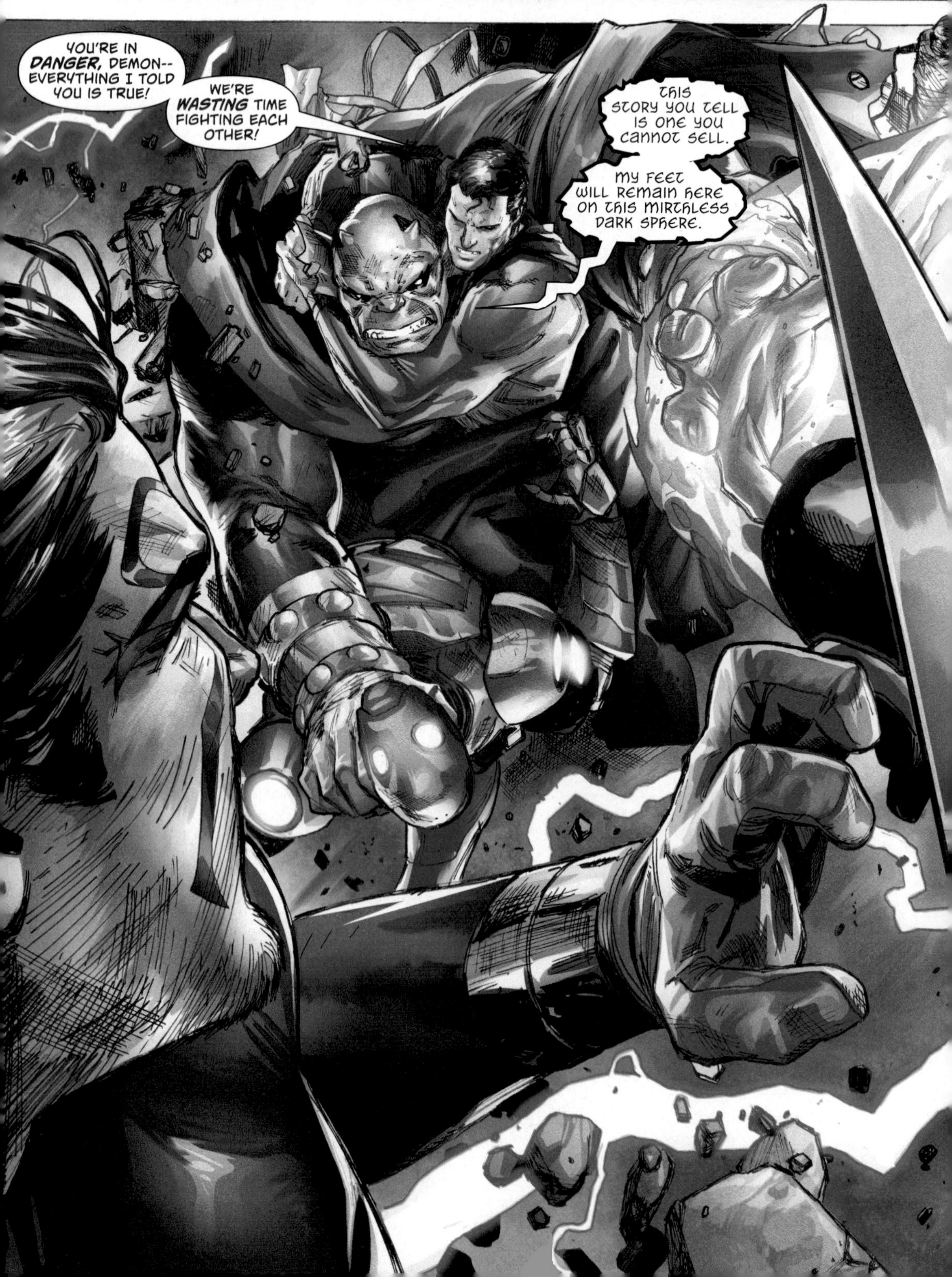
YOU'RE IN DANGER, DEMON-- EVERYTHING I TOLD YOU IS TRUE!
WE'RE WASTING TIME FIGHTING EACH OTHER!
THIS STORY YOU TELL IS ONE YOU CANNOT SELL.
MY FEET WILL REMAIN HERE ON THIS MIRTHLESS DARK SPHERE.

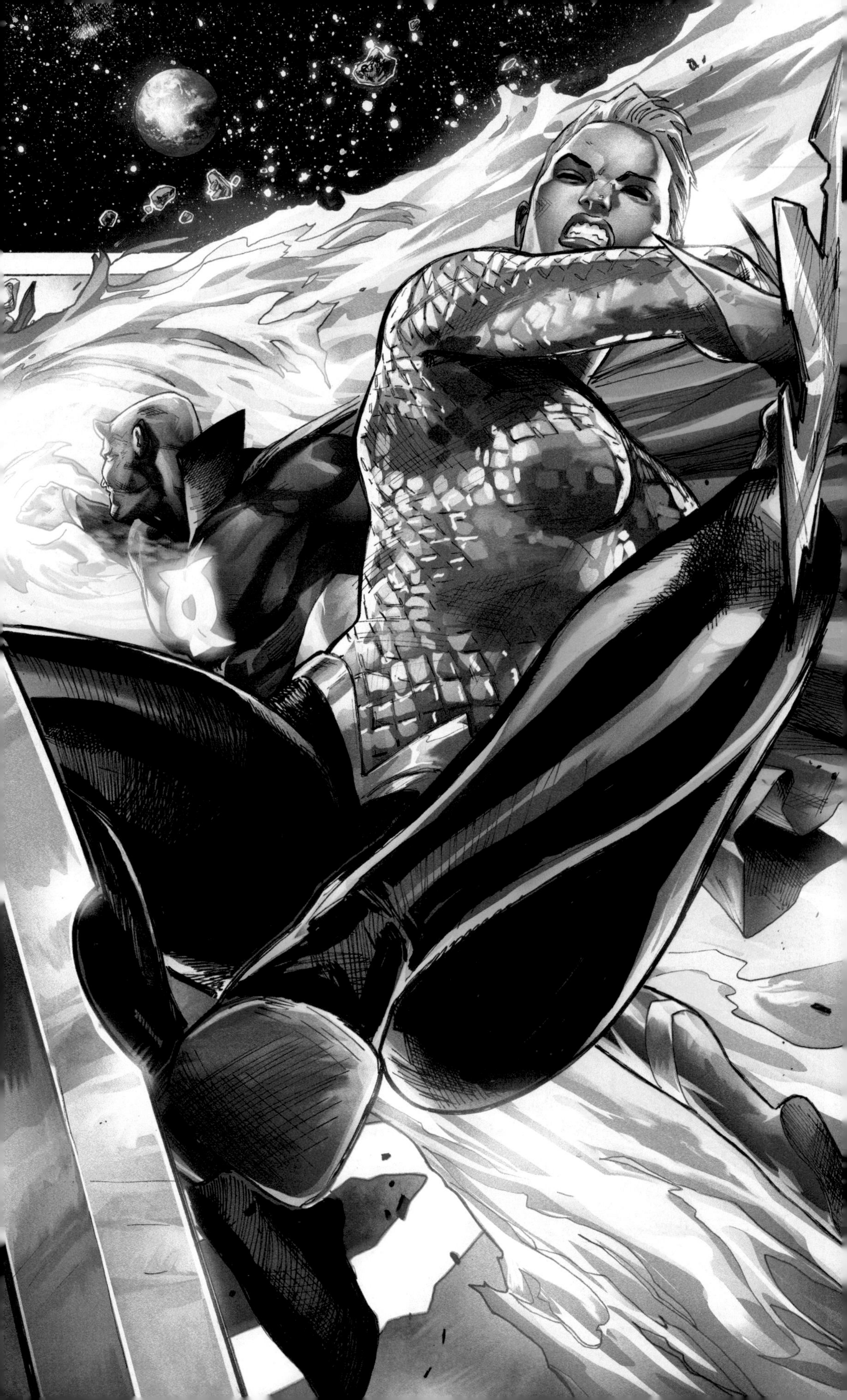

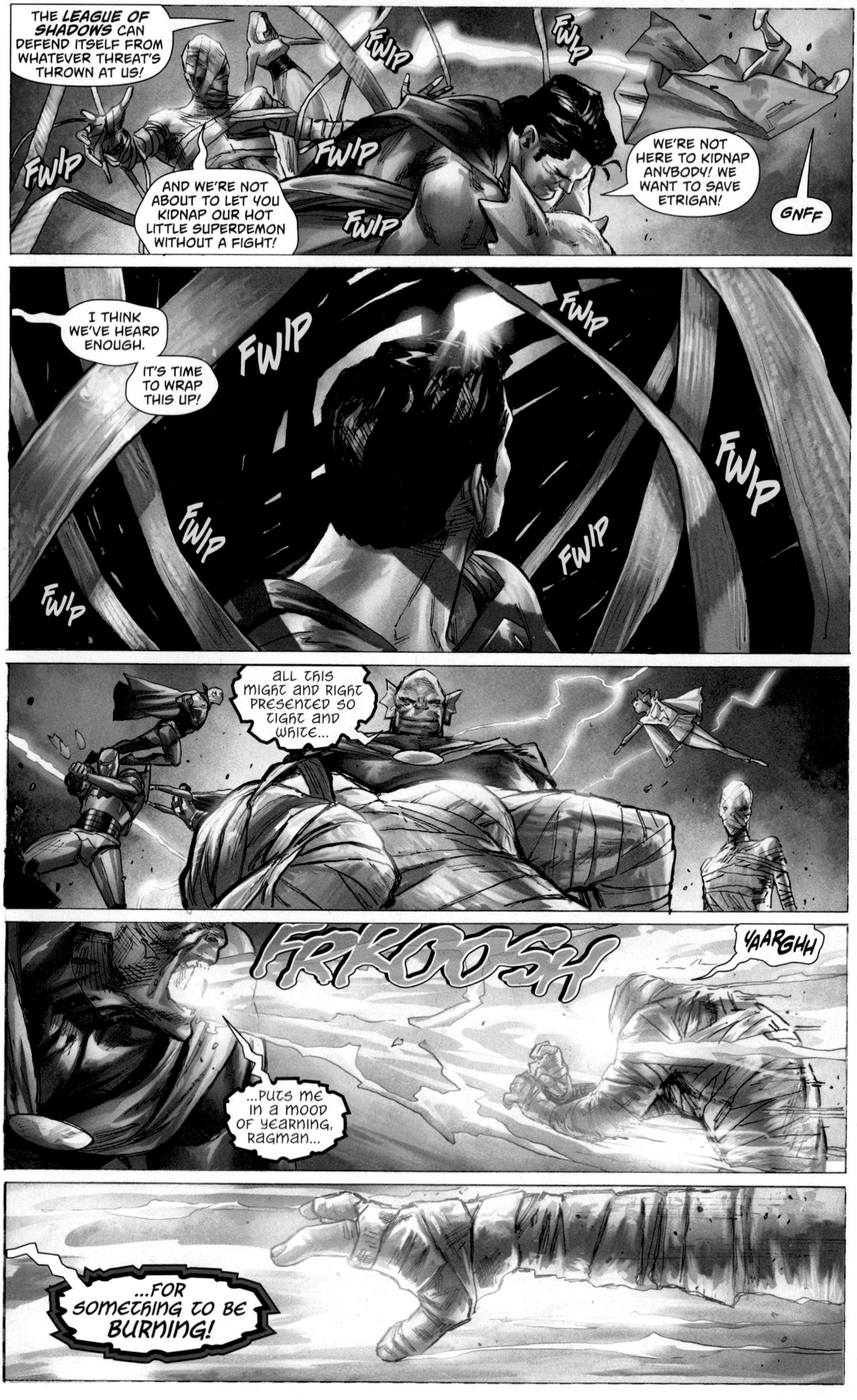
THE LEAGUE OF SHADOWS CAN DEFEND ITSELF FROM WHATEVER THREAT'S THROWN AT US!
FWIP
FWIP
FWIP
FWIP
AND WE'RE NOT ABOUT TO LET YOU KIDNAP OUR HOT LITTLE SUPERDEMON WITHOUT A FIGHT!
FWIP
WE'RE NOT HERE TO KIDNAP ANYBODY! WE WANT TO SAVE ETRIGAN!
GNFF
I THINK WE'VE HEARD ENOUGH.
IT'S TIME TO WRAP THIS UP!
FWIP
FWIP
FWIP
FWIP
FWIP
FWIP
ALL THIS MIGHT AND RIGHT PRESENTED SO TIGHT AND WHITE...
FRKOOSH
YAARGHH
...PUTS ME IN A MOOD OF YEARNING, RAGMAN...
...FOR SOMETHING TO BE BURNING!

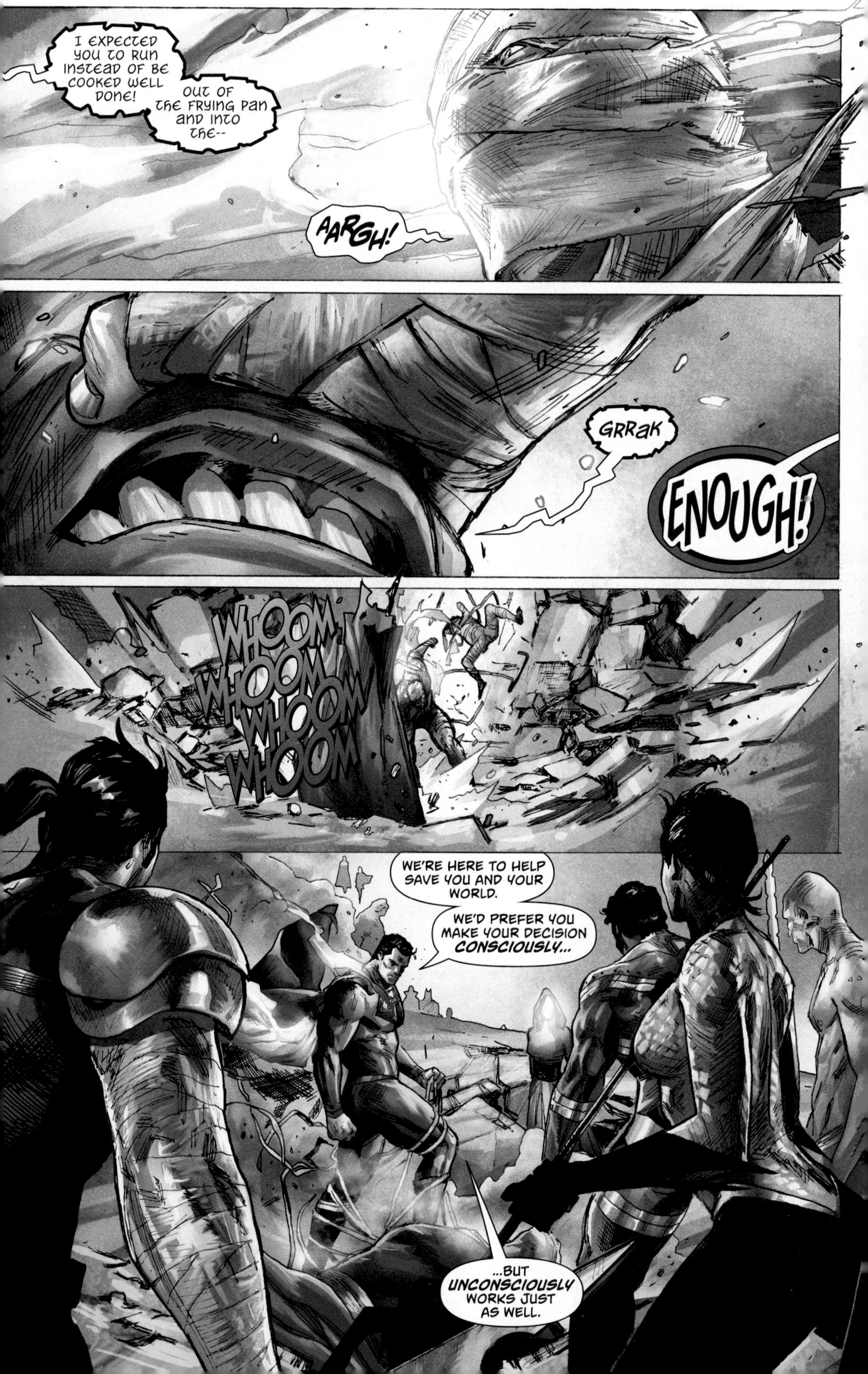
I EXPECTED YOU TO RUN INSTEAD OF BE COOKED WELL DONE!
OUT OF THE FRYING PAN AND INTO THE--
AARGH!
GRRAK
ENOUGH!
WHOOM WHOOM WHOOM WHOOM
WE'RE HERE TO HELP SAVE YOU AND YOUR WORLD.
WE'D PREFER YOU MAKE YOUR DECISION CONSCIOUSLY...
...BUT UNCONSCIOUSLY WORKS JUST AS WELL.

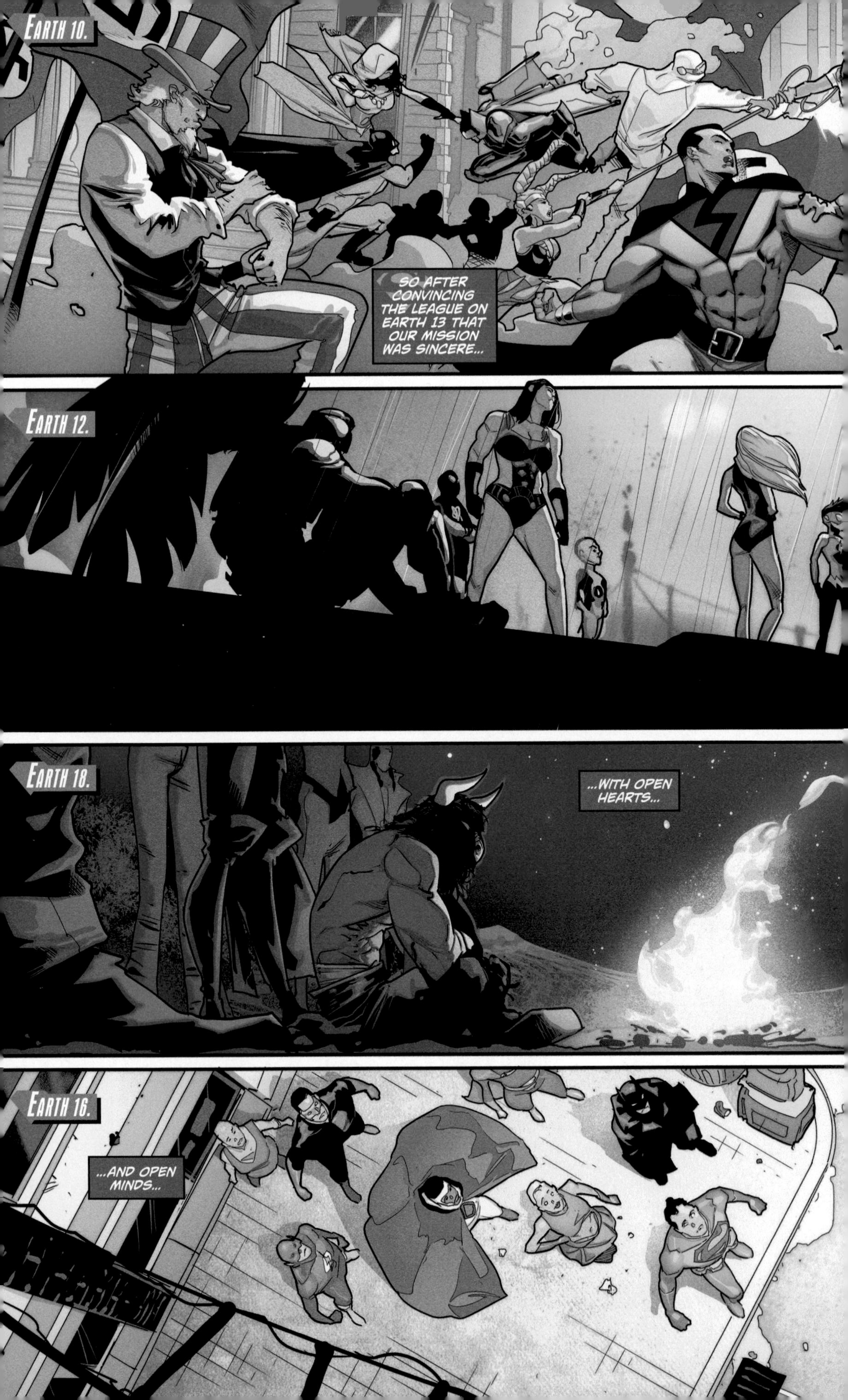
EARTH 10.
SO AFTER CONVINCING THE LEAGUE ON EARTH 13 THAT OUR MISSION WAS SINCERE...
EARTH 12.
EARTH 18.
...WITH OPEN HEARTS...
EARTH 16.
...AND OPEN MINDS...

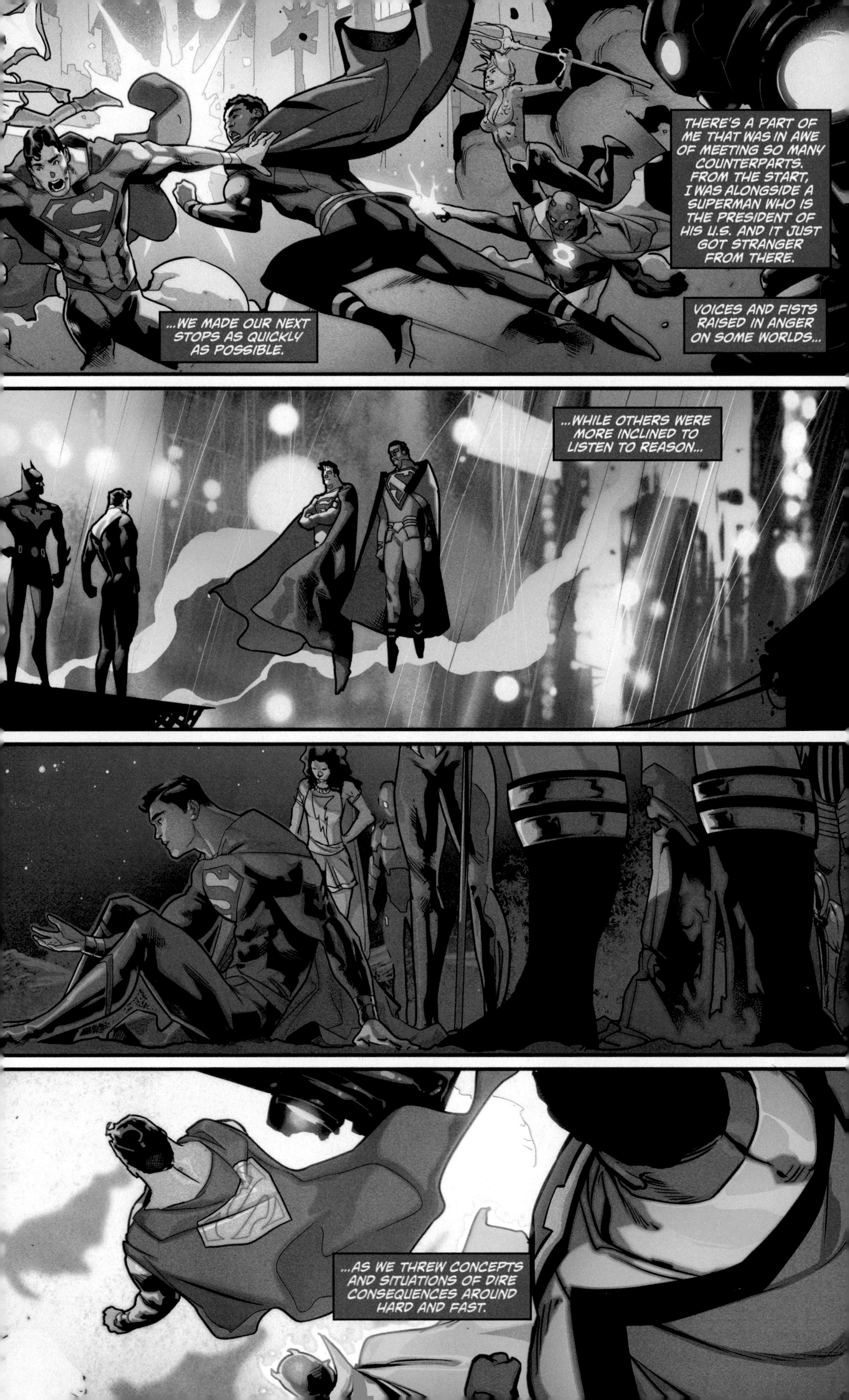
THERE'S A PART OF ME THAT WAS IN AWE OF MEETING SO MANY COUNTERPARTS. FROM THE START, I WAS ALONGSIDE A SUPERMAN WHO IS THE PRESIDENT OF HIS U.S. AND IT JUST GOT STRANGER FROM THERE.
VOICES AND FISTS RAISED IN ANGER ON SOME WORLDS...
...WE MADE OUR NEXT STOPS AS QUICKLY AS POSSIBLE.
...WHILE OTHERS WERE MORE INCLINED TO LISTEN TO REASON...
...AS WE THREW CONCEPTS AND SITUATIONS OF DIRE CONSEQUENCES AROUND HARD AND FAST.

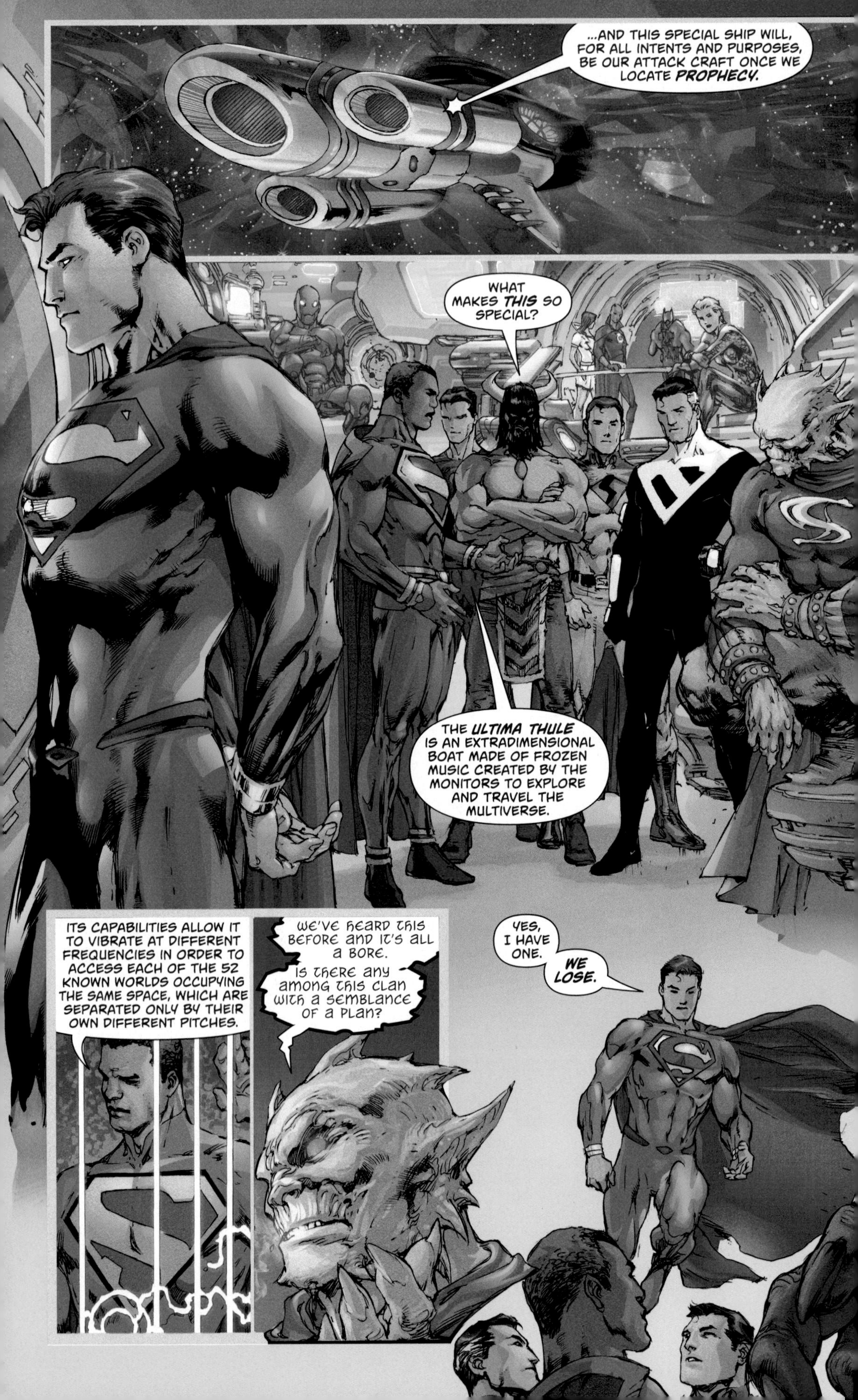
...AND THIS SPECIAL SHIP WILL, FOR ALL INTENTS AND PURPOSES, BE OUR ATTACK CRAFT ONCE WE LOCATE PROPHECY.
WHAT MAKES THIS SO SPECIAL?
THE ULTIMA THULE IS AN EXTRADIMENSIONAL BOAT MADE OF FROZEN MUSIC CREATED BY THE MONITORS TO EXPLORE AND TRAVEL THE MULTIVERSE.
ITS CAPABILITIES ALLOW IT TO VIBRATE AT DIFFERENT FREQUENCIES IN ORDER TO ACCESS EACH OF THE 52 KNOWN WORLDS OCCUPYING THE SAME SPACE, WHICH ARE SEPARATED ONLY BY THEIR OWN DIFFERENT PITCHES.
WE'VE HEARD THIS BEFORE AND IT'S ALL A BORE.
IS THERE ANY AMONG THIS CLAN WITH A SEMBLANCE OF A PLAN?
YES, I HAVE ONE. WE LOSE.

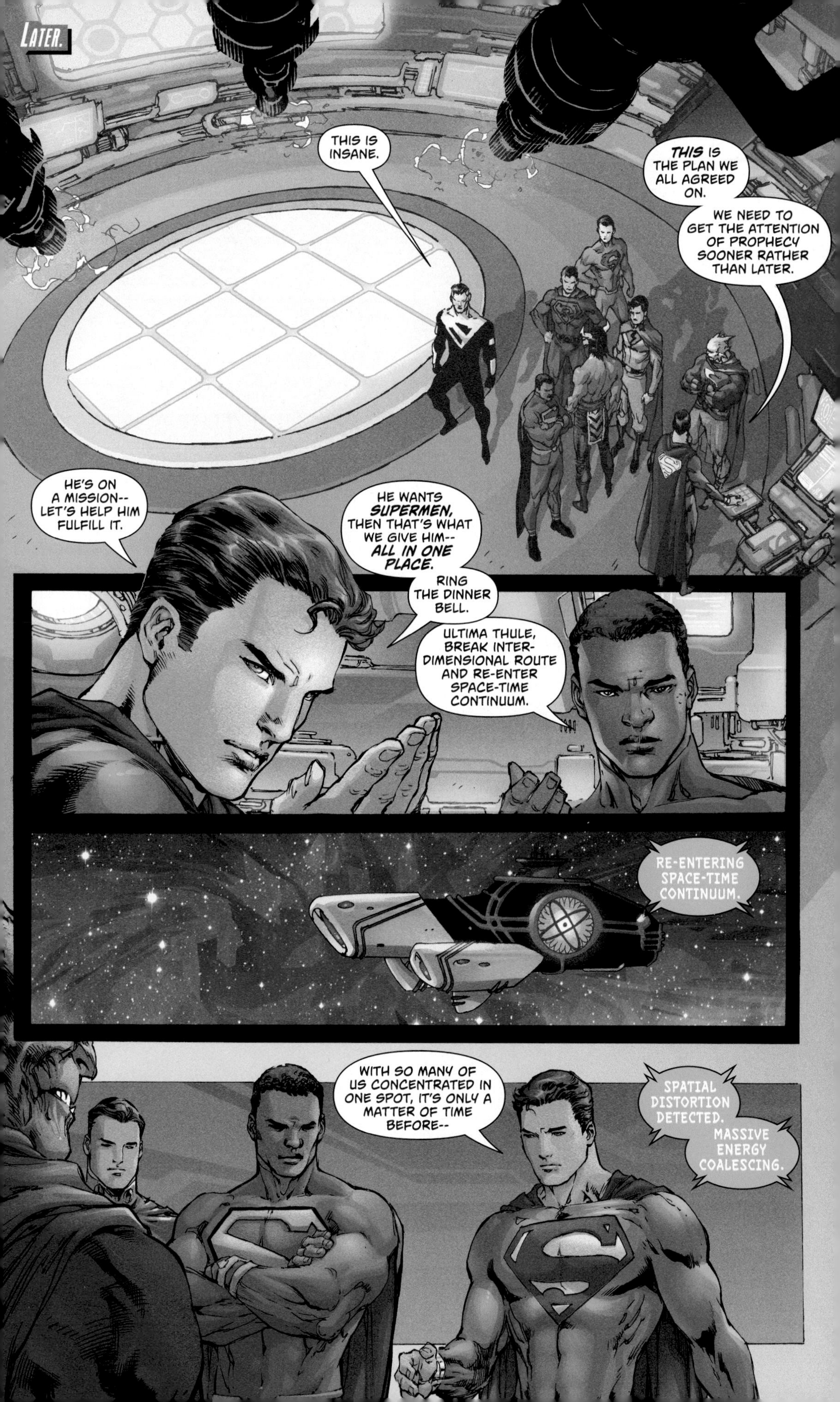
LATER.
THIS IS INSANE.
THIS IS THE PLAN WE ALL AGREED ON.
WE NEED TO GET THE ATTENTION OF PROPHECY SOONER RATHER THAN LATER.
HE'S ON A MISSION-- LET'S HELP HIM FULFILL IT.
HE WANTS SUPERMEN, THEN THAT'S WHAT WE GIVE HIM-- ALL IN ONE PLACE.
RING THE DINNER BELL.
ULTIMA THULE, BREAK INTER-DIMENSIONAL ROUTE AND RE-ENTER SPACE-TIME CONTINUUM.
RE-ENTERING SPACE-TIME CONTINUUM.
WITH SO MANY OF US CONCENTRATED IN ONE SPOT, IT'S ONLY A MATTER OF TIME BEFORE--
SPATIAL DISTORTION DETECTED.
MASSIVE ENERGY COALESCING.

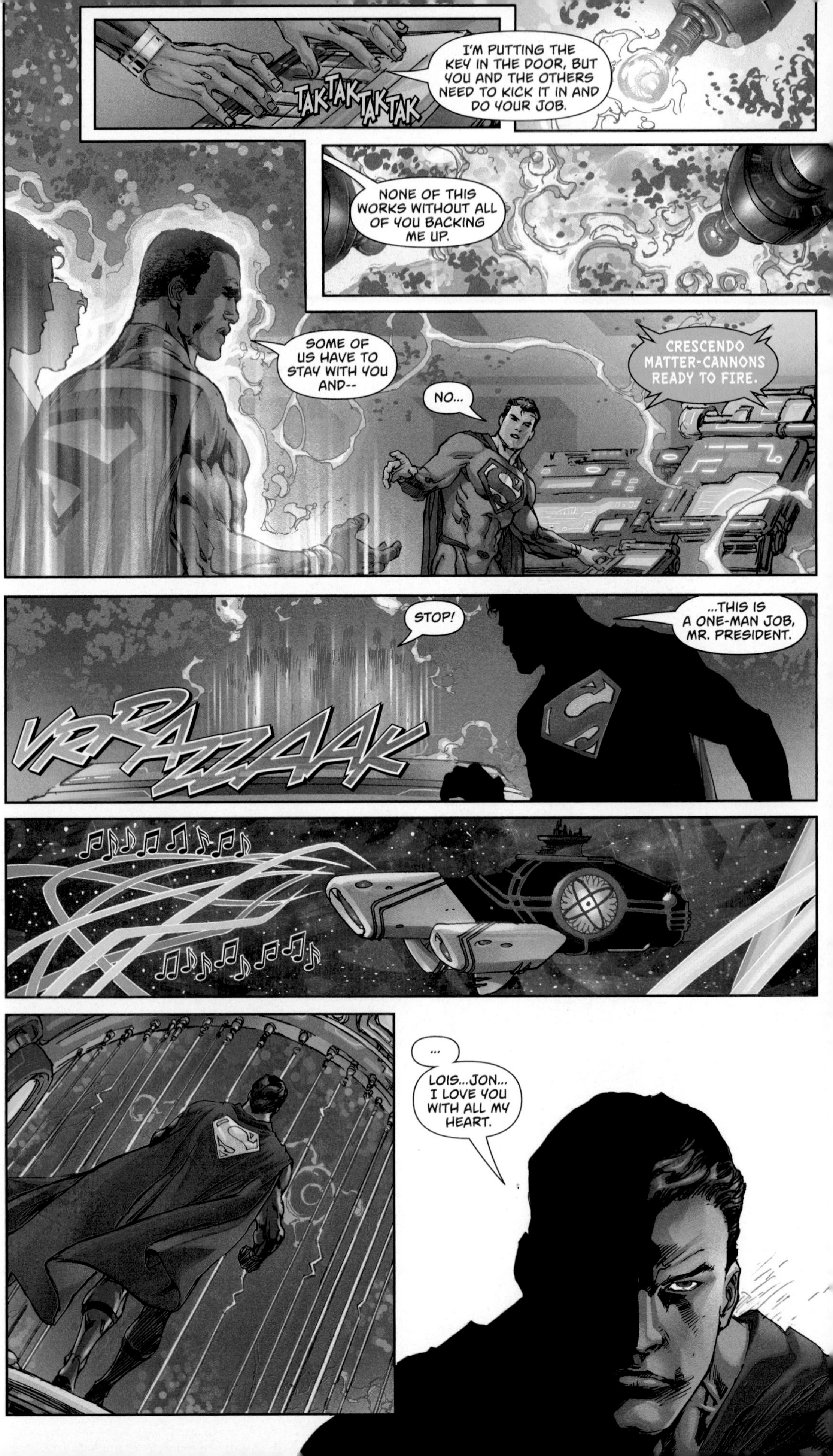
TAKTAKTAKTAK
I'M PUTTING THE KEY IN THE DOOR, BUT YOU AND THE OTHERS NEED TO KICK IT IN AND DO YOUR JOB.
NONE OF THIS WORKS WITHOUT ALL OF YOU BACKING ME UP.
SOME OF US HAVE TO STAY WITH YOU AND--
CRESCENDO MATTER-CANNONS READY TO FIRE.
NO...
STOP!
...THIS IS A ONE-MAN JOB, MR. PRESIDENT.
VRRAZZAAK
...
LOIS...JON... I LOVE YOU WITH ALL MY HEART.

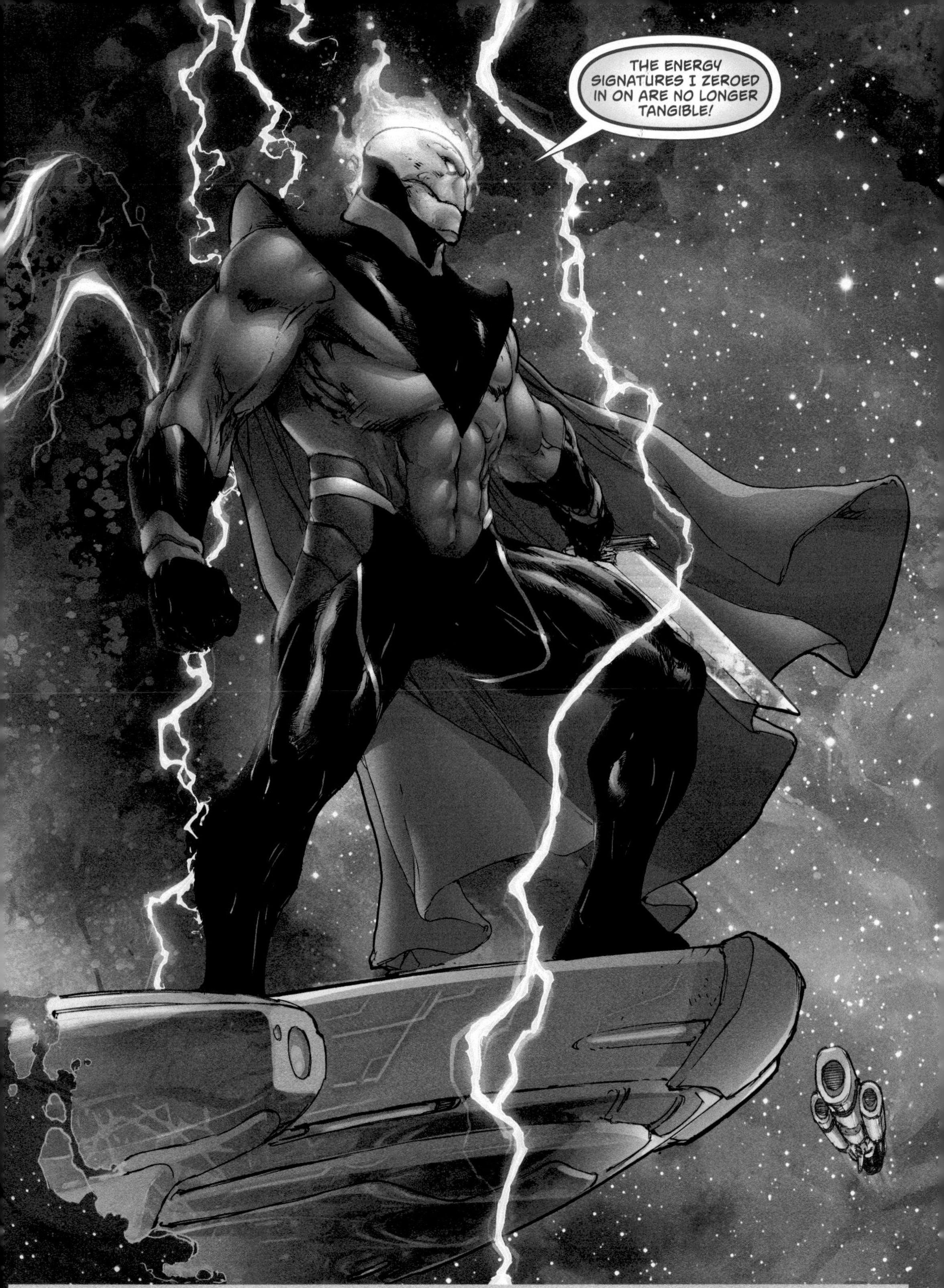
THE ENERGY SIGNATURES I ZEROED IN ON ARE NO LONGER TANGIBLE!

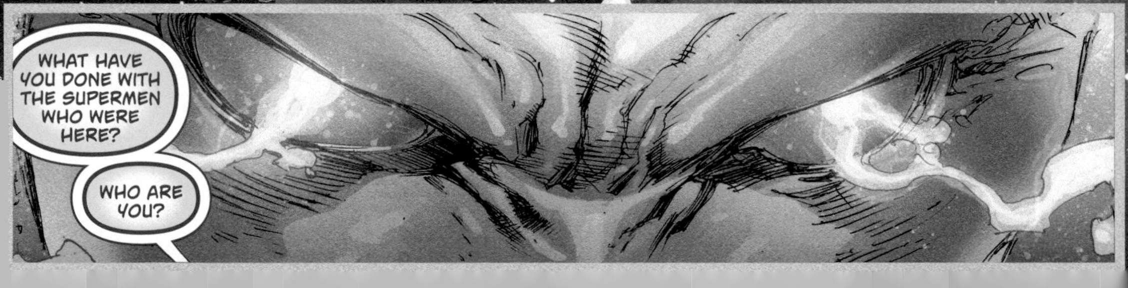
WHAT HAVE YOU DONE WITH THE SUPERMEN WHO WERE HERE?
WHO ARE YOU?

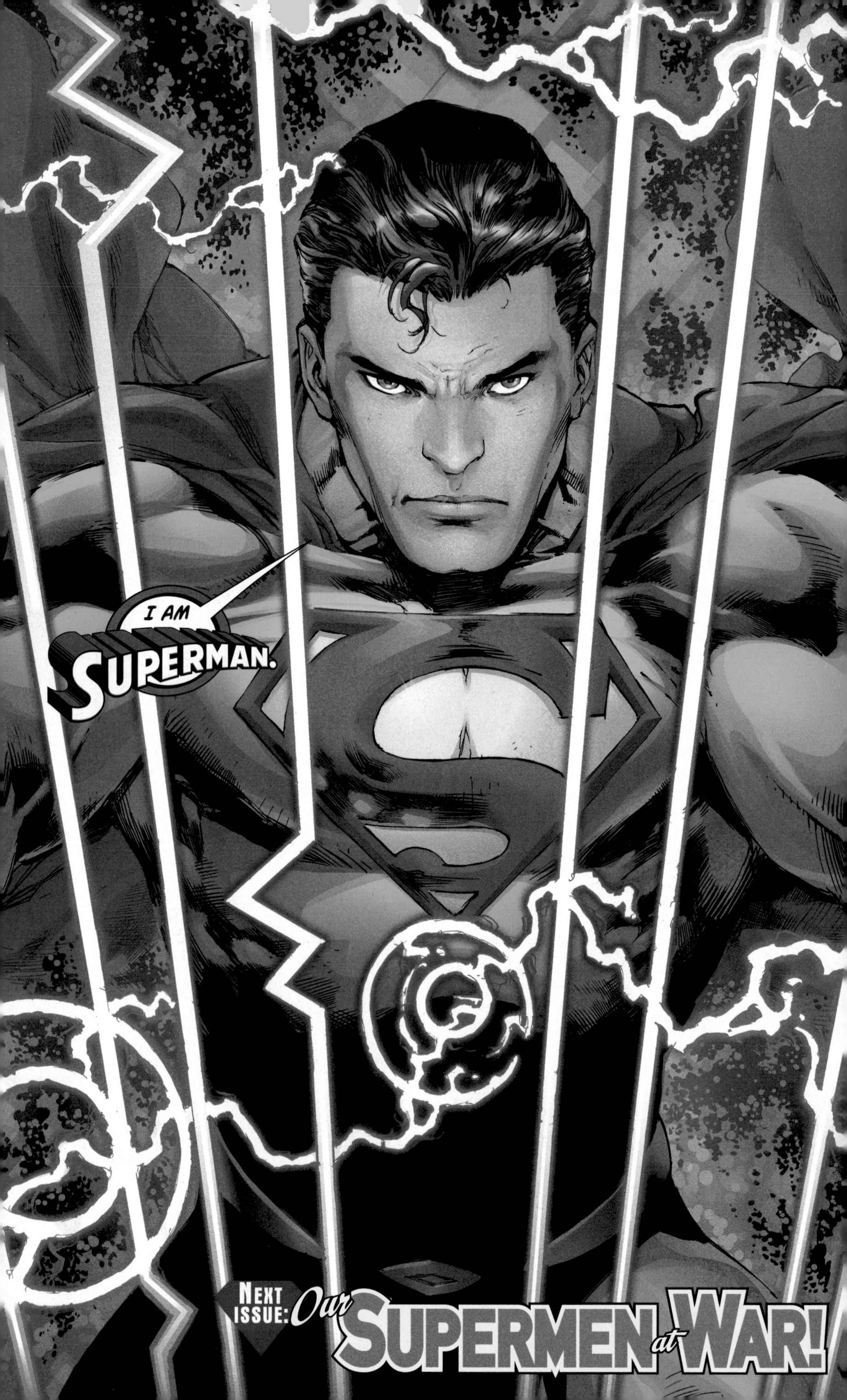
I AM SUPERMAN.
NEXT ISSUE: Our SUPERMEN at WAR!

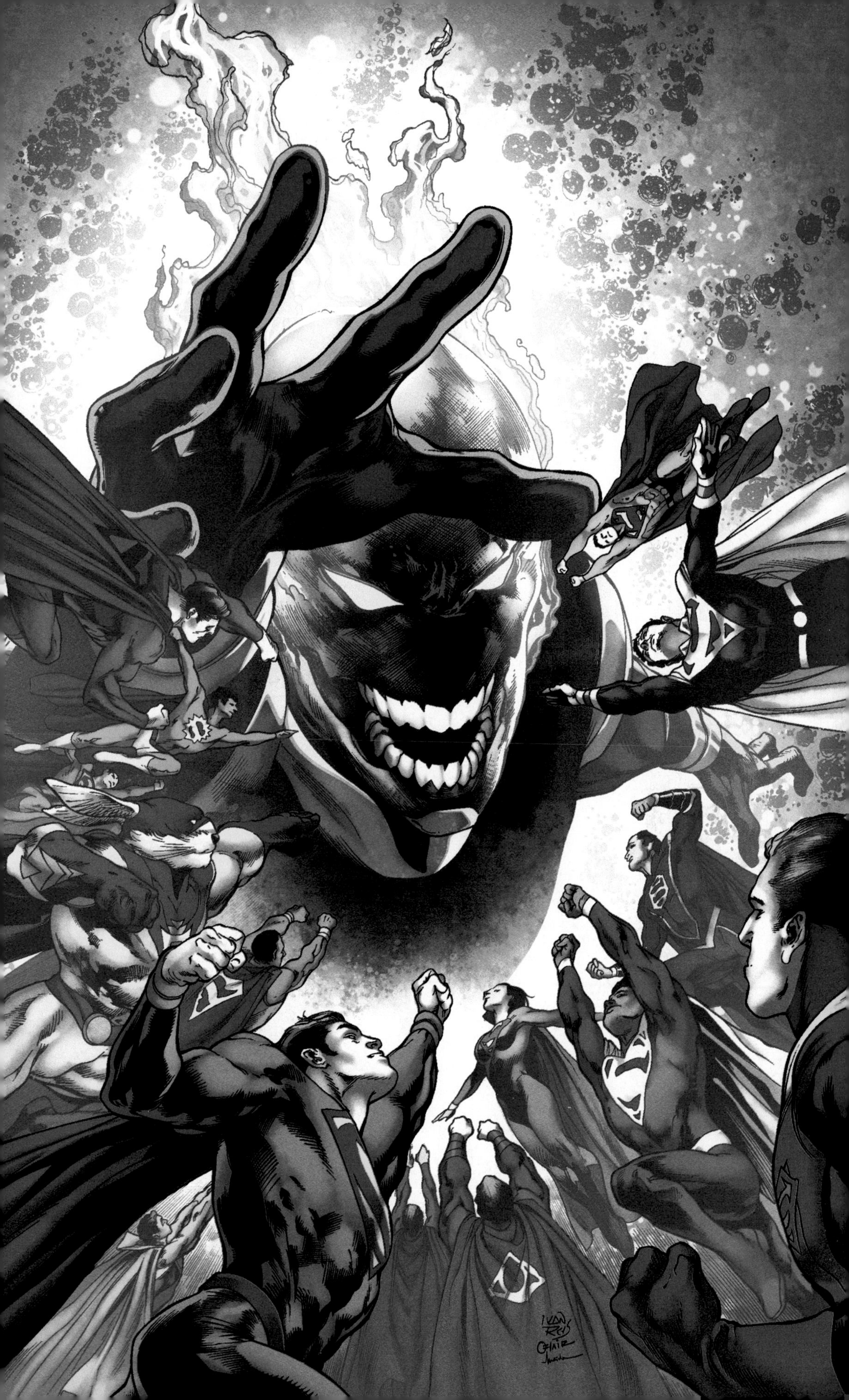

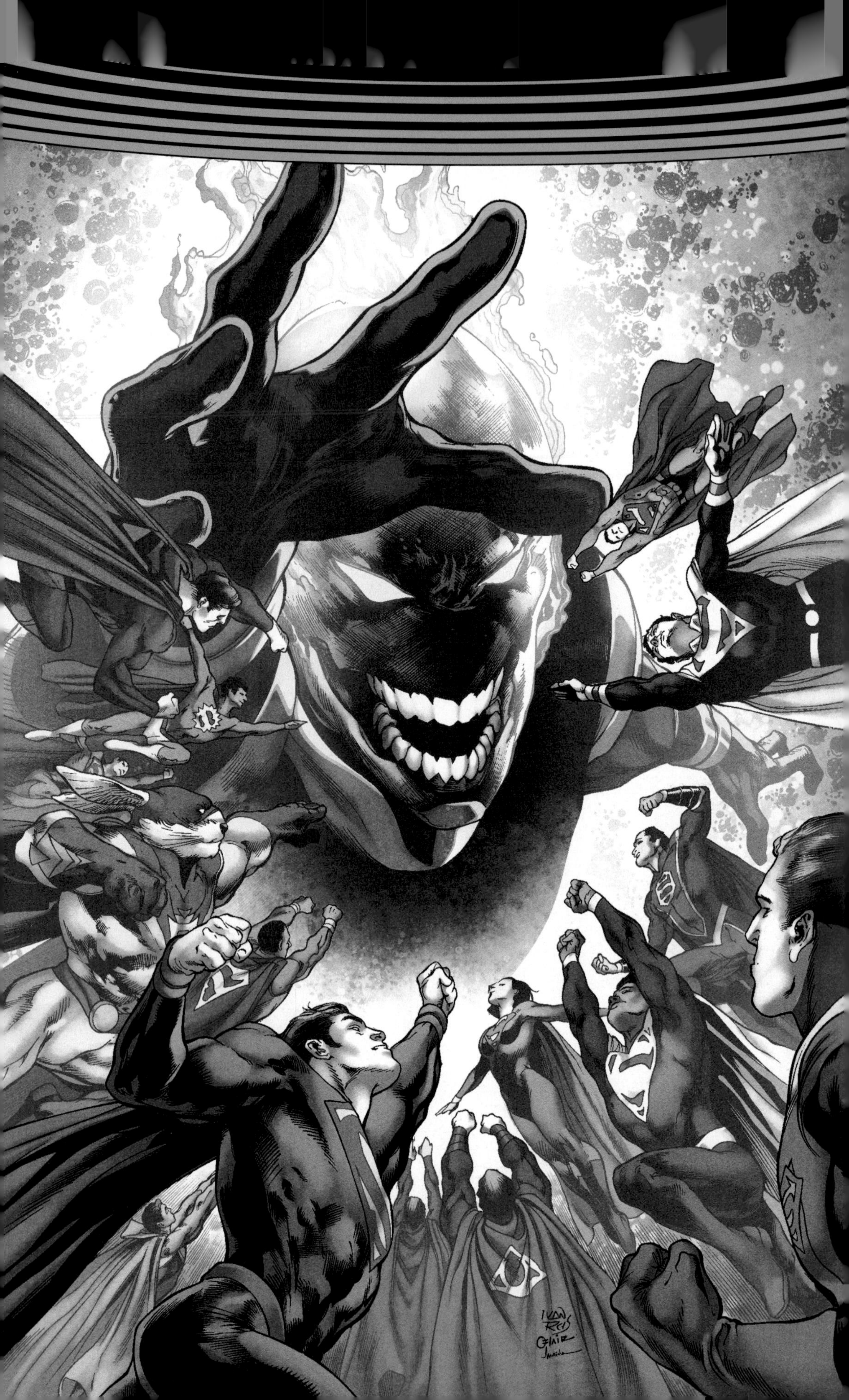

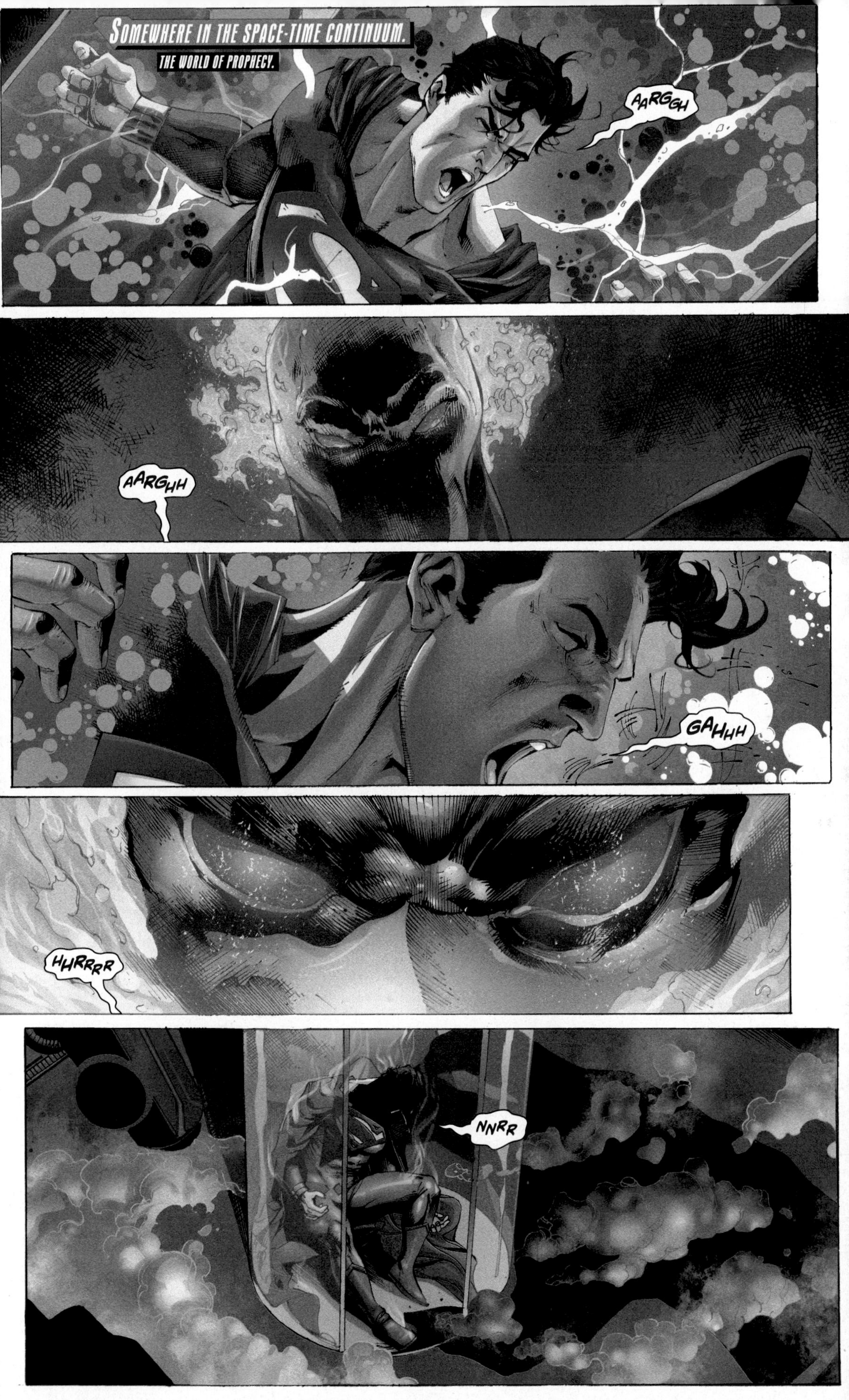
SOMEWHERE IN THE SPACE-TIME CONTINUUM.
THE WORLD OF PROPHECY.
AARGGH
AARGHH
GAHHH
HHRRRR
NNRR

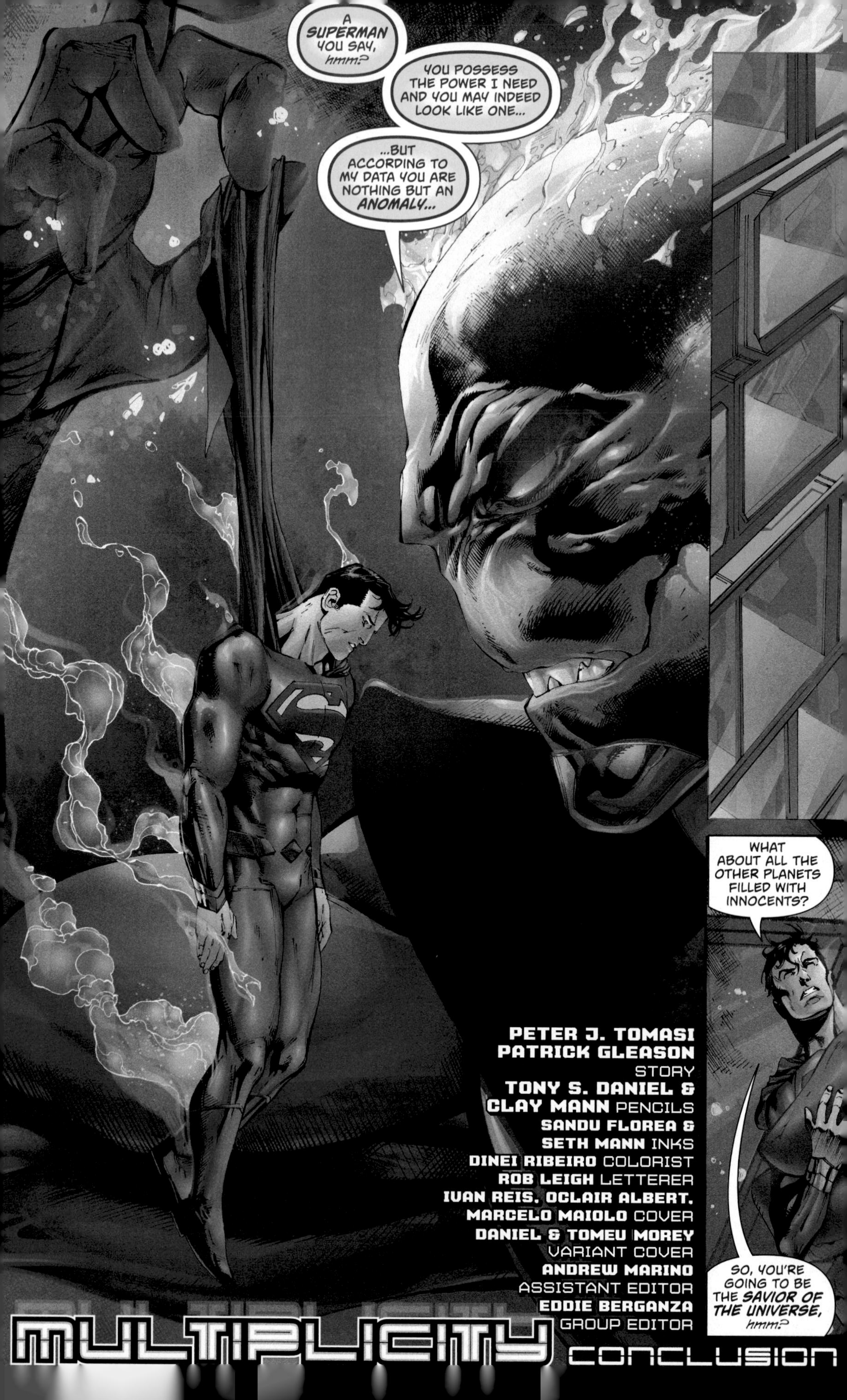
A SUPERMAN YOU SAY, hmm?
YOU POSSESS THE POWER I NEED AND YOU MAY INDEED LOOK LIKE ONE...
...BUT ACCORDING TO MY DATA YOU ARE NOTHING BUT AN ANOMALY...
WHAT ABOUT ALL THE OTHER PLANETS FILLED WITH INNOCENTS?
SO, YOU'RE GOING TO BE THE SAVIOR OF THE UNIVERSE, hmm?
PETER J. TOMASI
PATRICK GLEASON
STORY
TONY S. DANIEL &
CLAY MANN PENCILS
SANDU FLOREA &
SETH MANN INKS
DINEI RIBEIRO COLORIST
ROB LEIGH LETTERER
IVAN REIS, OCLAIR ALBERT,
MARCELO MAIOLO COVER
DANIEL & TOMEU MOREY
VARIANT COVER
ANDREW MARINO
ASSISTANT EDITOR
EDDIE BERGANZA
GROUP EDITOR
MULTIPLICITY
CONCLUSION

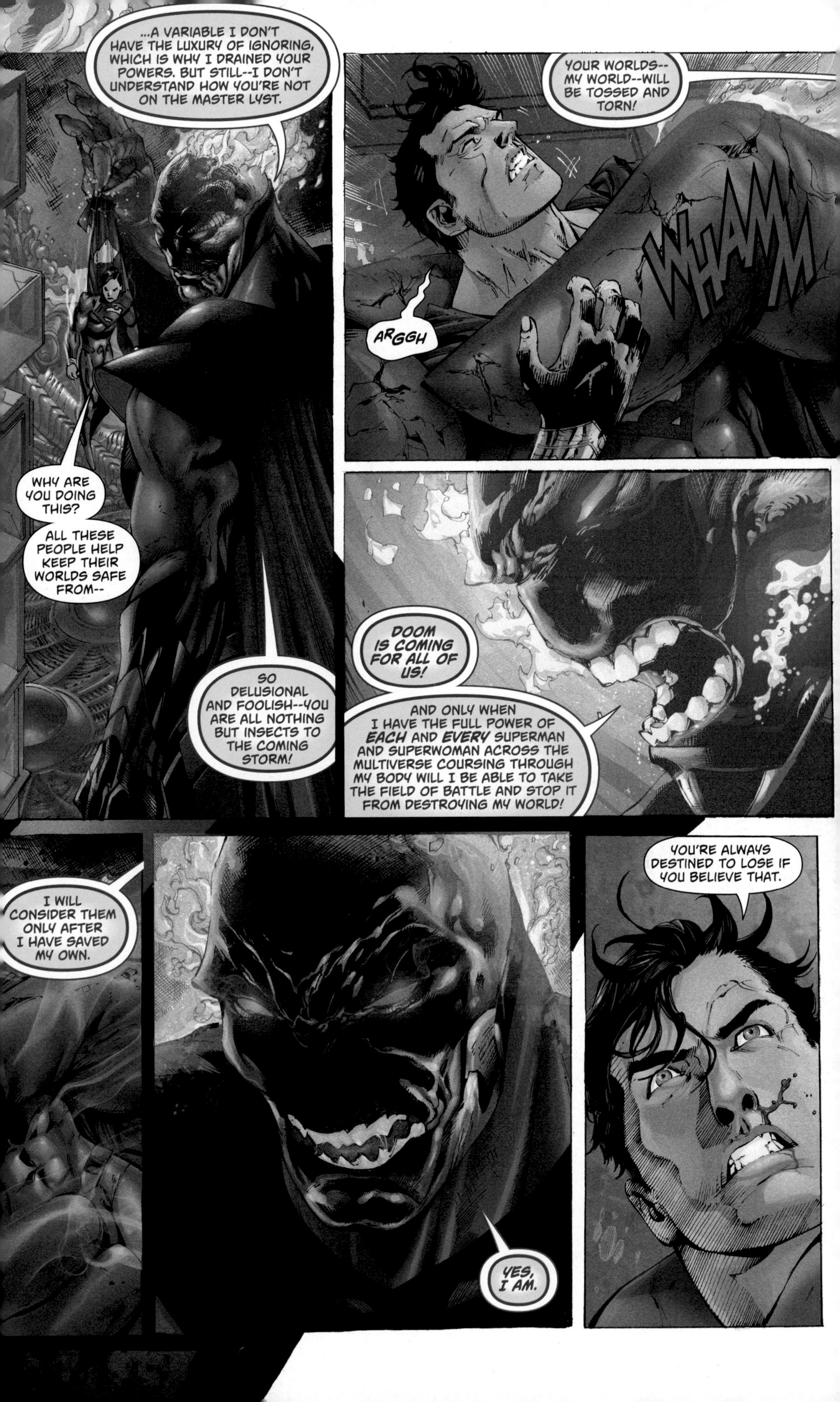
...A VARIABLE I DON'T HAVE THE LUXURY OF IGNORING, WHICH IS WHY I DRAINED YOUR POWERS. BUT STILL--I DON'T UNDERSTAND HOW YOU'RE NOT ON THE MASTER LYST.
WHY ARE YOU DOING THIS?
ALL THESE PEOPLE HELP KEEP THEIR WORLDS SAFE FROM--
SO DELUSIONAL AND FOOLISH--YOU ARE ALL NOTHING BUT INSECTS TO THE COMING STORM!
YOUR WORLDS--MY WORLD--WILL BE TOSSED AND TORN!
WHAM
ARGGH
DOOM IS COMING FOR ALL OF US!
AND ONLY WHEN I HAVE THE FULL POWER OF EACH AND EVERY SUPERMAN AND SUPERWOMAN ACROSS THE MULTIVERSE COURSING THROUGH MY BODY WILL I BE ABLE TO TAKE THE FIELD OF BATTLE AND STOP IT FROM DESTROYING MY WORLD!
I WILL CONSIDER THEM ONLY AFTER I HAVE SAVED MY OWN.
YES, I AM.
YOU'RE ALWAYS DESTINED TO LOSE IF YOU BELIEVE THAT.

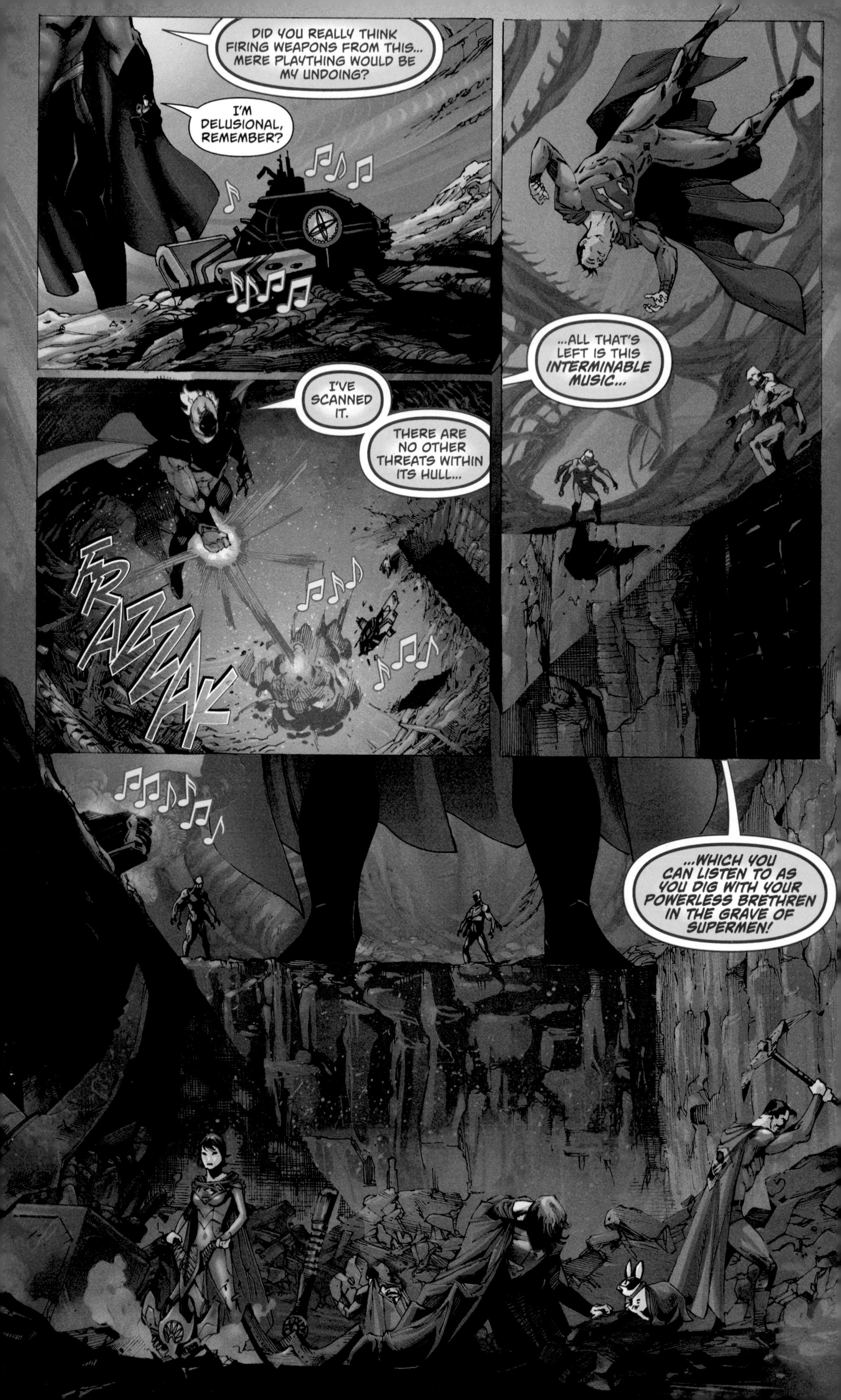

DID YOU REALLY THINK FIRING WEAPONS FROM THIS... MERE PLAYTHING WOULD BE MY UNDOING?
I'M DELUSIONAL, REMEMBER?
I'VE SCANNED IT.
THERE ARE NO OTHER THREATS WITHIN ITS HULL...
FRAZZZAK
...ALL THAT'S LEFT IS THIS INTERMINABLE MUSIC...
...WHICH YOU CAN LISTEN TO AS YOU DIG WITH YOUR POWERLESS BRETHREN IN THE GRAVE OF SUPERMEN!

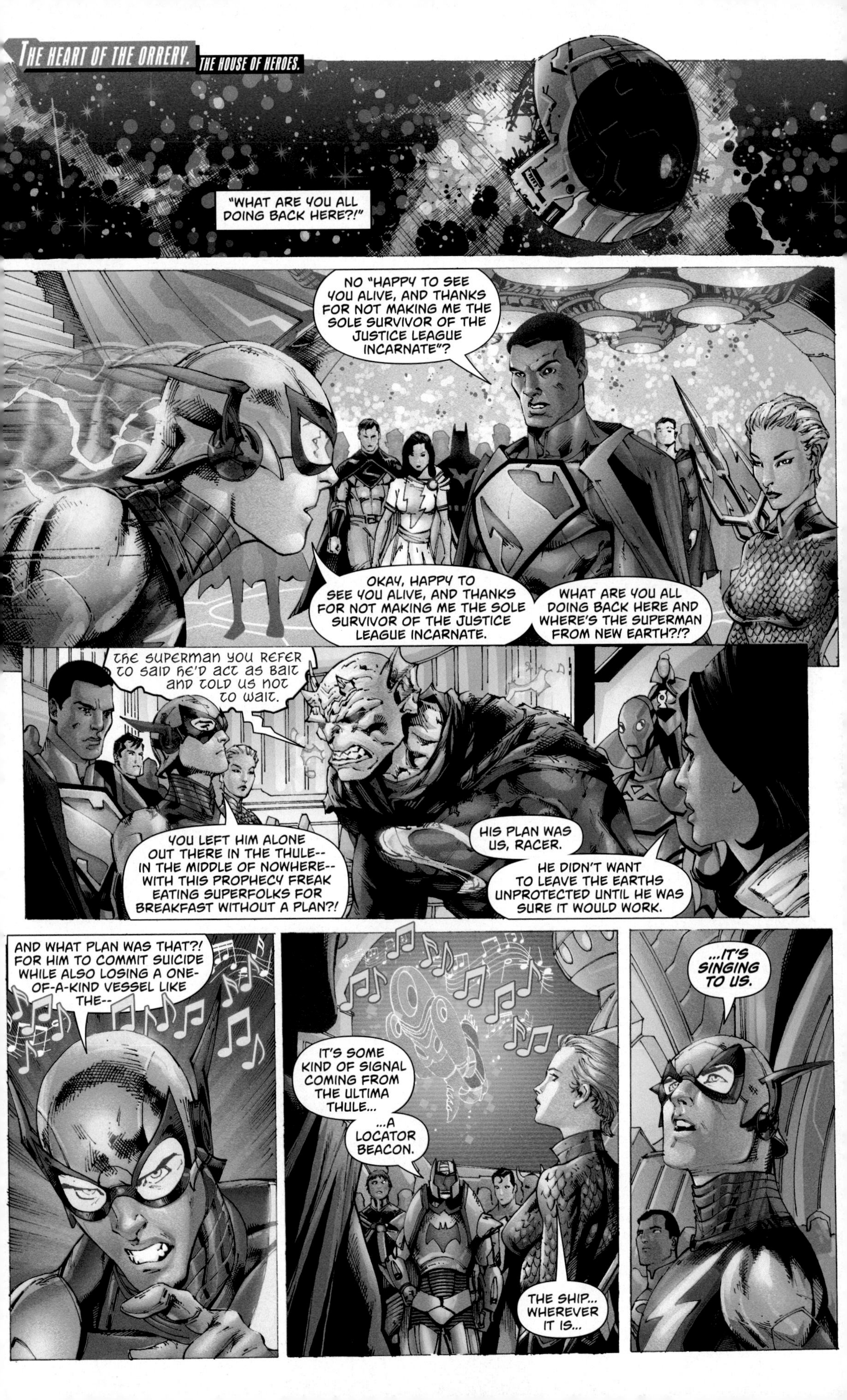
THE HEART OF THE ORRERY.
THE HOUSE OF HEROES.
"WHAT ARE YOU ALL DOING BACK HERE?!"
NO "HAPPY TO SEE YOU ALIVE, AND THANKS FOR NOT MAKING ME THE SOLE SURVIVOR OF THE JUSTICE LEAGUE INCARNATE"?
OKAY, HAPPY TO SEE YOU ALIVE, AND THANKS FOR NOT MAKING ME THE SOLE SURVIVOR OF THE JUSTICE LEAGUE INCARNATE.
WHAT ARE YOU ALL DOING BACK HERE AND WHERE'S THE SUPERMAN FROM NEW EARTH?!?
THE SUPERMAN YOU REFER TO SAID HE'D ACT AS BAIT AND TOLD US NOT TO WAIT.
YOU LEFT HIM ALONE OUT THERE IN THE THULE-- IN THE MIDDLE OF NOWHERE-- WITH THIS PROPHECY FREAK EATING SUPERFOLKS FOR BREAKFAST WITHOUT A PLAN?!
HIS PLAN WAS US, RACER.
HE DIDN'T WANT TO LEAVE THE EARTHS UNPROTECTED UNTIL HE WAS SURE IT WOULD WORK.
AND WHAT PLAN WAS THAT?! FOR HIM TO COMMIT SUICIDE WHILE ALSO LOSING A ONE-OF-A-KIND VESSEL LIKE THE--
IT'S SOME KIND OF SIGNAL COMING FROM THE ULTIMA THULE...
...A LOCATOR BEACON.
THE SHIP... WHEREVER IT IS...
...IT'S SINGING TO US.

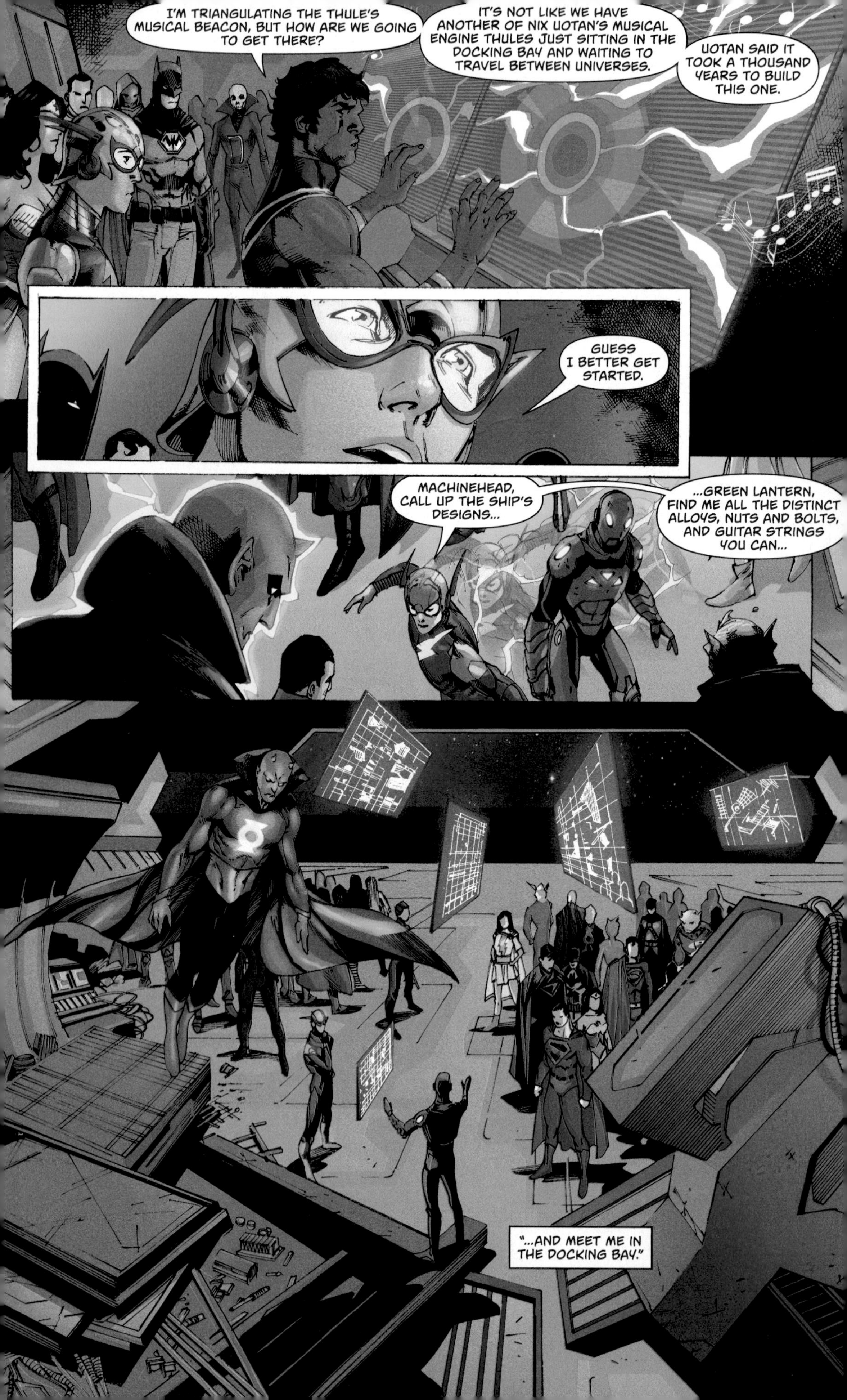
I'M TRIANGULATING THE THULE'S MUSICAL BEACON, BUT HOW ARE WE GOING TO GET THERE?
IT'S NOT LIKE WE HAVE ANOTHER OF NIX UOTAN'S MUSICAL ENGINE THULES JUST SITTING IN THE DOCKING BAY AND WAITING TO TRAVEL BETWEEN UNIVERSES.
UOTAN SAID IT TOOK A THOUSAND YEARS TO BUILD THIS ONE.
GUESS I BETTER GET STARTED.
MACHINEHEAD, CALL UP THE SHIP'S DESIGNS...
...GREEN LANTERN, FIND ME ALL THE DISTINCT ALLOYS, NUTS AND BOLTS, AND GUITAR STRINGS YOU CAN...
"...AND MEET ME IN THE DOCKING BAY."

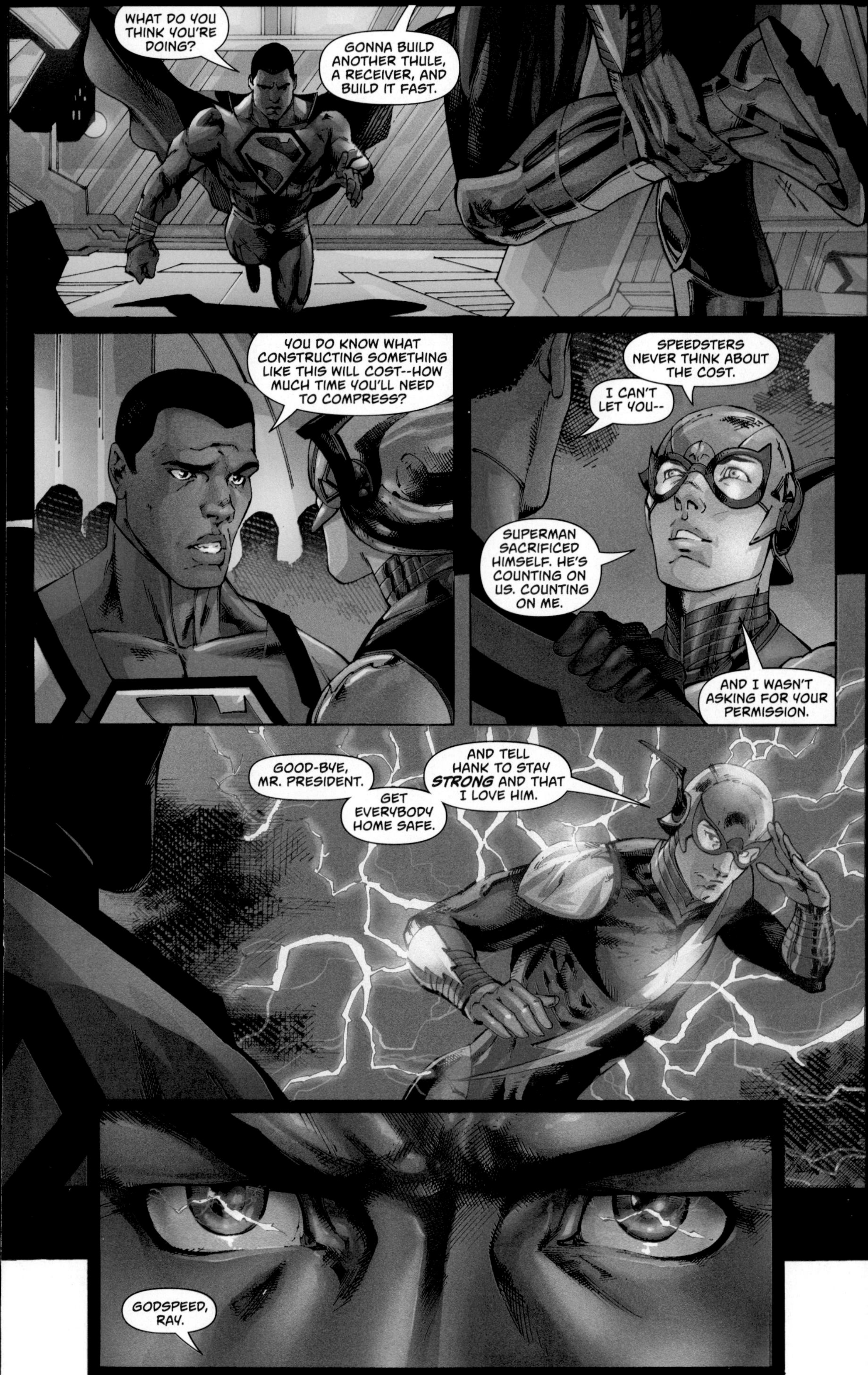
WHAT DO YOU THINK YOU'RE DOING?
GONNA BUILD ANOTHER THULE, A RECEIVER, AND BUILD IT FAST.
YOU DO KNOW WHAT CONSTRUCTING SOMETHING LIKE THIS WILL COST--HOW MUCH TIME YOU'LL NEED TO COMPRESS?
I CAN'T LET YOU--
SPEEDSTERS NEVER THINK ABOUT THE COST.
SUPERMAN SACRIFICED HIMSELF. HE'S COUNTING ON US. COUNTING ON ME.
AND I WASN'T ASKING FOR YOUR PERMISSION.
GOOD-BYE, MR. PRESIDENT.
GET EVERYBODY HOME SAFE.
AND TELL HANK TO STAY STRONG AND THAT I LOVE HIM.
GODSPEED, RAY.

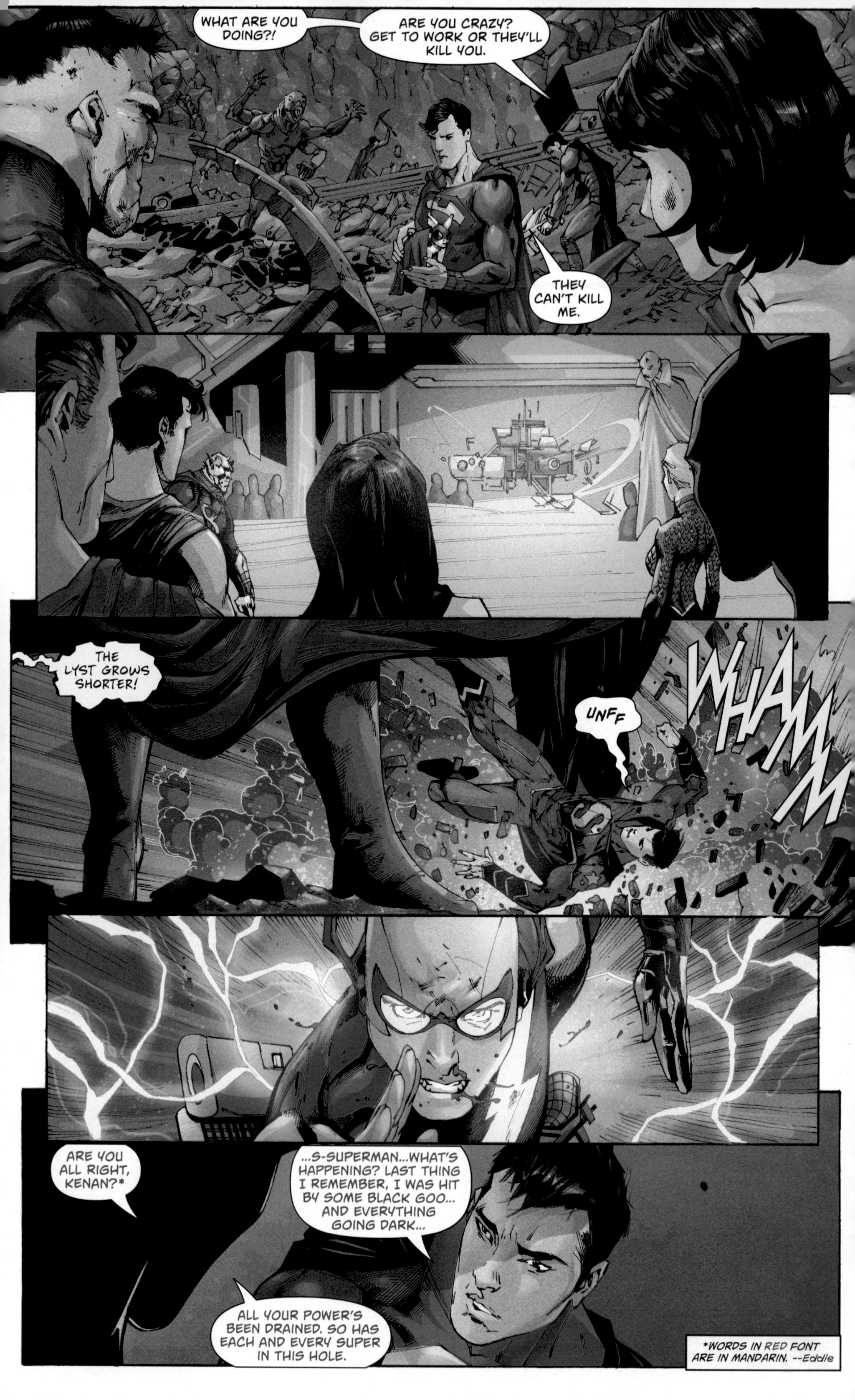
WHAT ARE YOU DOING?!
ARE YOU CRAZY? GET TO WORK OR THEY'LL KILL YOU.
THEY CAN'T KILL ME.
THE LYST GROWS SHORTER!
UNFF
WHAMM
ARE YOU ALL RIGHT, KENAN?*
...S-SUPERMAN...WHAT'S HAPPENING? LAST THING I REMEMBER, I WAS HIT BY SOME BLACK GOO... AND EVERYTHING GOING DARK...
ALL YOUR POWER'S BEEN DRAINED. SO HAS EACH AND EVERY SUPER IN THIS HOLE.
*WORDS IN RED FONT ARE IN MANDARIN. --Eddie

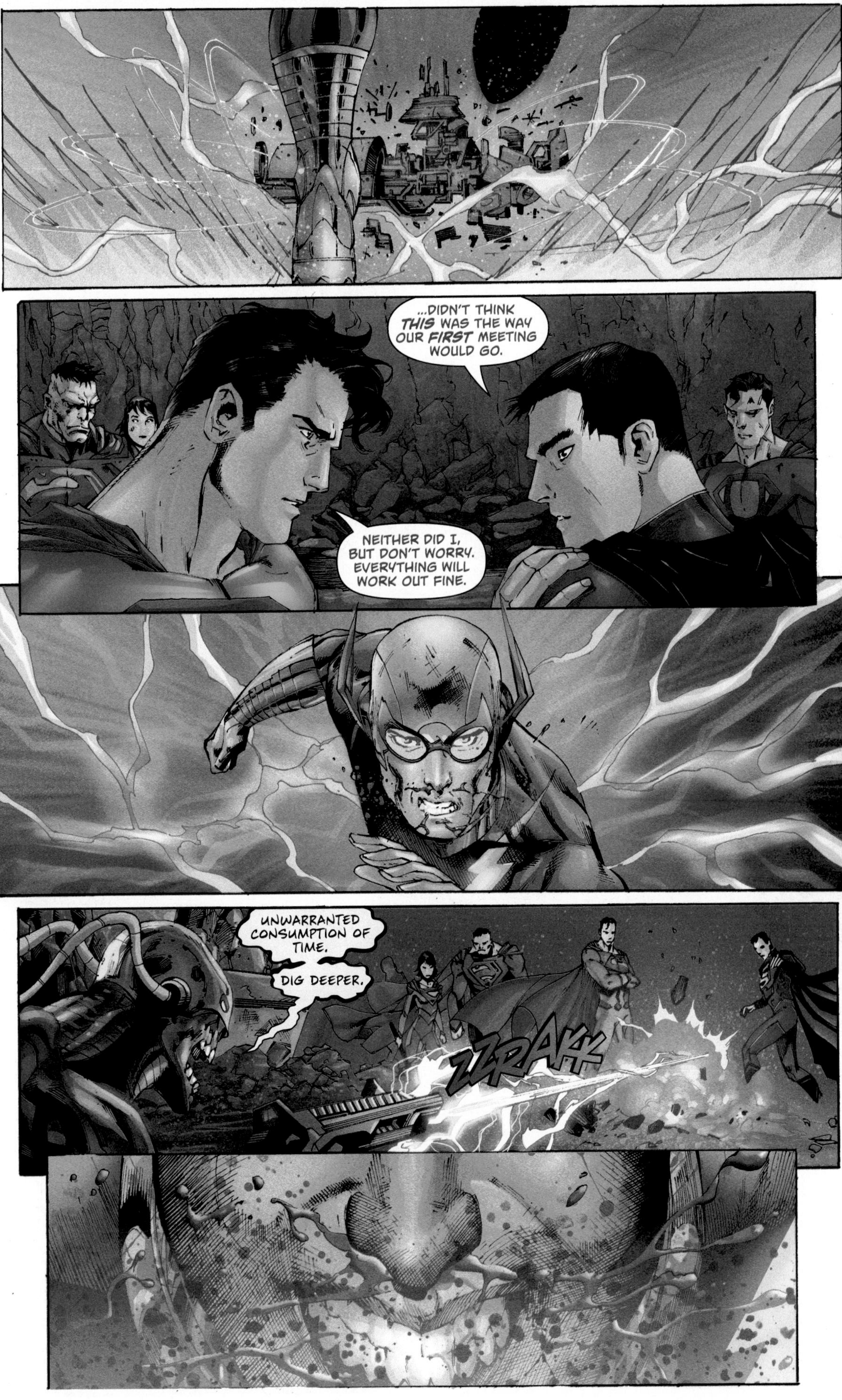
...DIDN'T THINK THIS WAS THE WAY OUR FIRST MEETING WOULD GO.
NEITHER DID I, BUT DON'T WORRY. EVERYTHING WILL WORK OUT FINE.
UNWARRANTED CONSUMPTION OF TIME.
DIG DEEPER.
ZZRAKK

I HATE TO ASK YOU THIS, BUT HOW IS *THIS* GOING TO WORK OUT FINE IF NONE OF US HAVE POWERS?

WE'VE BEEN TOSSED IN THIS GRAVE LIKE GARBAGE.

AND HOW IS IT THEY CAN'T KILL *YOU*?

YOU MISUNDERSTOOD WHAT I SAID, THAT BEAST MIGHT BE ABLE TO KILL ME, BUT *HE CAN'T KILL US.*

GREAT VATHLO!

RED RACER DID IT!

YOU'RE *SUPERMEN* AND *SUPERWOMEN.*

WE'RE ALL CREATED *EQUAL,* BECAUSE WE WANT TO HELP, AND NOTHING WILL EVER DESTROY THAT AS LONG AS THERE'S ONE PERSON LEFT TAKING A BREATH WITH AN "S" ON THEIR CHEST.

BUT HOW DID PROPHECY GET YOU?

RAY!

WHERE ARE YOU?!

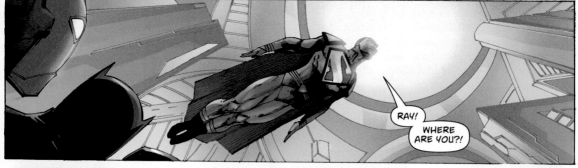

I GOT HIM, ACTUALLY. I ACTED AS BAIT.

WHY WOULD YOU DO THAT?

TO BREAK YOU ALL OUT, OF COURSE.

FREE YOU AND HELP GET YOUR POWERS BACK.

ALL BY YOURSELF, *hmm?*

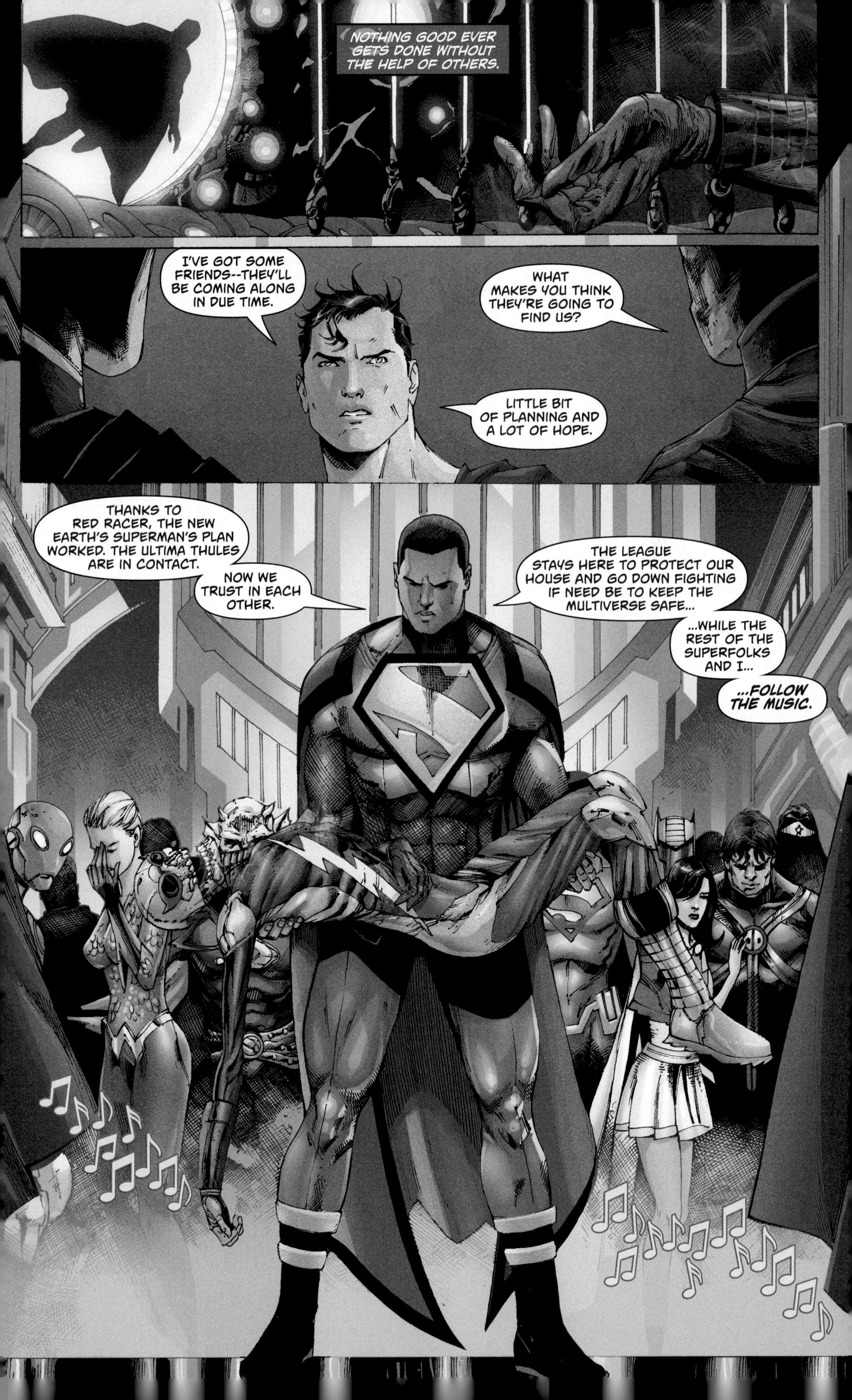
NOTHING GOOD EVER GETS DONE WITHOUT THE HELP OF OTHERS.
I'VE GOT SOME FRIENDS--THEY'LL BE COMING ALONG IN DUE TIME.
WHAT MAKES YOU THINK THEY'RE GOING TO FIND US?
LITTLE BIT OF PLANNING AND A LOT OF HOPE.
THANKS TO RED RACER, THE NEW EARTH'S SUPERMAN'S PLAN WORKED. THE ULTIMA THULES ARE IN CONTACT.
NOW WE TRUST IN EACH OTHER.
THE LEAGUE STAYS HERE TO PROTECT OUR HOUSE AND GO DOWN FIGHTING IF NEED BE TO KEEP THE MULTIVERSE SAFE...
...WHILE THE REST OF THE SUPERFOLKS AND I...
...FOLLOW THE MUSIC.

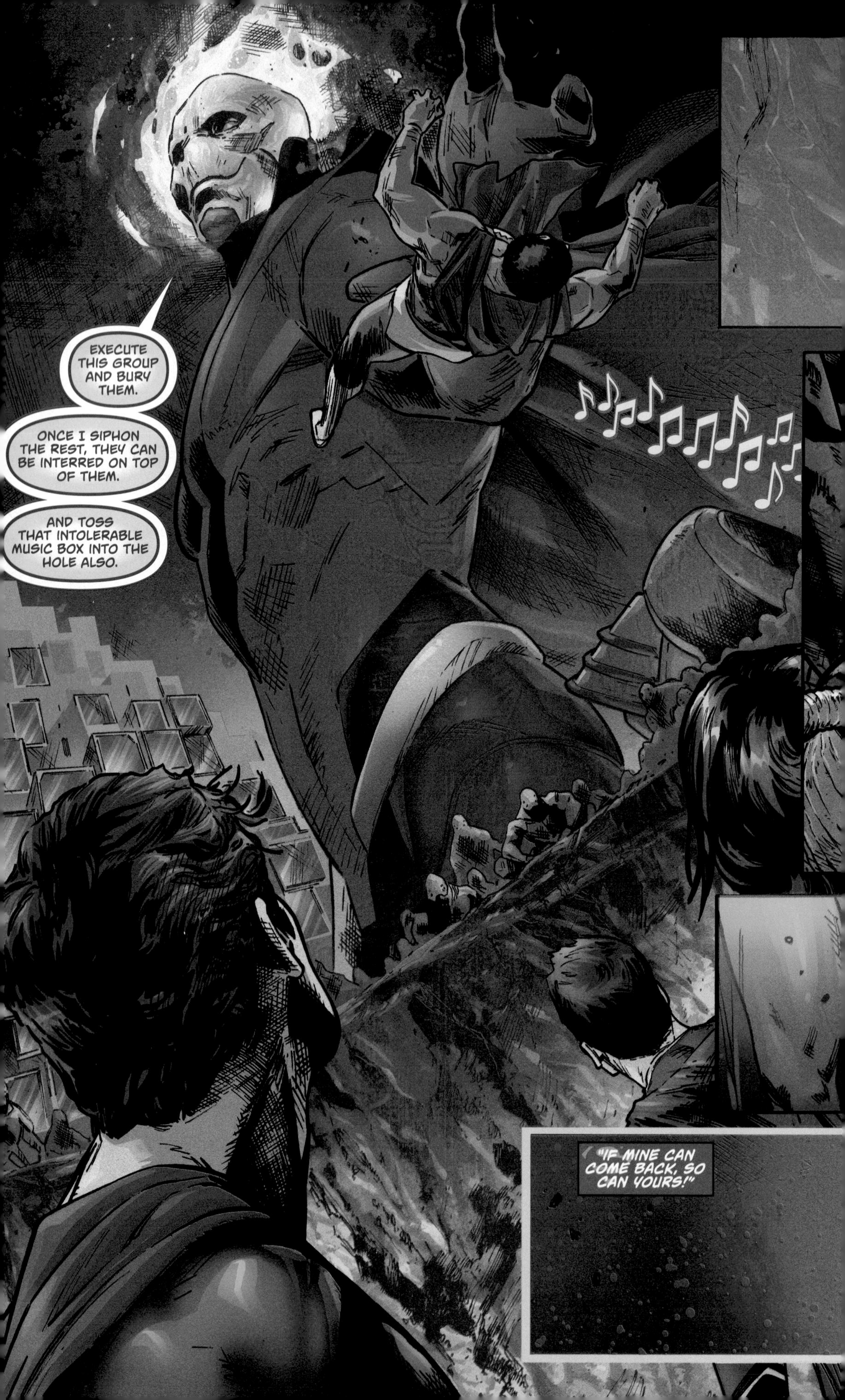
EXECUTE THIS GROUP AND BURY THEM.
ONCE I SIPHON THE REST, THEY CAN BE INTERRED ON TOP OF THEM.
AND TOSS THAT INTOLERABLE MUSIC BOX INTO THE HOLE ALSO.
"IF MINE CAN COME BACK, SO CAN YOURS!"

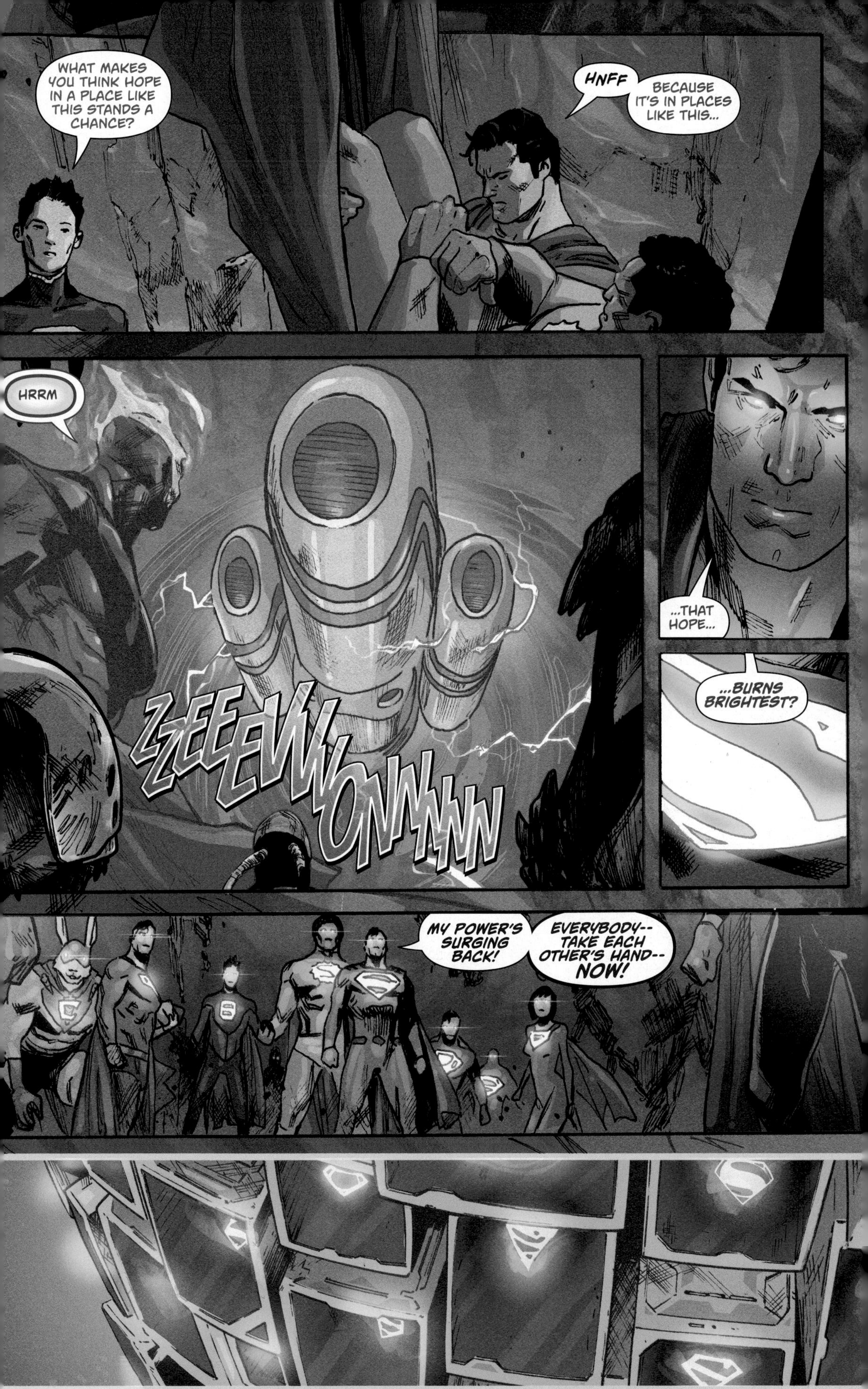
WHAT MAKES YOU THINK HOPE IN A PLACE LIKE THIS STANDS A CHANCE?
HNFF
BECAUSE IT'S IN PLACES LIKE THIS...
HRRM
...THAT HOPE...
...BURNS BRIGHTEST?
MY POWER'S SURGING BACK!
EVERYBODY-- TAKE EACH OTHER'S HAND-- NOW!

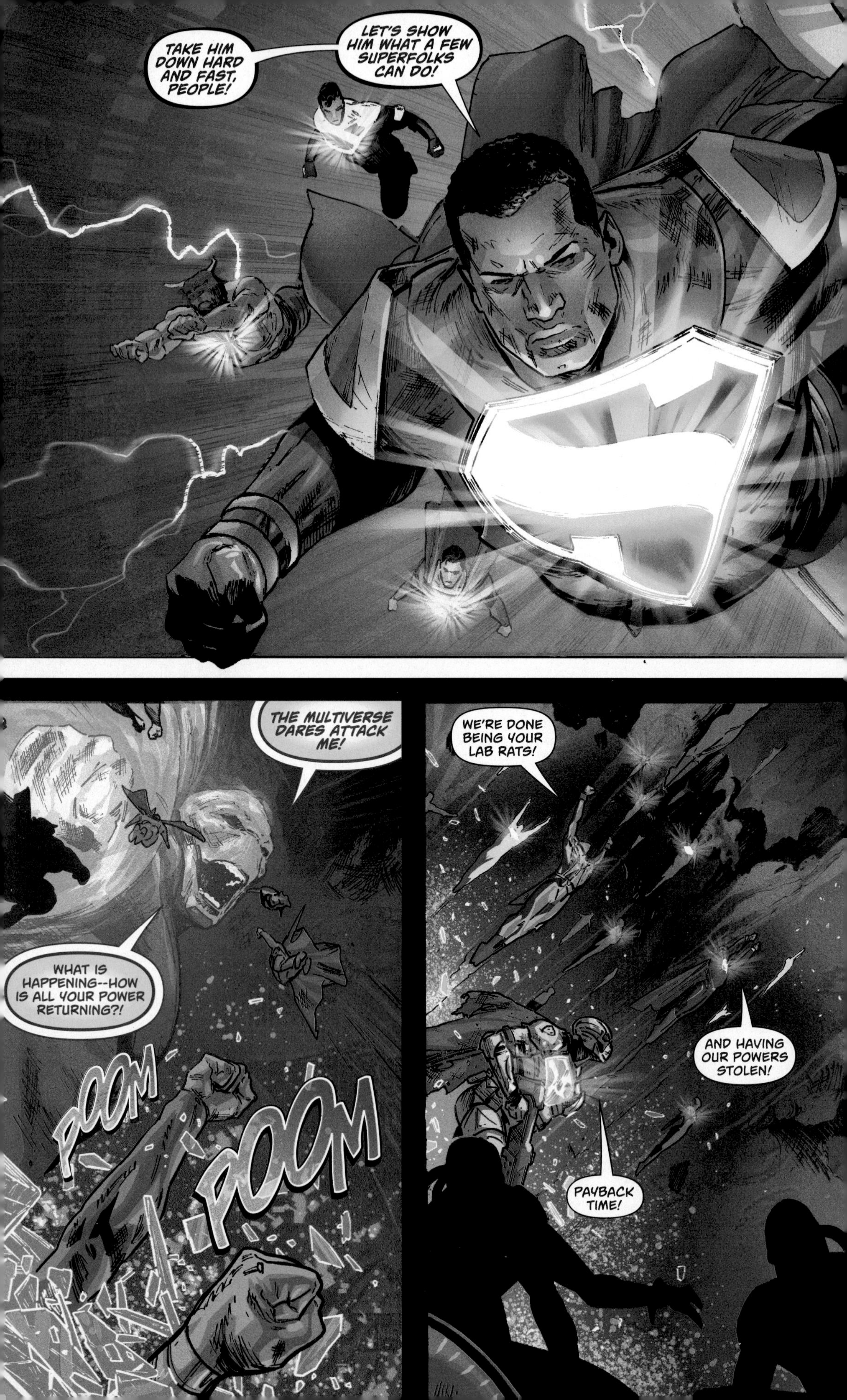
TAKE HIM DOWN HARD AND FAST, PEOPLE!
LET'S SHOW HIM WHAT A FEW SUPERFOLKS CAN DO!
THE MULTIVERSE DARES ATTACK ME!
WHAT IS HAPPENING--HOW IS ALL YOUR POWER RETURNING?!
POOM
POOM
WE'RE DONE BEING YOUR LAB RATS!
AND HAVING OUR POWERS STOLEN!
PAYBACK TIME!

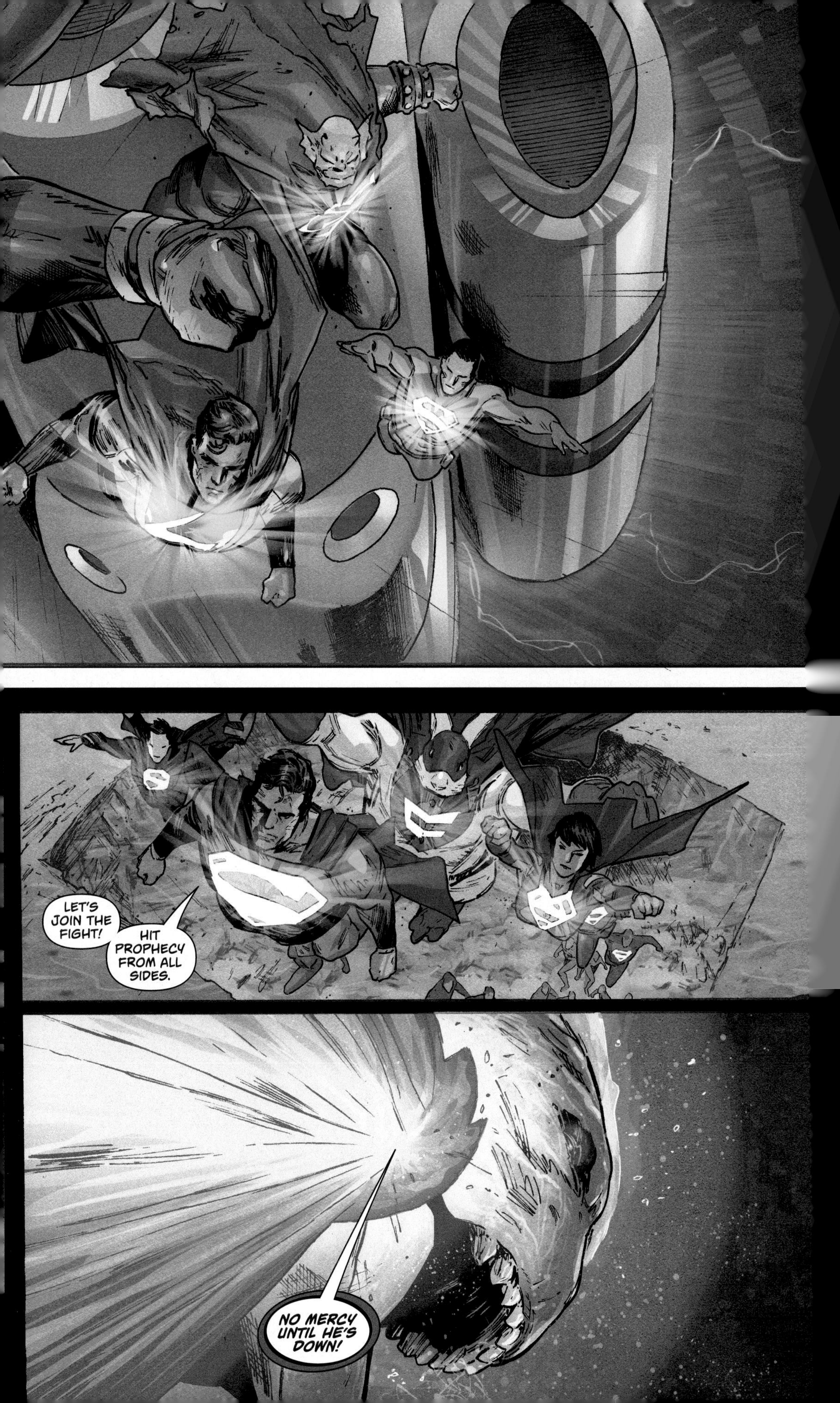
LET'S JOIN THE FIGHT!
HIT PROPHECY FROM ALL SIDES.
NO MERCY UNTIL HE'S DOWN!

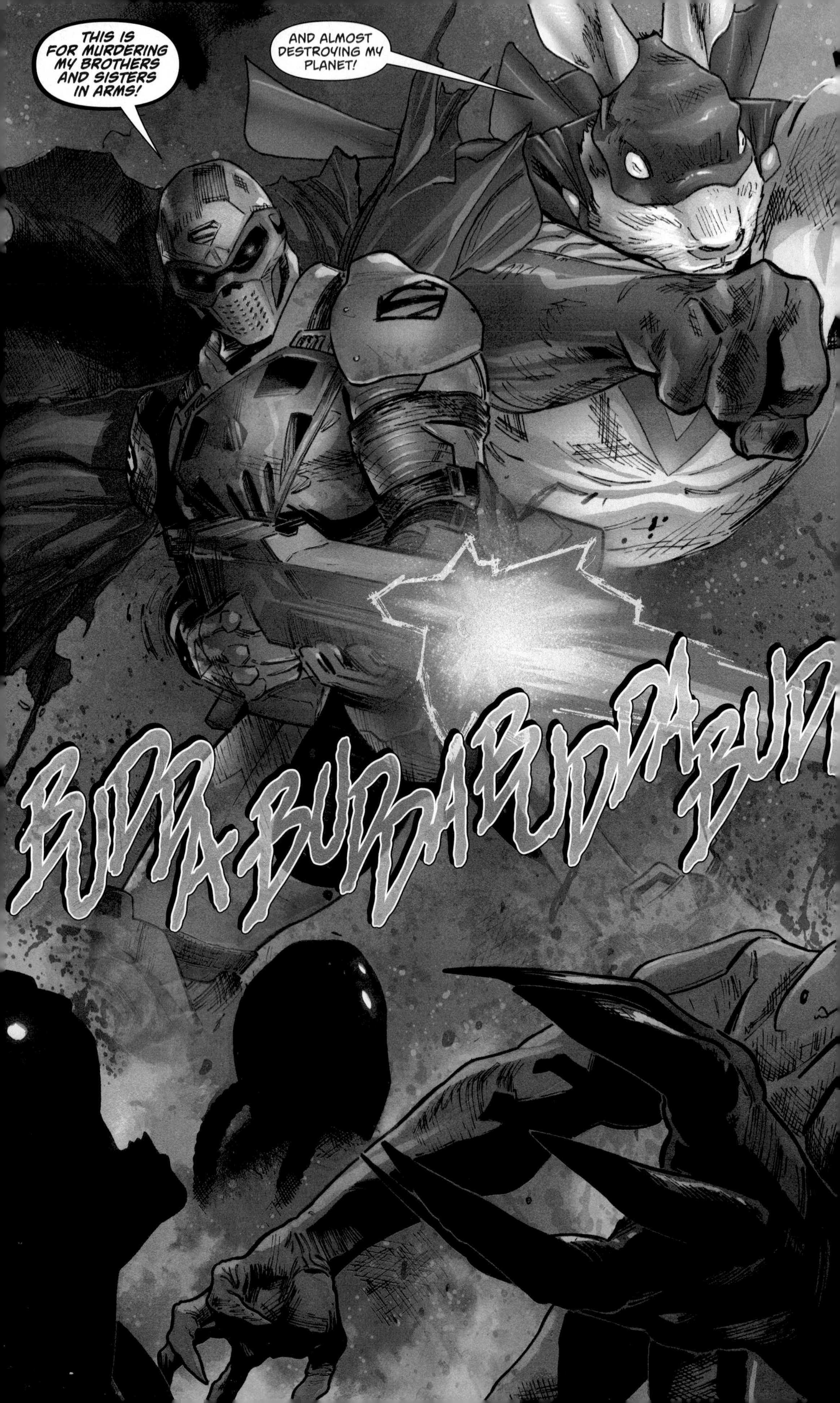
THIS IS FOR MURDERING MY BROTHERS AND SISTERS IN ARMS!
AND ALMOST DESTROYING MY PLANET!
BUDDA BUDDA BUDDA BUD

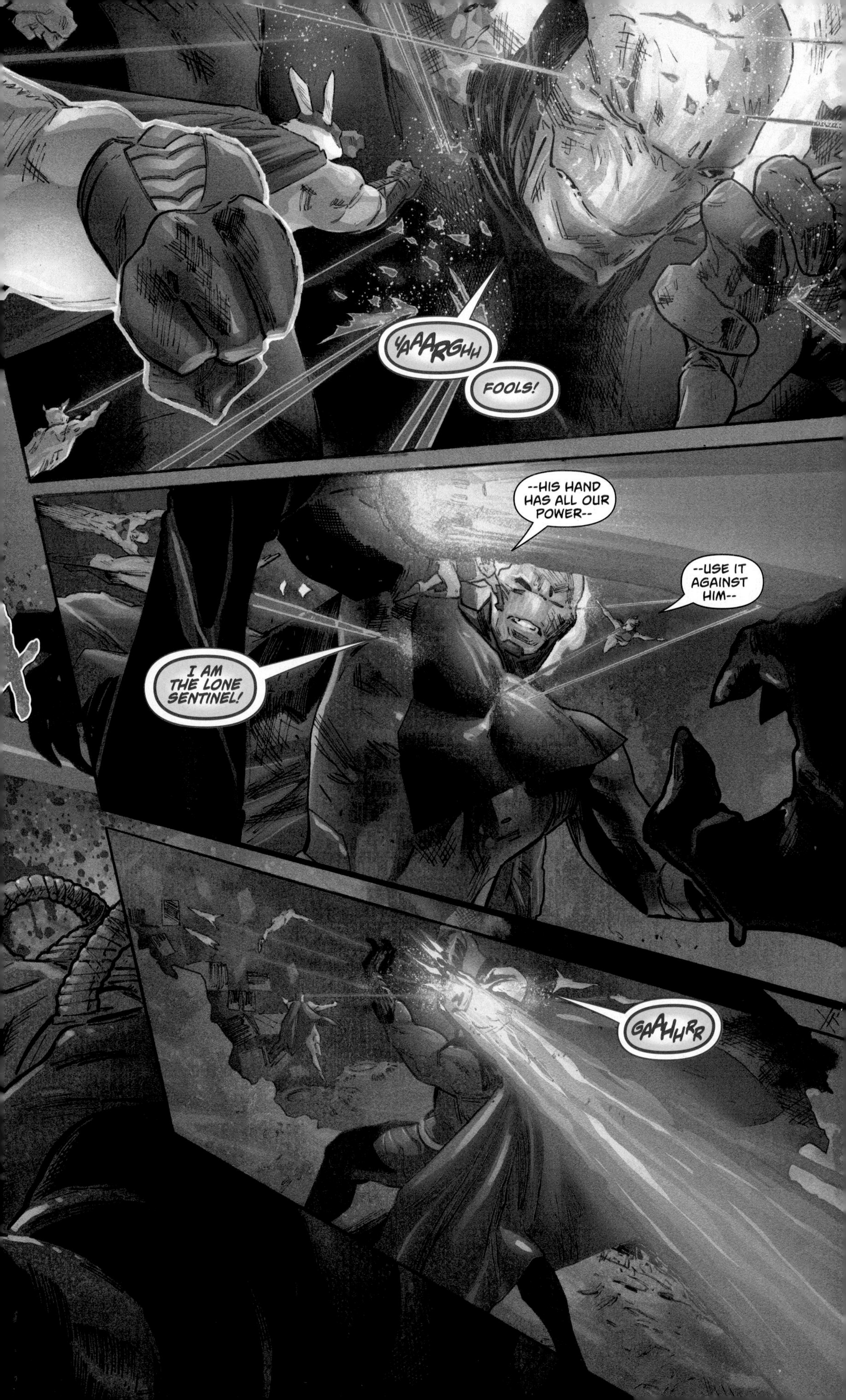
YAAARGHH
FOOLS!
--HIS HAND HAS ALL OUR POWER--
I AM THE LONE SENTINEL!
--USE IT AGAINST HIM--
GAAHHRR

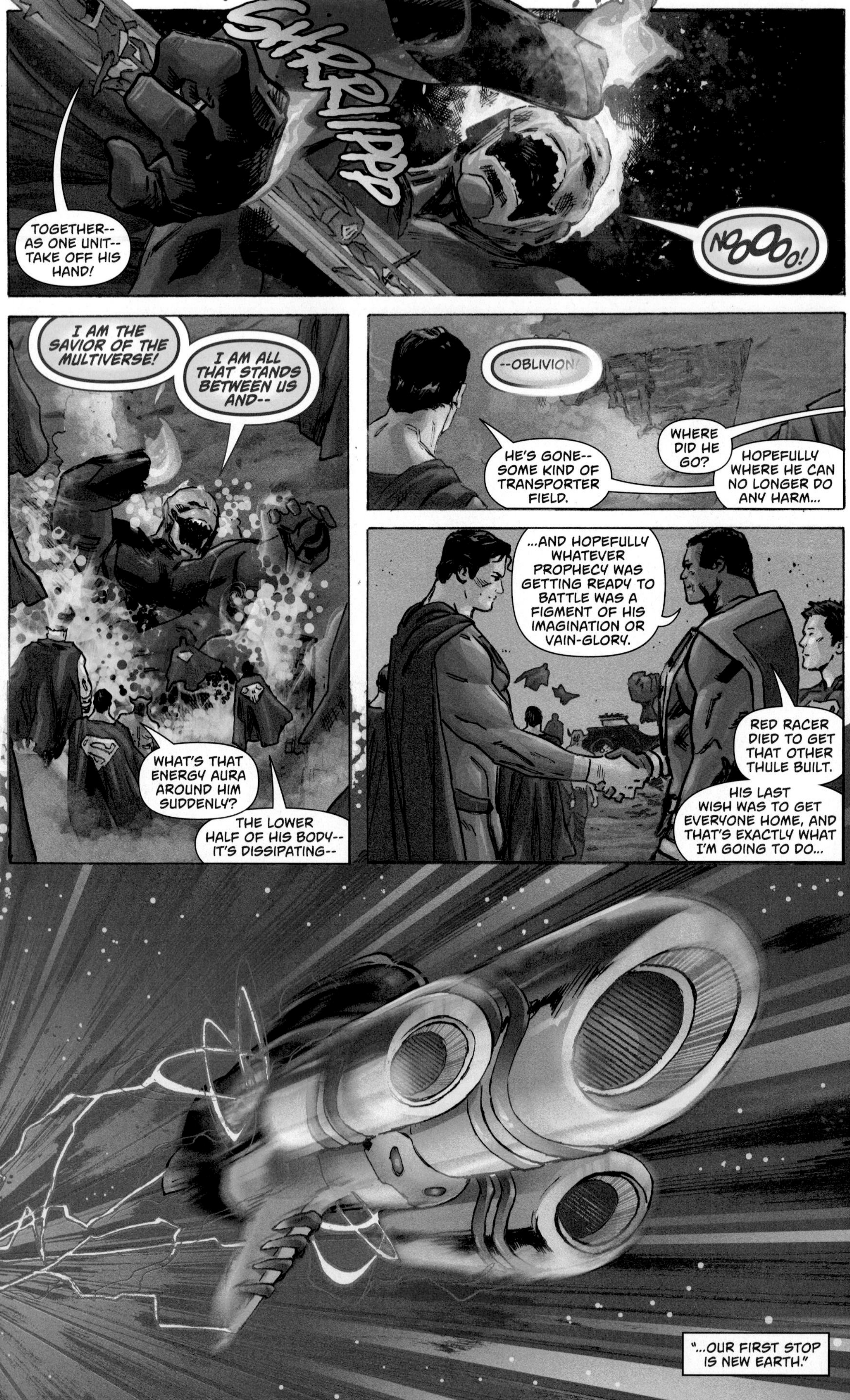

SHRRIPPP
TOGETHER-- AS ONE UNIT-- TAKE OFF HIS HAND!
NOOOOO!
I AM THE SAVIOR OF THE MULTIVERSE!
I AM ALL THAT STANDS BETWEEN US AND--
WHAT'S THAT ENERGY AURA AROUND HIM SUDDENLY?
THE LOWER HALF OF HIS BODY-- IT'S DISSIPATING--
--OBLIVION!
HE'S GONE-- SOME KIND OF TRANSPORTER FIELD.
WHERE DID HE GO?
HOPEFULLY WHERE HE CAN NO LONGER DO ANY HARM...
...AND HOPEFULLY WHATEVER PROPHECY WAS GETTING READY TO BATTLE WAS A FIGMENT OF HIS IMAGINATION OR VAIN-GLORY.
RED RACER DIED TO GET THAT OTHER THULE BUILT.
HIS LAST WISH WAS TO GET EVERYONE HOME, AND THAT'S EXACTLY WHAT I'M GOING TO DO...
"...OUR FIRST STOP IS NEW EARTH."

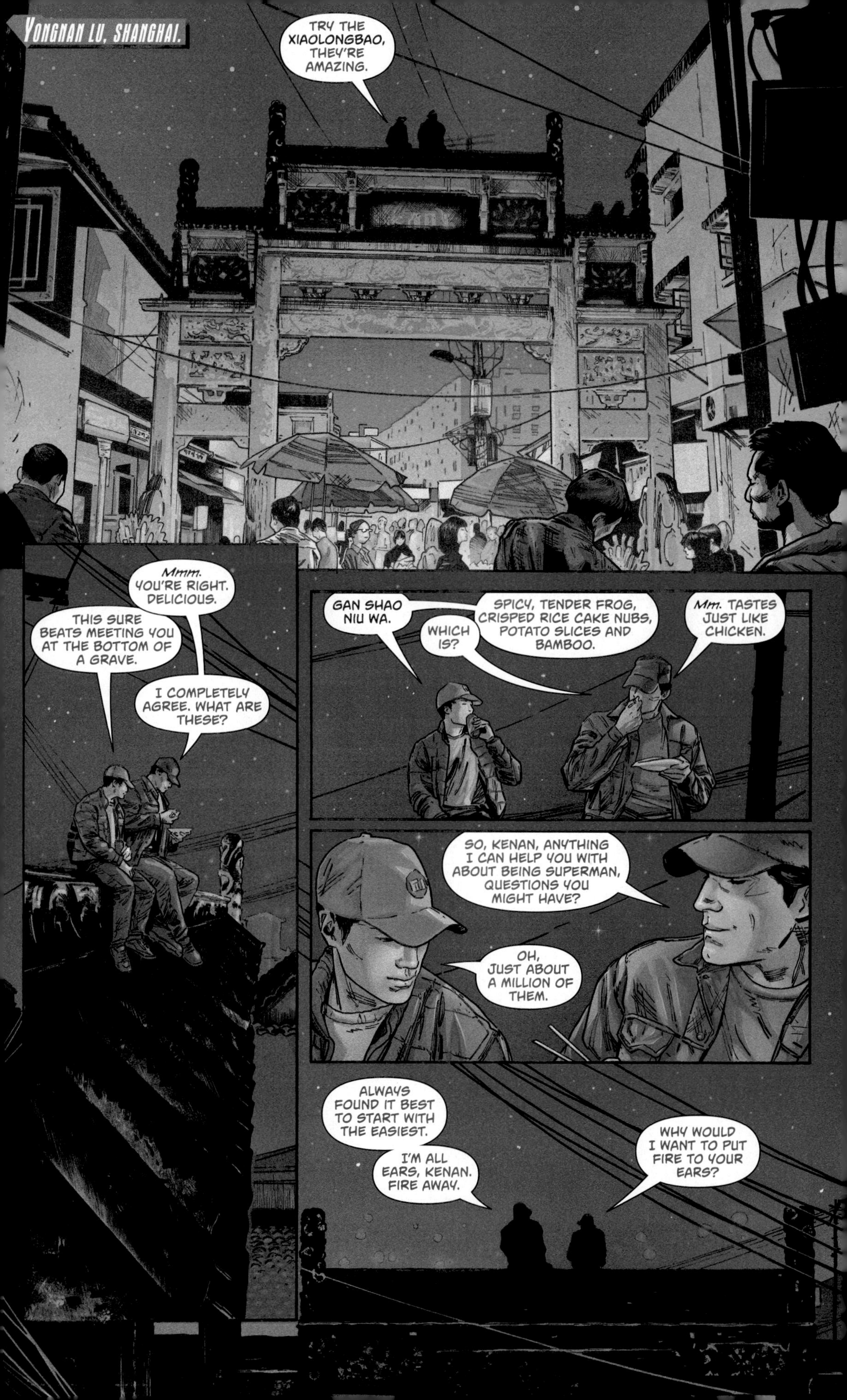
YONGNAN LU, SHANGHAI.
TRY THE XIAOLONGBAO, THEY'RE AMAZING.
Mmm. YOU'RE RIGHT. DELICIOUS.
THIS SURE BEATS MEETING YOU AT THE BOTTOM OF A GRAVE.
I COMPLETELY AGREE. WHAT ARE THESE?
GAN SHAO NIU WA.
WHICH IS?
SPICY, TENDER FROG, CRISPED RICE CAKE NUBS, POTATO SLICES AND BAMBOO.
Mm. TASTES JUST LIKE CHICKEN.
SO, KENAN, ANYTHING I CAN HELP YOU WITH ABOUT BEING SUPERMAN, QUESTIONS YOU MIGHT HAVE?
OH, JUST ABOUT A MILLION OF THEM.
ALWAYS FOUND IT BEST TO START WITH THE EASIEST.
I'M ALL EARS, KENAN. FIRE AWAY.
WHY WOULD I WANT TO PUT FIRE TO YOUR EARS?

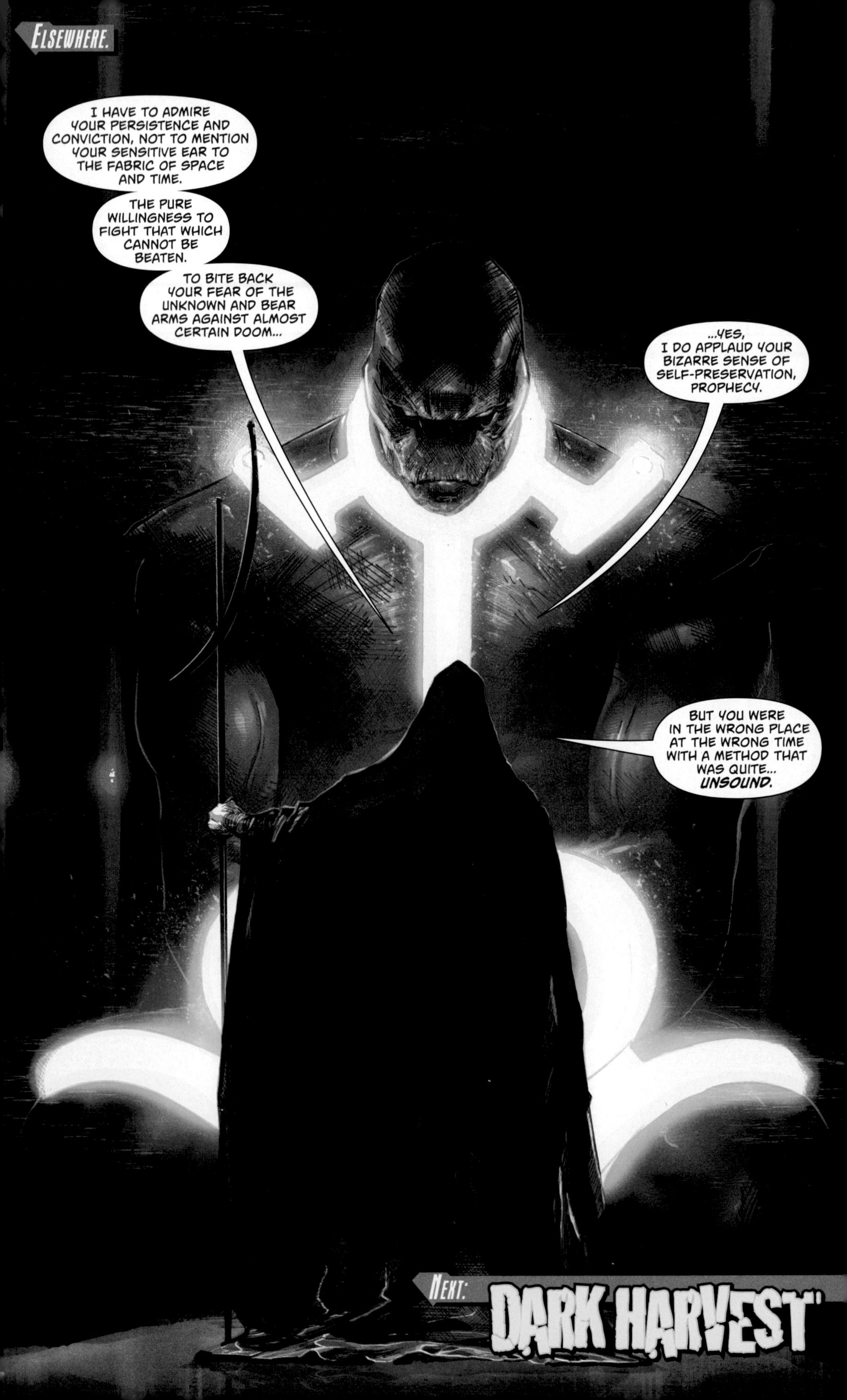
ELSEWHERE.
I HAVE TO ADMIRE YOUR PERSISTENCE AND CONVICTION, NOT TO MENTION YOUR SENSITIVE EAR TO THE FABRIC OF SPACE AND TIME.
THE PURE WILLINGNESS TO FIGHT THAT WHICH CANNOT BE BEATEN.
TO BITE BACK YOUR FEAR OF THE UNKNOWN AND BEAR ARMS AGAINST ALMOST CERTAIN DOOM...
...YES, I DO APPLAUD YOUR BIZARRE SENSE OF SELF-PRESERVATION, PROPHECY.
BUT YOU WERE IN THE WRONG PLACE AT THE WRONG TIME WITH A METHOD THAT WAS QUITE... *UNSOUND*.
NEXT: DARK HARVEST

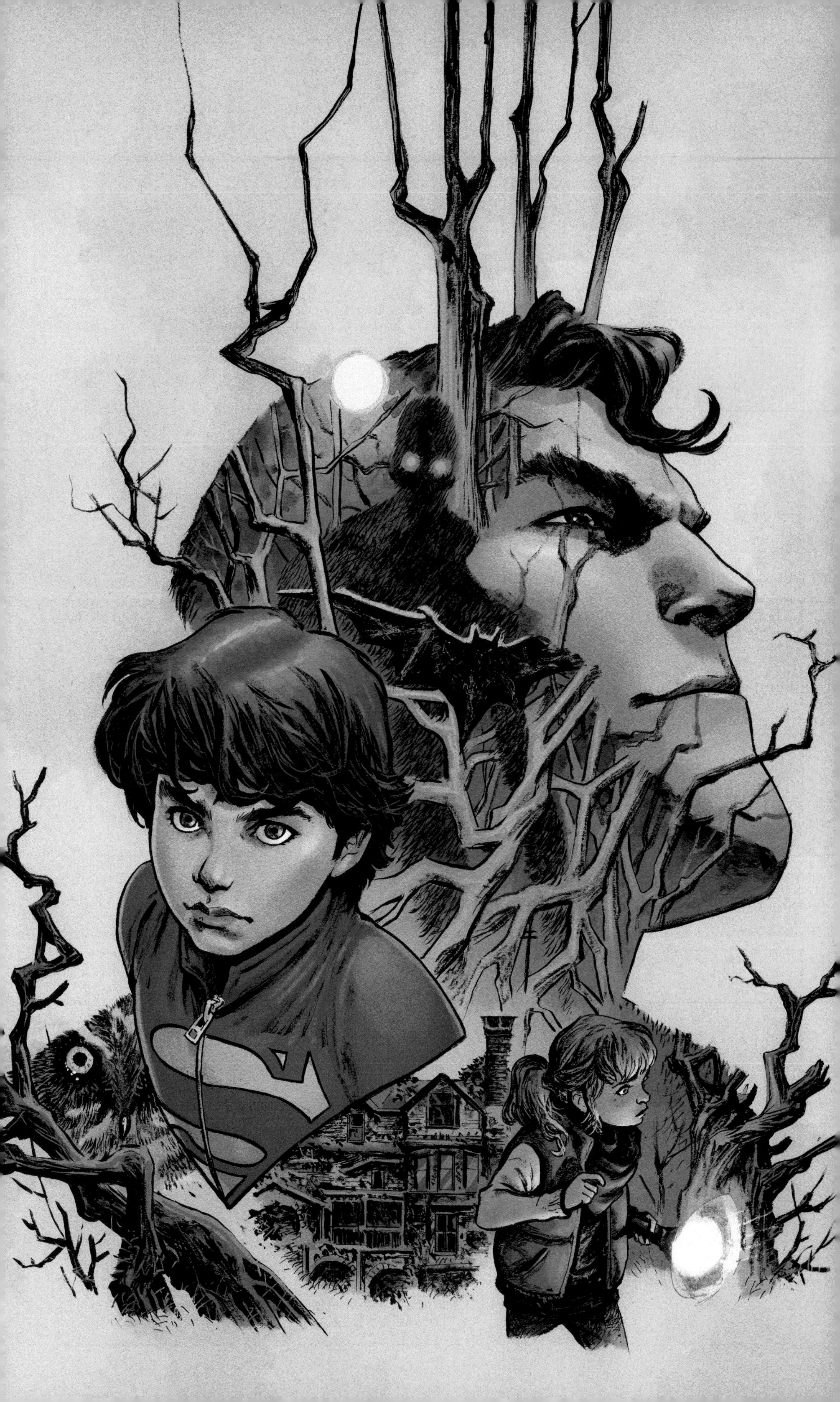

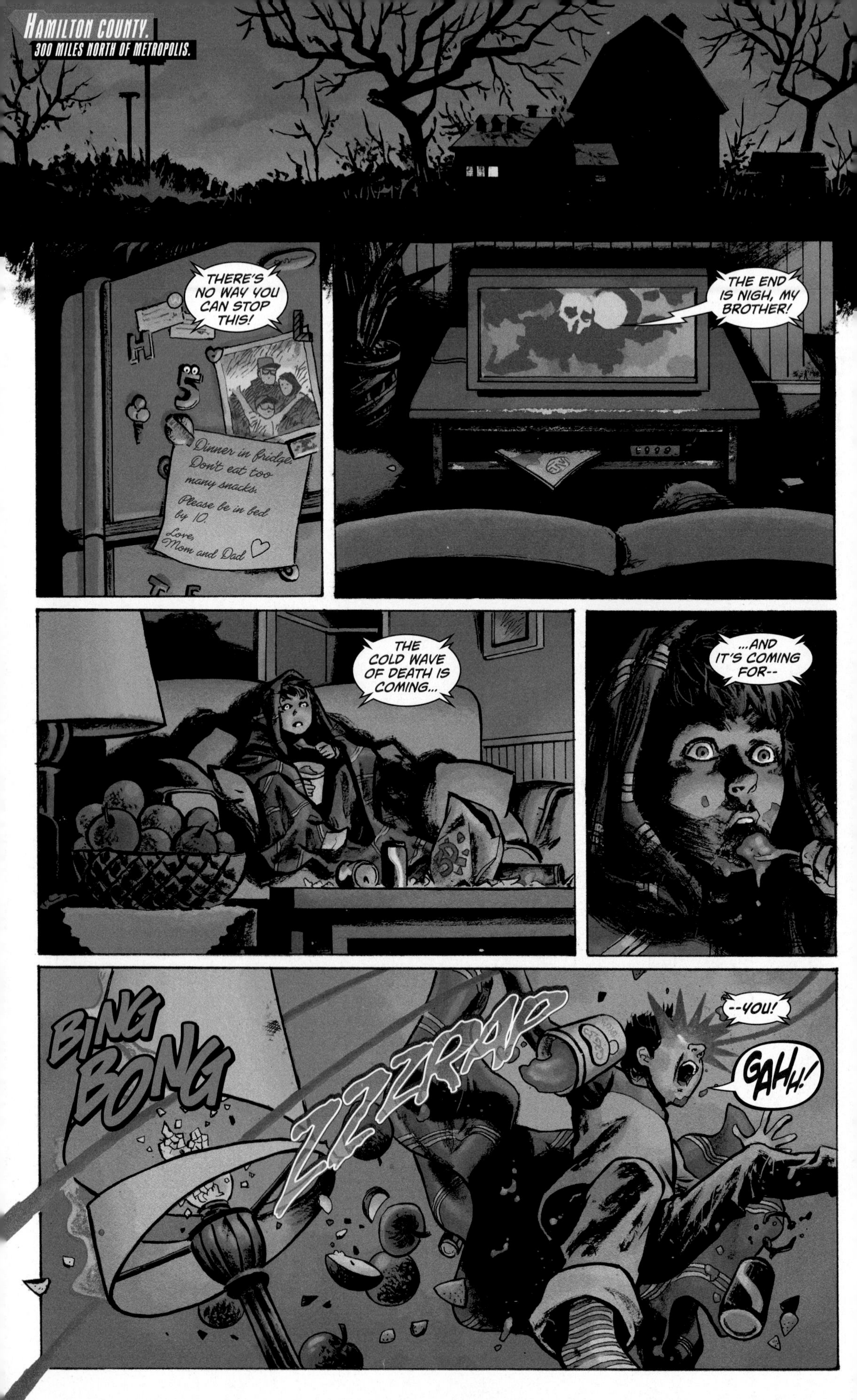

HAMILTON COUNTY.
300 MILES NORTH OF METROPOLIS.
THERE'S NO WAY YOU CAN STOP THIS!
Dinner in fridge. Don't eat too many snacks. Please be in bed by 10. Love, Mom and Dad
THE END IS NIGH, MY BROTHER!
THE COLD WAVE OF DEATH IS COMING...
...AND IT'S COMING FOR--
BING BONG
ZZZRRAP
--YOU!
GAHH!

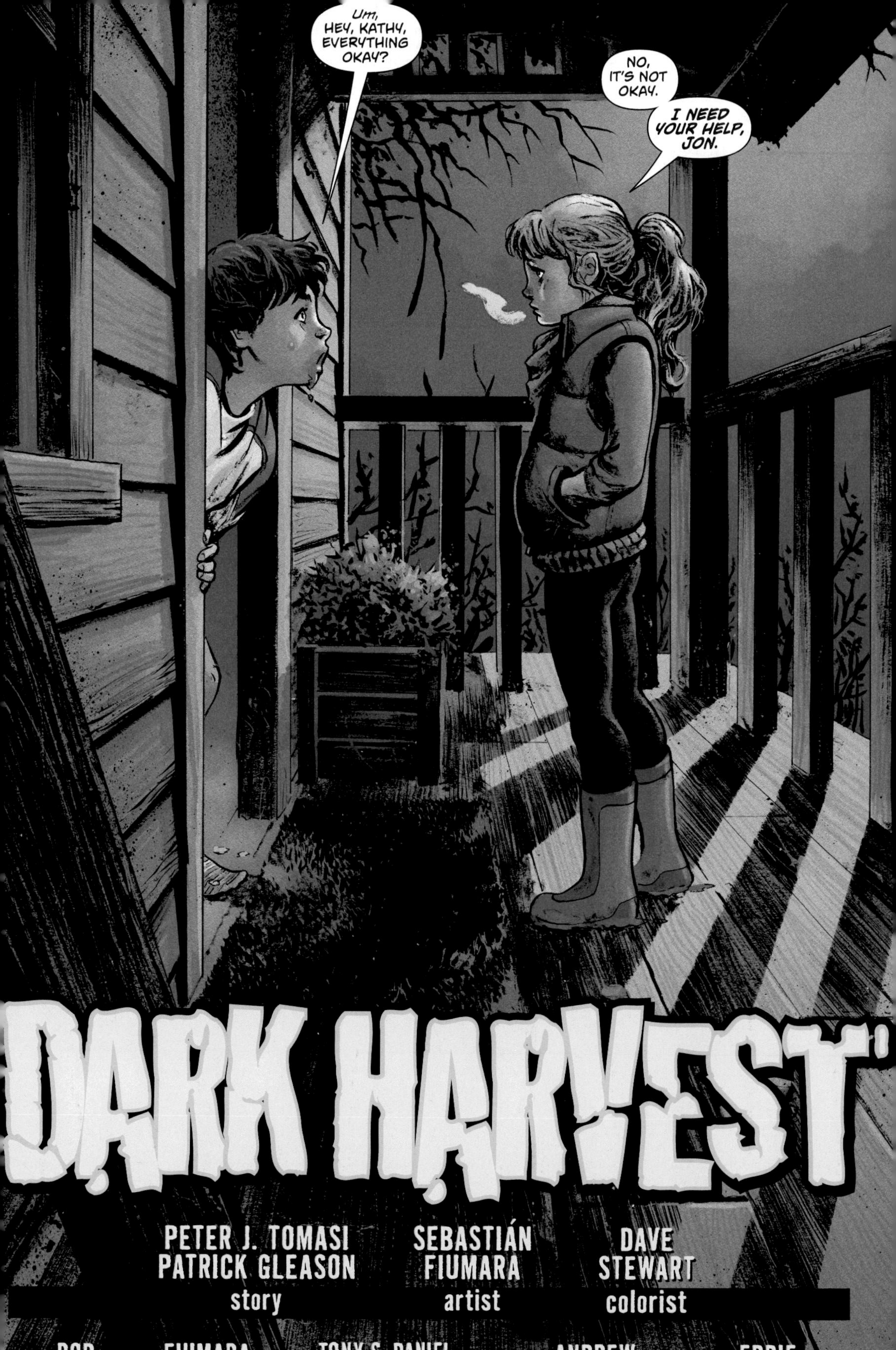

Um, HEY, KATHY, EVERYTHING OKAY?
NO, IT'S NOT OKAY.
I NEED YOUR HELP, JON.
DARK HARVEST

PETER J. TOMASI
PATRICK GLEASON
story

SEBASTIÁN FIUMARA
artist

DAVE STEWART
colorist

ROB LEIGH
letterer

FIUMARA & STEWART
cover

TONY S. DANIEL & TOMEU MOREY
variant cover

ANDREW MARINO
assistant editor

EDDIE BERGANZA
editor

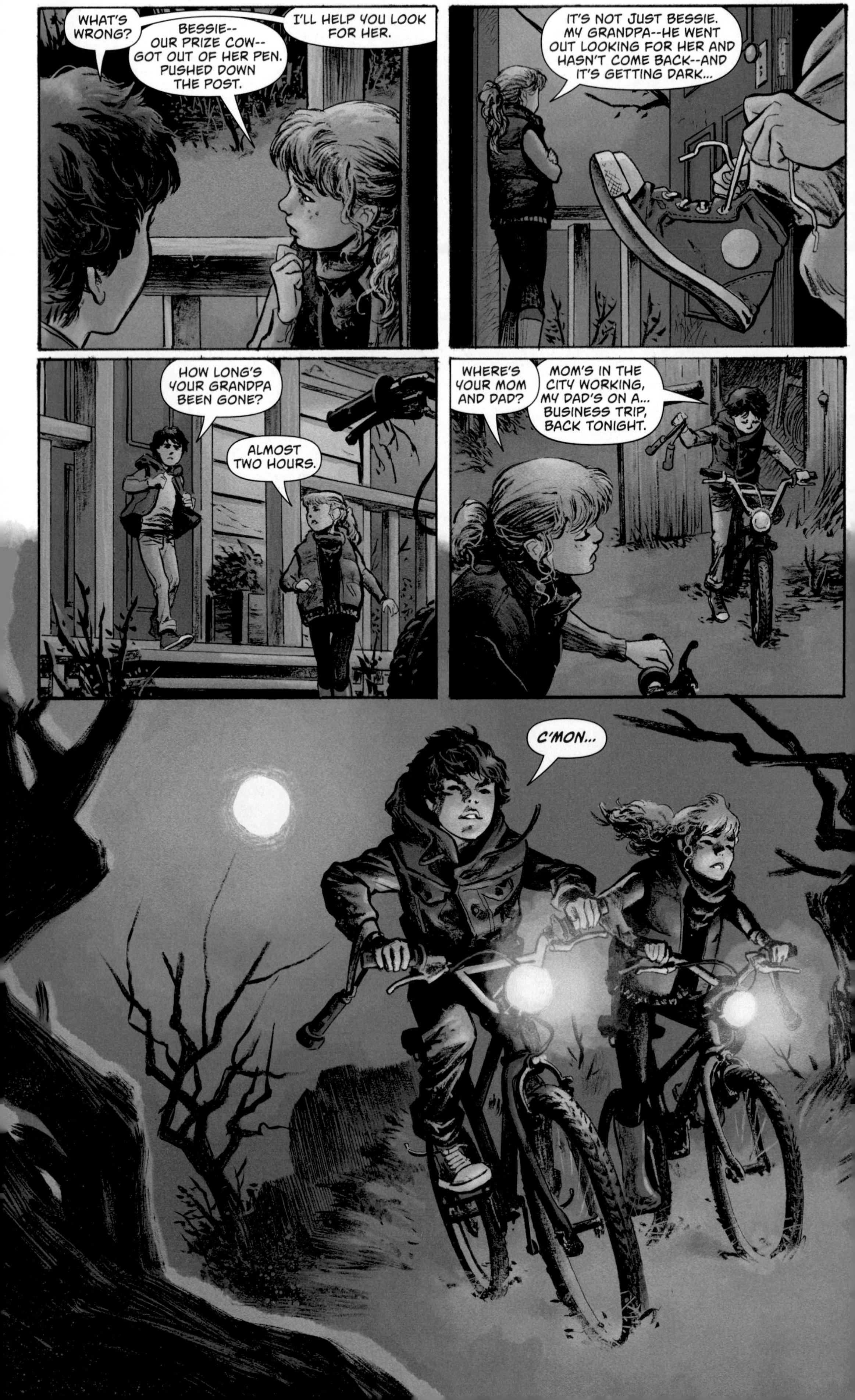
WHAT'S WRONG?
BESSIE-- OUR PRIZE COW-- GOT OUT OF HER PEN. PUSHED DOWN THE POST.
I'LL HELP YOU LOOK FOR HER.
IT'S NOT JUST BESSIE. MY GRANDPA--HE WENT OUT LOOKING FOR HER AND HASN'T COME BACK--AND IT'S GETTING DARK...
HOW LONG'S YOUR GRANDPA BEEN GONE?
ALMOST TWO HOURS.
WHERE'S YOUR MOM AND DAD?
MOM'S IN THE CITY WORKING, MY DAD'S ON A... BUSINESS TRIP, BACK TONIGHT.
C'MON...

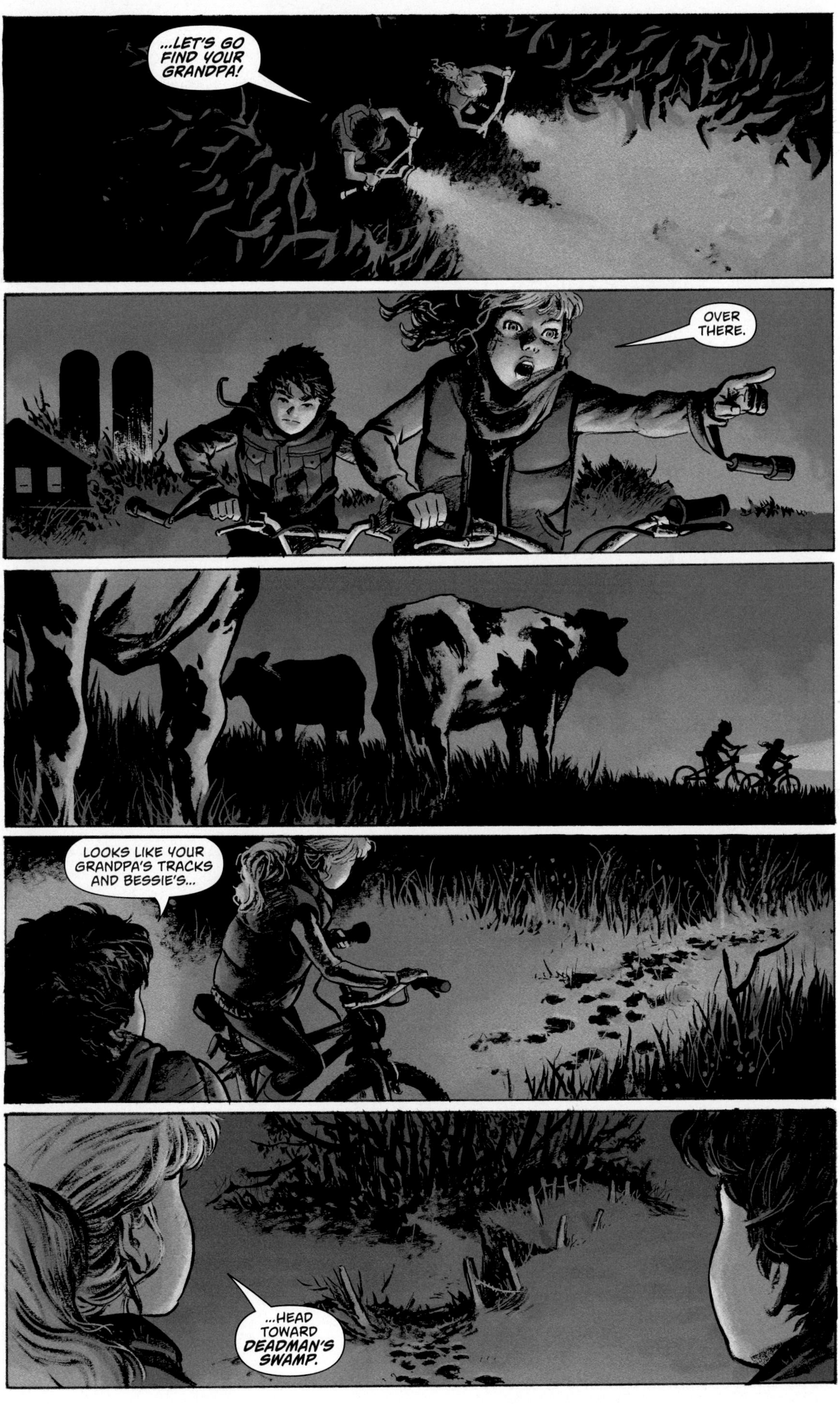
...LET'S GO FIND YOUR GRANDPA!
OVER THERE.
LOOKS LIKE YOUR GRANDPA'S TRACKS AND BESSIE'S...
...HEAD TOWARD DEADMAN'S SWAMP.

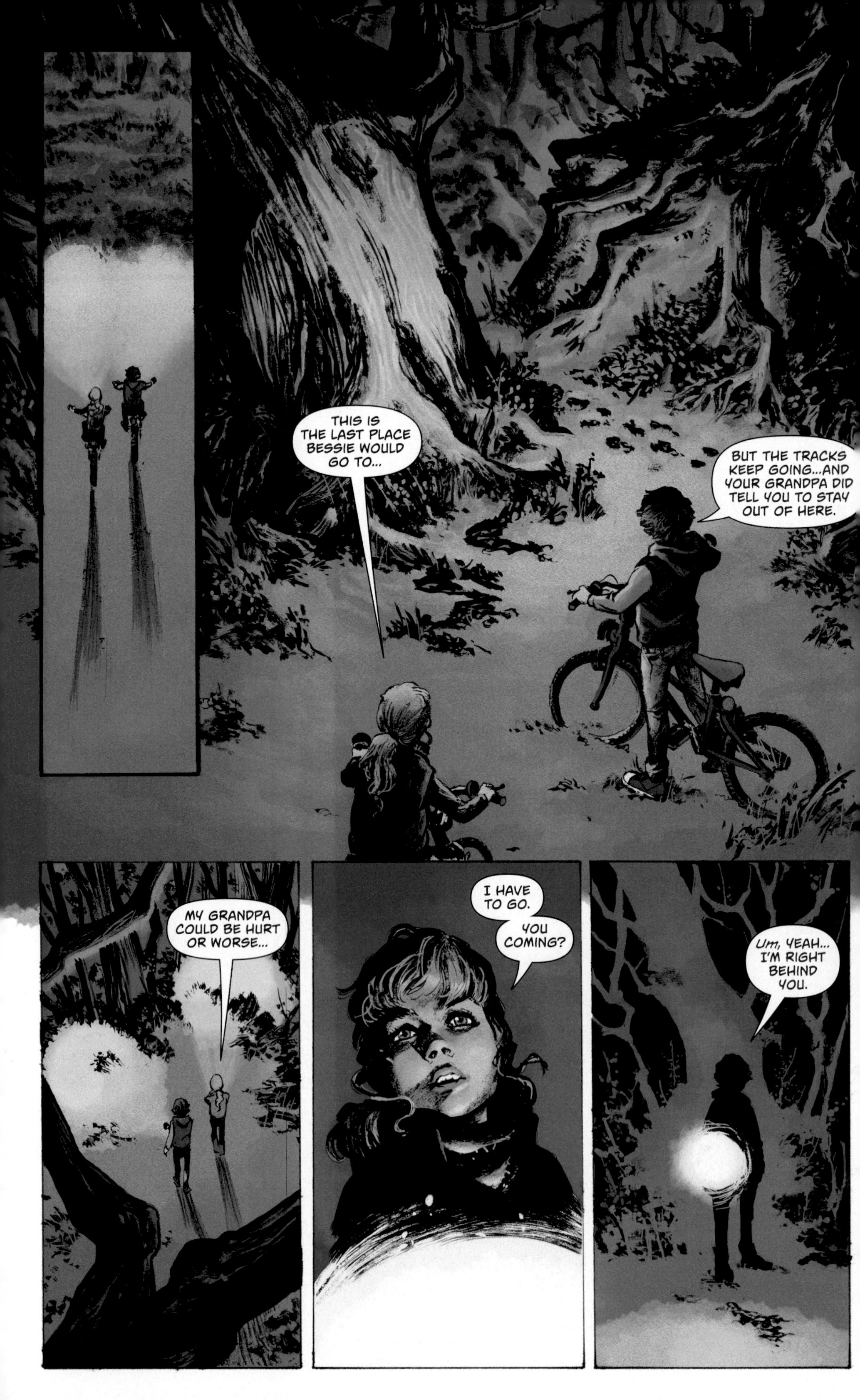
THIS IS THE LAST PLACE BESSIE WOULD GO TO...
BUT THE TRACKS KEEP GOING...AND YOUR GRANDPA DID TELL YOU TO STAY OUT OF HERE.
MY GRANDPA COULD BE HURT OR WORSE...
I HAVE TO GO.
YOU COMING?
UM, YEAH... I'M RIGHT BEHIND YOU.

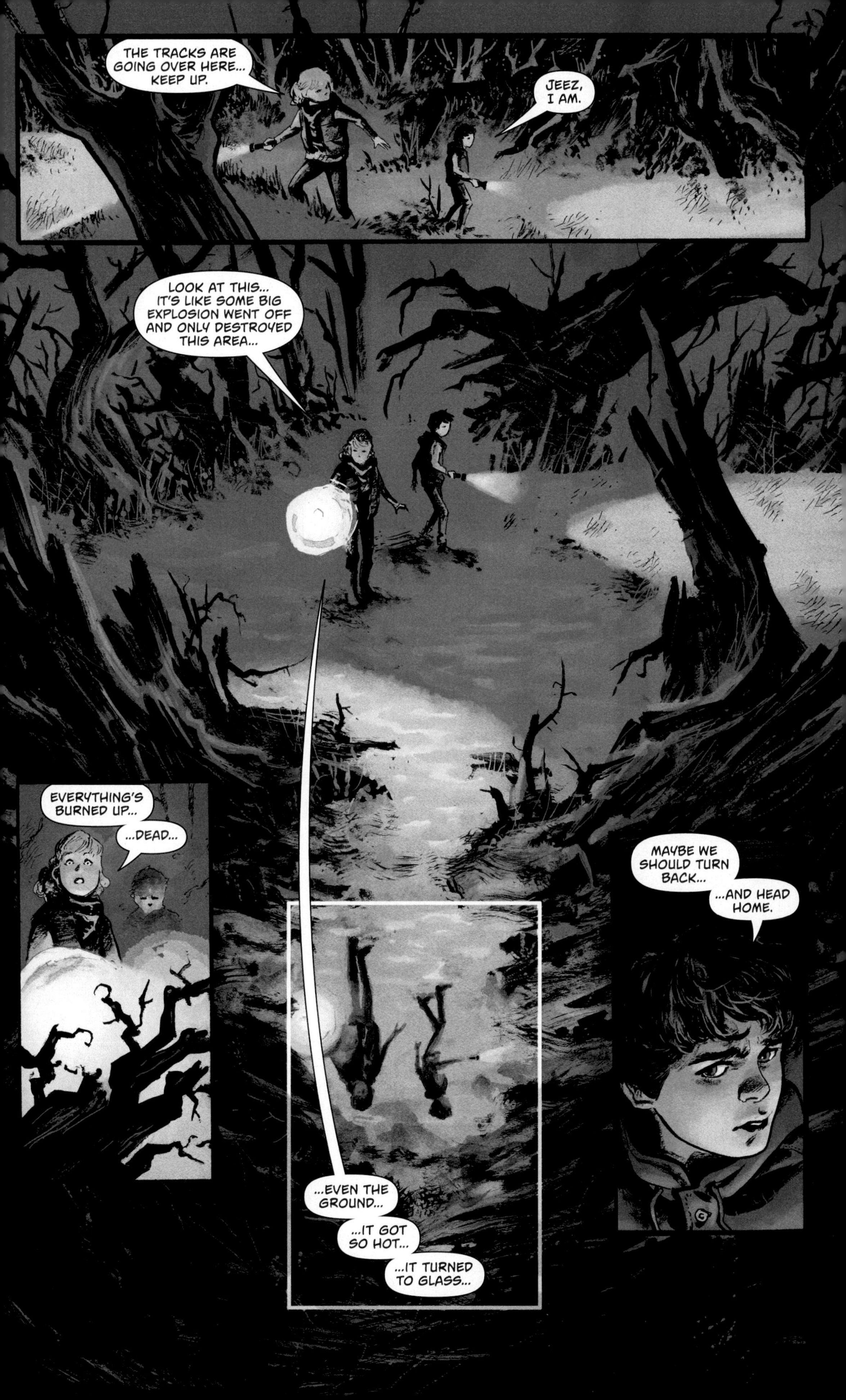
THE TRACKS ARE GOING OVER HERE... KEEP UP.
JEEZ, I AM.
LOOK AT THIS... IT'S LIKE SOME BIG EXPLOSION WENT OFF AND ONLY DESTROYED THIS AREA...
EVERYTHING'S BURNED UP...
...DEAD...
...EVEN THE GROUND...
...IT GOT SO HOT...
...IT TURNED TO GLASS...
MAYBE WE SHOULD TURN BACK...
...AND HEAD HOME.

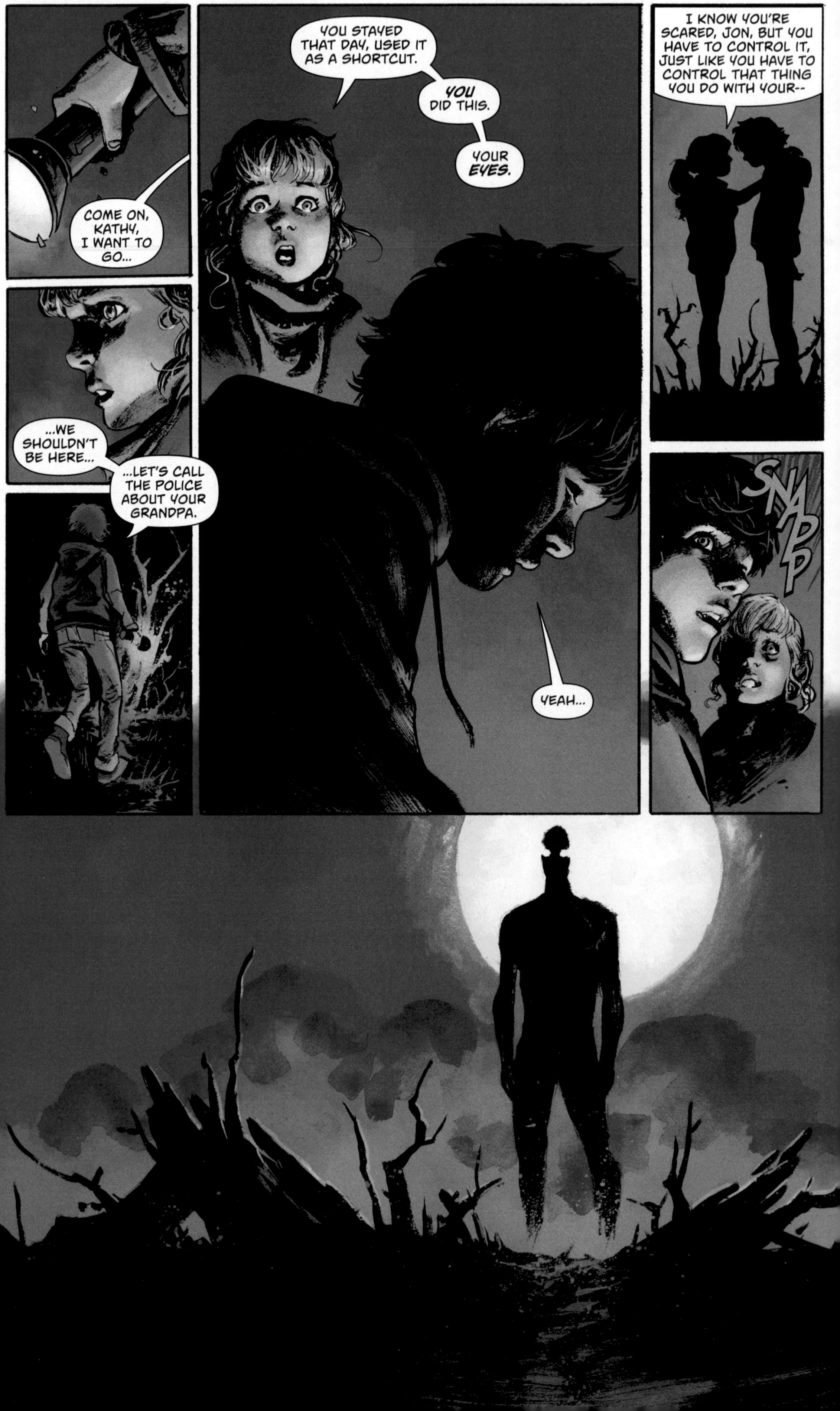
COME ON, KATHY, I WANT TO GO...
...WE SHOULDN'T BE HERE...
...LET'S CALL THE POLICE ABOUT YOUR GRANDPA.
YOU STAYED THAT DAY, USED IT AS A SHORTCUT.
YOU DID THIS.
YOUR EYES.
YEAH...
I KNOW YOU'RE SCARED, JON, BUT YOU HAVE TO CONTROL IT, JUST LIKE YOU HAVE TO CONTROL THAT THING YOU DO WITH YOUR--
SNAP

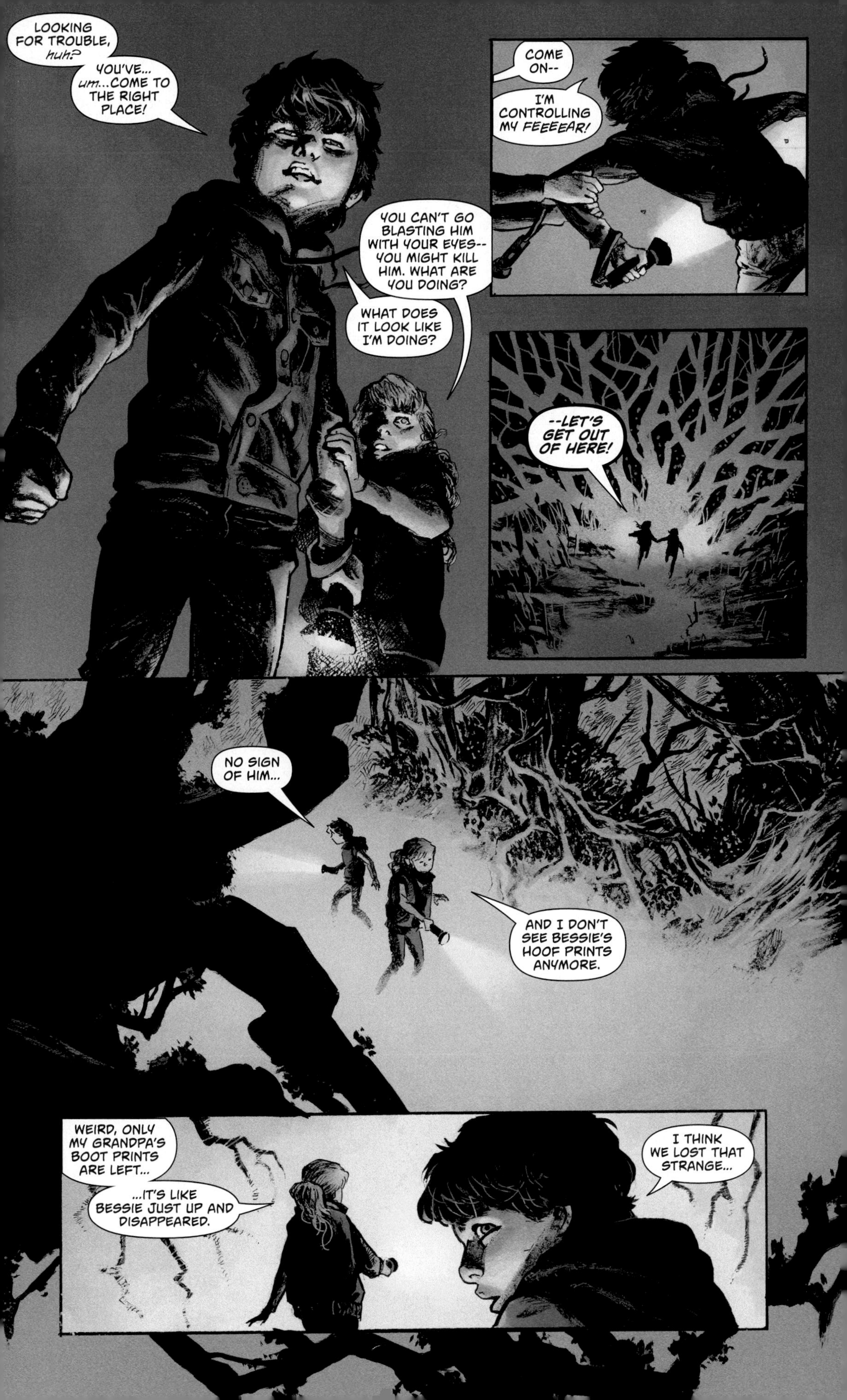
LOOKING FOR TROUBLE, *huh?*
YOU'VE... *um*...COME TO THE RIGHT PLACE!
COME ON--
I'M CONTROLLING MY *FEEEEAR!*
YOU CAN'T GO BLASTING HIM WITH YOUR EYES--YOU MIGHT KILL HIM. WHAT ARE YOU DOING?
WHAT DOES IT LOOK LIKE I'M DOING?
--LET'S GET OUT OF HERE!
NO SIGN OF HIM...
AND I DON'T SEE BESSIE'S HOOF PRINTS ANYMORE.
WEIRD, ONLY MY GRANDPA'S BOOT PRINTS ARE LEFT...
...IT'S LIKE BESSIE JUST UP AND DISAPPEARED.
I THINK WE LOST THAT STRANGE...

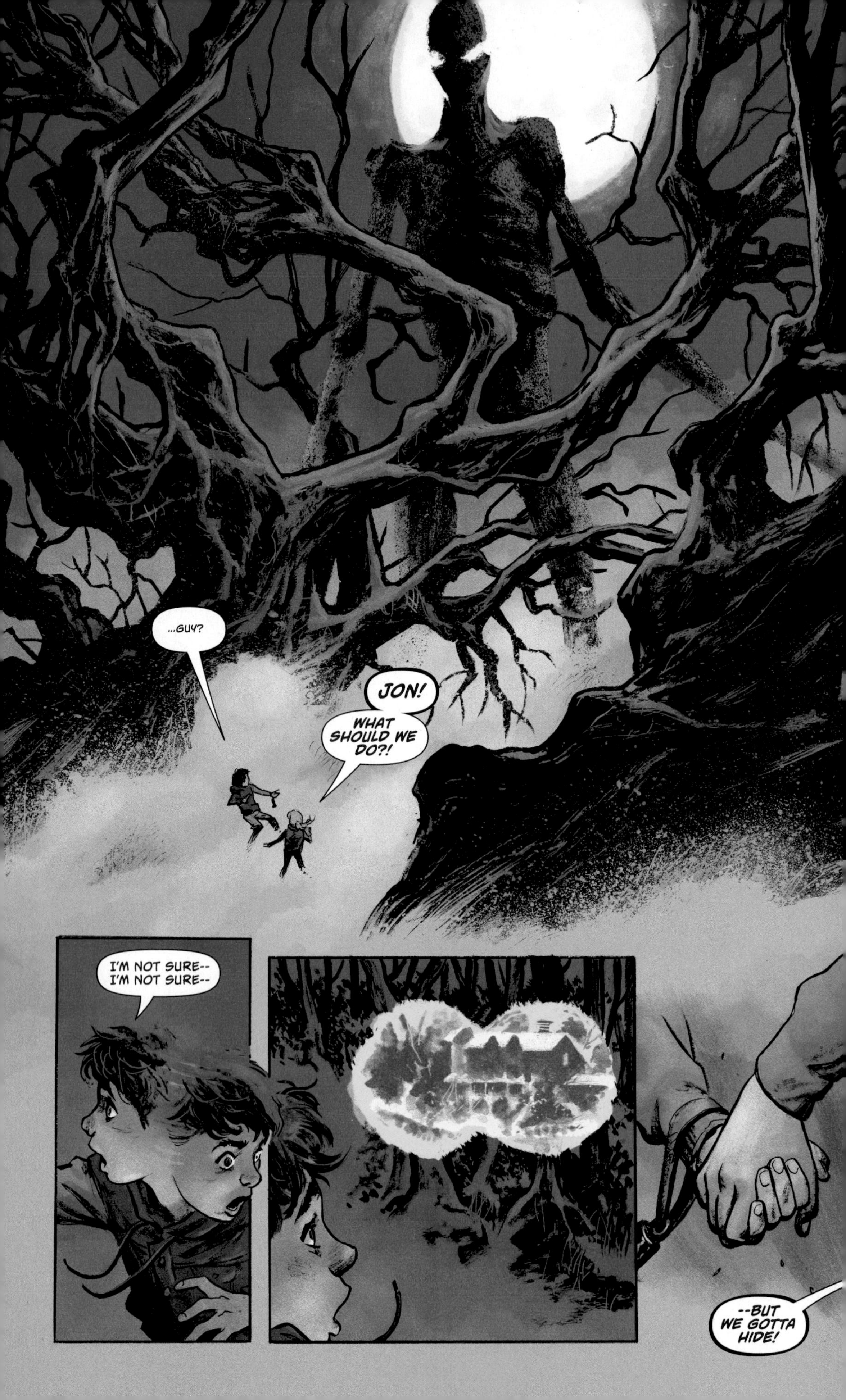
...GUY?
JON!
WHAT SHOULD WE DO?!
I'M NOT SURE-- I'M NOT SURE--
--BUT WE GOTTA HIDE!

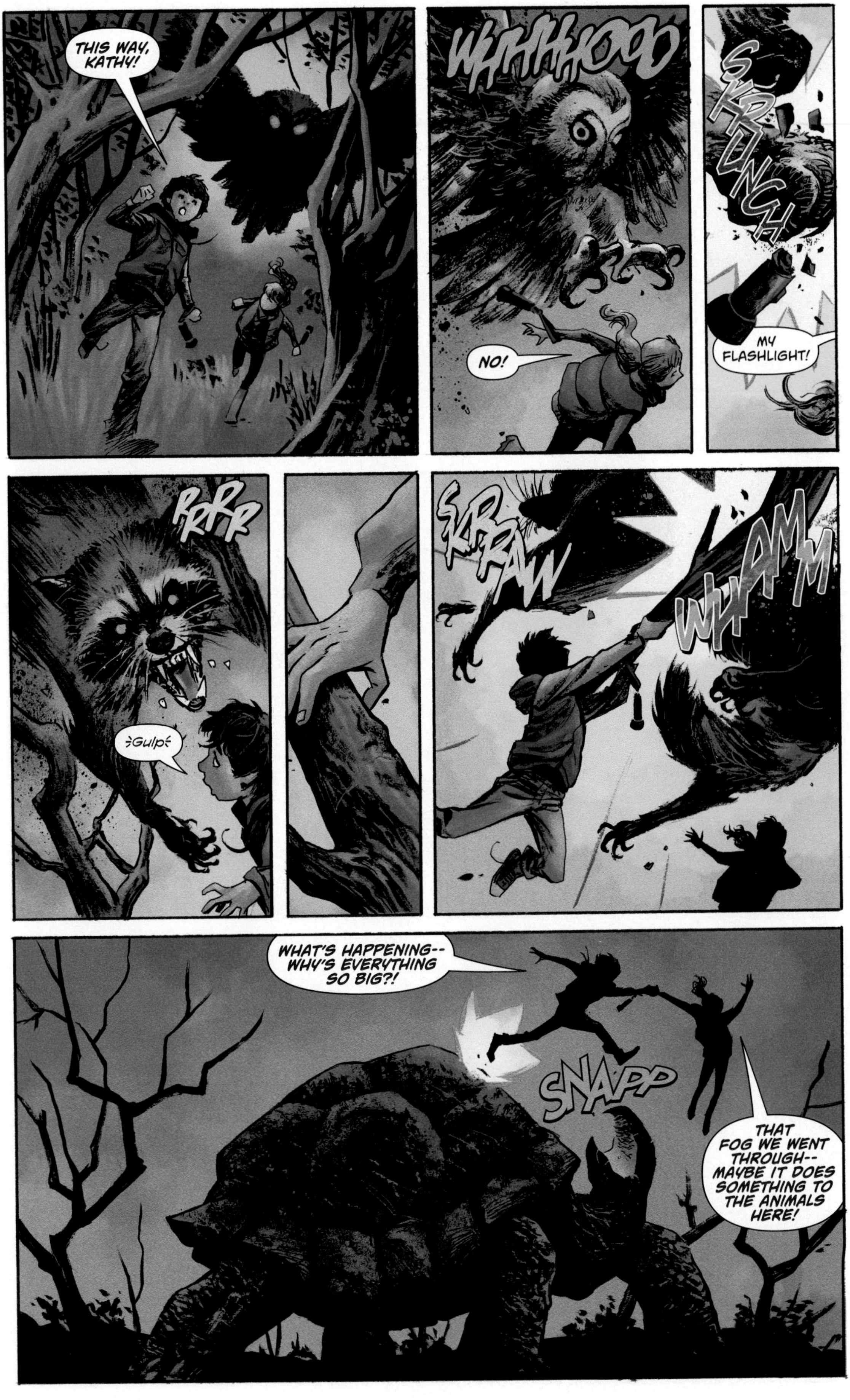
THIS WAY, KATHY!
WHHHOOO
NO!
SKRUNCH
MY FLASHLIGHT!
RRRR
Gulp
SKRRAW
WHAMM
WHAT'S HAPPENING-- WHY'S EVERYTHING SO BIG?!
SNAPP
THAT FOG WE WENT THROUGH-- MAYBE IT DOES SOMETHING TO THE ANIMALS HERE!

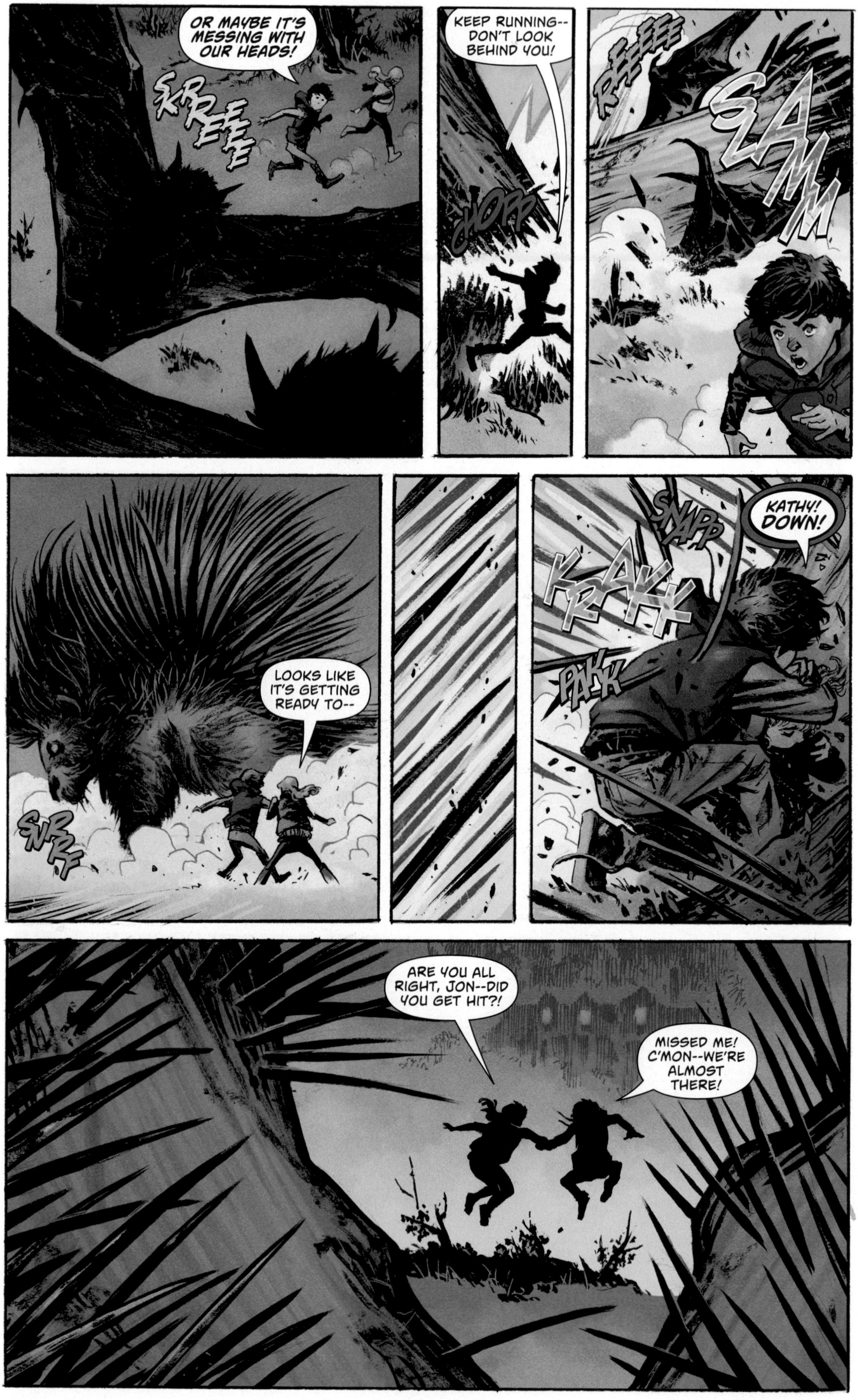
OR MAYBE IT'S MESSING WITH OUR HEADS!
SKREEEE
KEEP RUNNING-- DON'T LOOK BEHIND YOU!
CHOPP
REEEEE
SLAMM
LOOKS LIKE IT'S GETTING READY TO--
SNRK
KATHY! DOWN!
SNAPP
KRAKK
PAKK
ARE YOU ALL RIGHT, JON--DID YOU GET HIT?!
MISSED ME! C'MON--WE'RE ALMOST THERE!

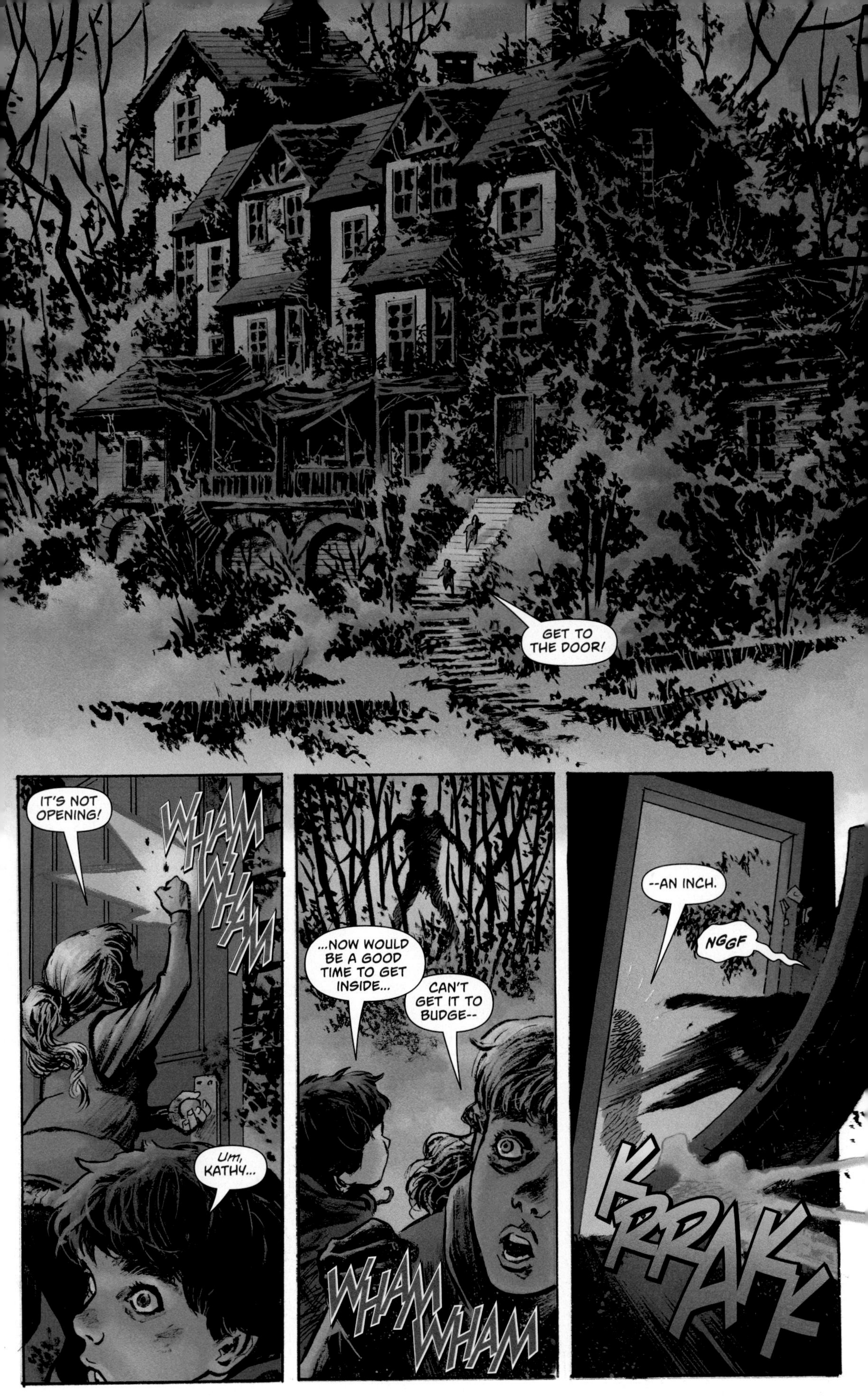
GET TO THE DOOR!
IT'S NOT OPENING!
WHAM WHAM WHAM
UM, KATHY...
...NOW WOULD BE A GOOD TIME TO GET INSIDE...
CAN'T GET IT TO BUDGE--
WHAM WHAM
--AN INCH.
NGGF
KRRAK

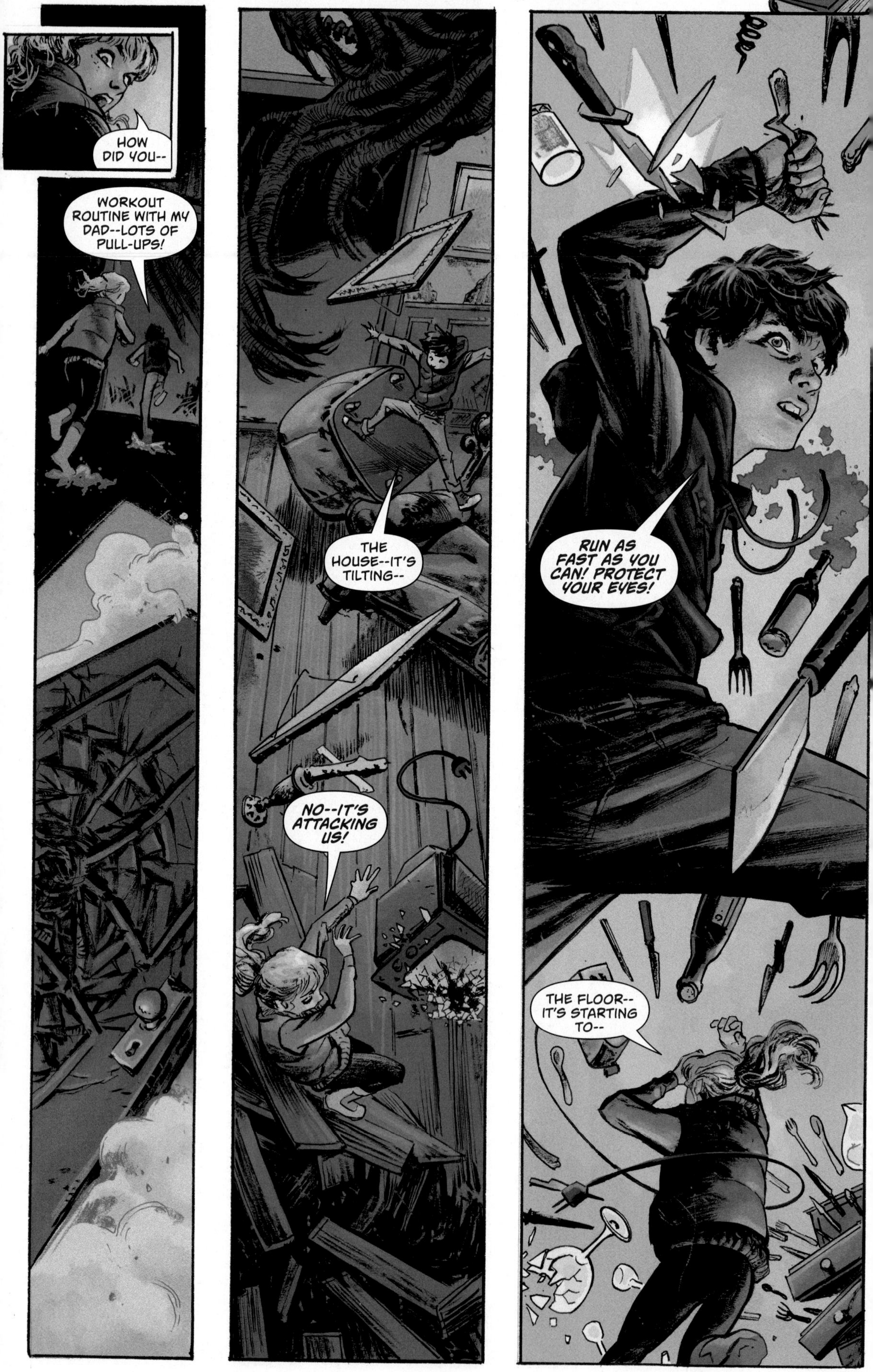
HOW DID YOU--
WORKOUT ROUTINE WITH MY DAD--LOTS OF PULL-UPS!
THE HOUSE--IT'S TILTING--
NO--IT'S ATTACKING US!
RUN AS FAST AS YOU CAN! PROTECT YOUR EYES!
THE FLOOR--IT'S STARTING TO--

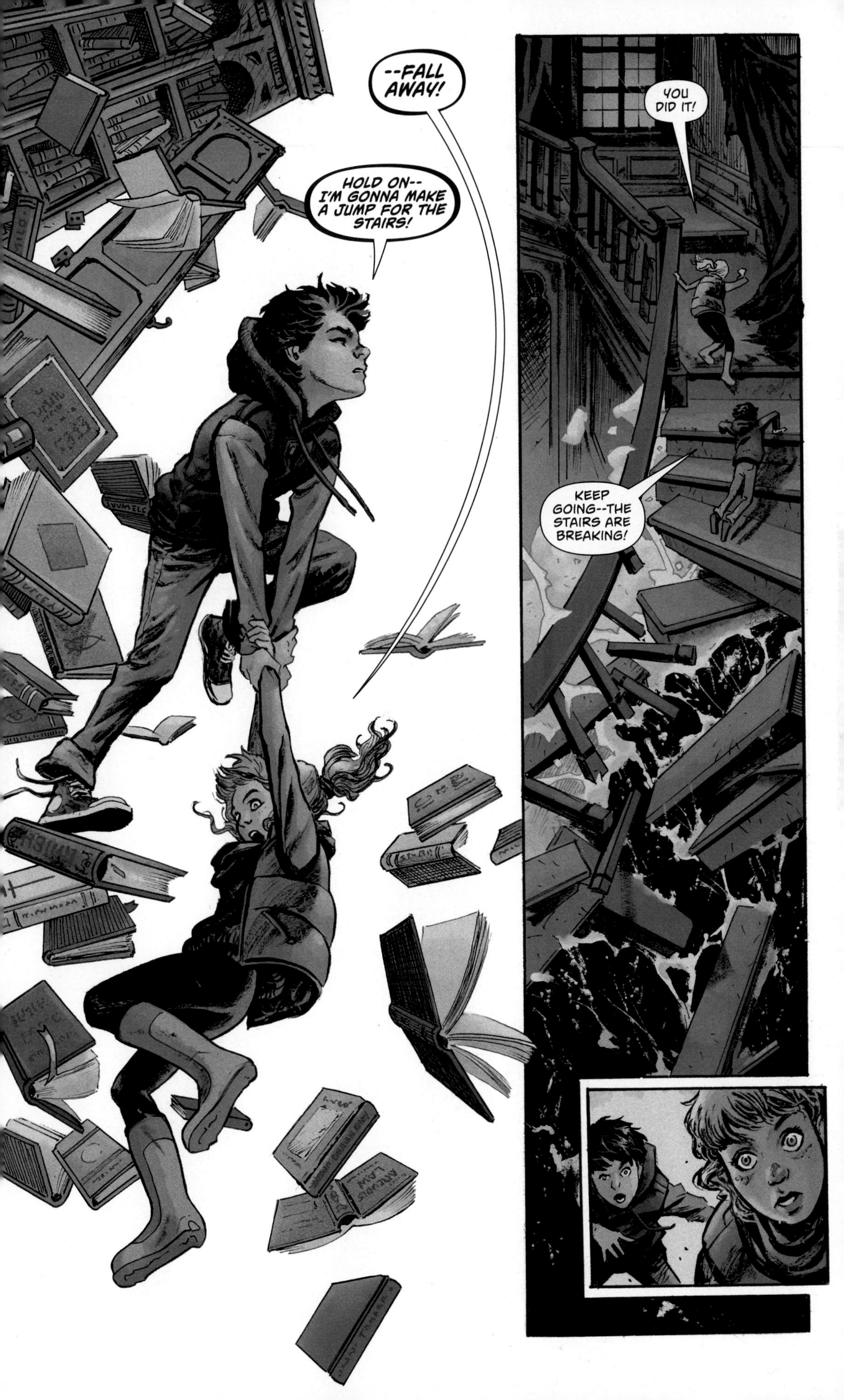
HOLD ON-- I'M GONNA MAKE A JUMP FOR THE STAIRS!
--FALL AWAY!
YOU DID IT!
KEEP GOING--THE STAIRS ARE BREAKING!

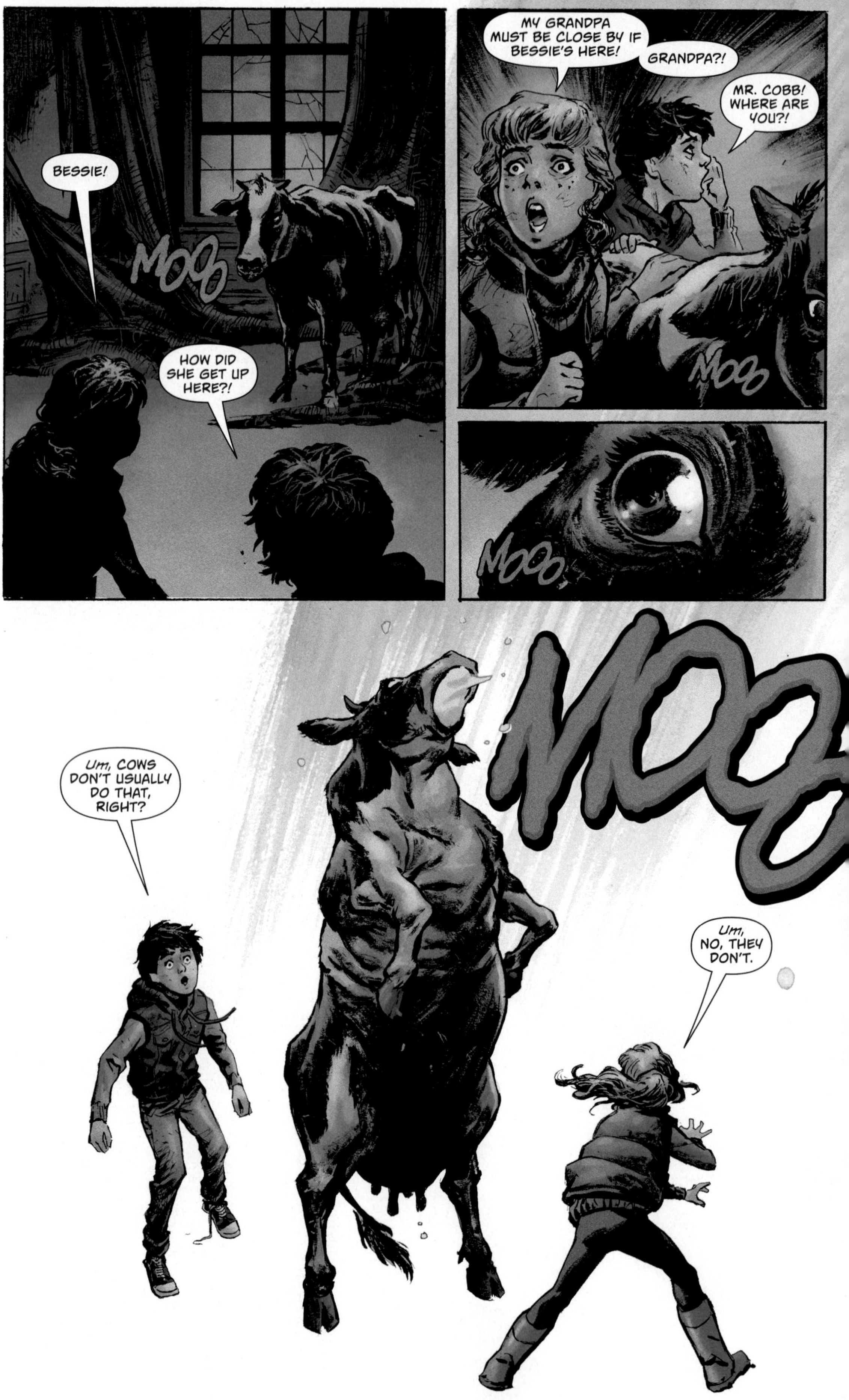
BESSIE!
MOOO
HOW DID SHE GET UP HERE?!
MY GRANDPA MUST BE CLOSE BY IF BESSIE'S HERE!
GRANDPA?!
MR. COBB! WHERE ARE YOU?!
MOOO
MOOO
MOOO
UM, COWS DON'T USUALLY DO THAT, RIGHT?
UM, NO, THEY DON'T.

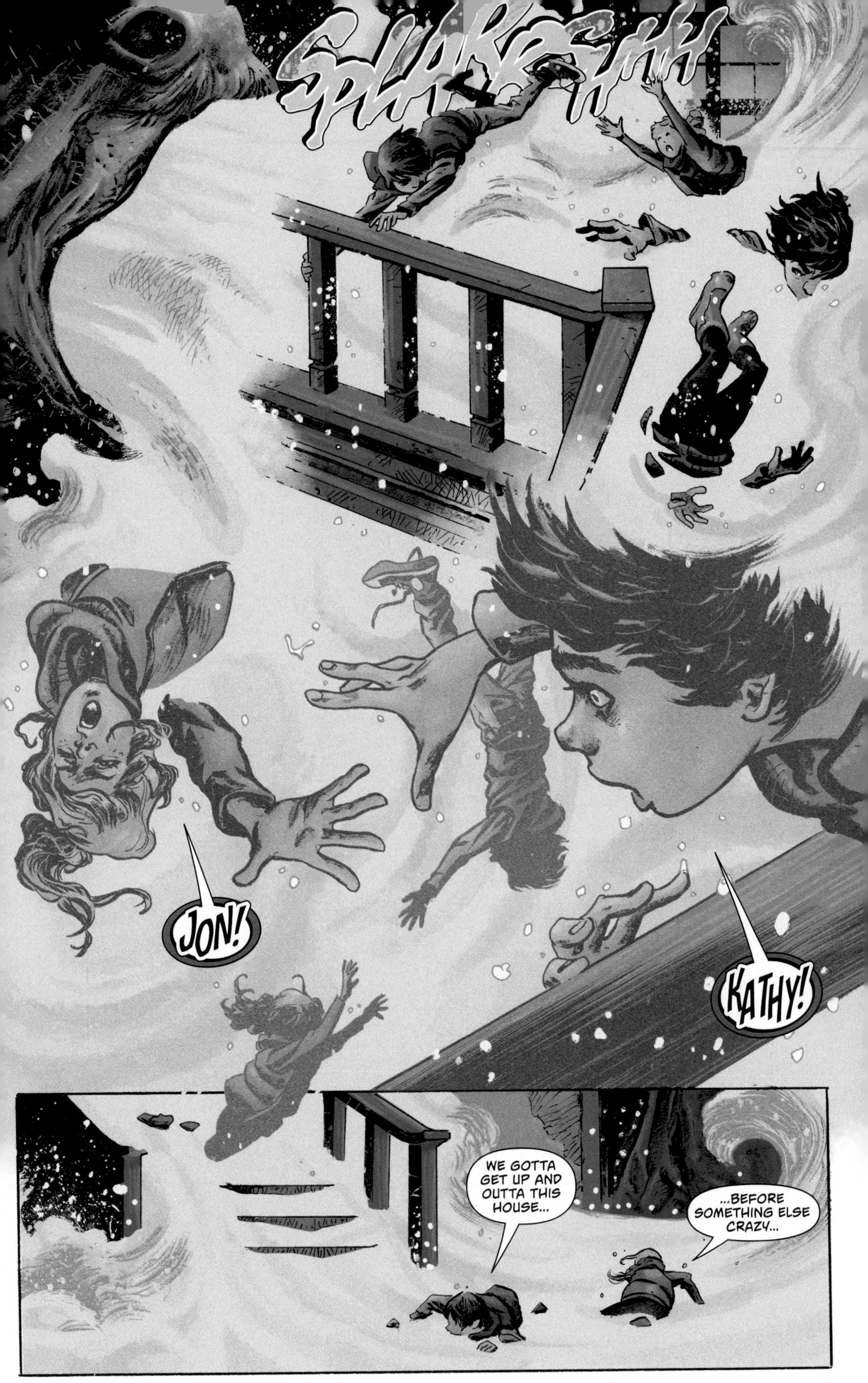
SPLAKRSHHH
JON!
KATHY!
WE GOTTA GET UP AND OUTTA THIS HOUSE...
...BEFORE SOMETHING ELSE CRAZY...

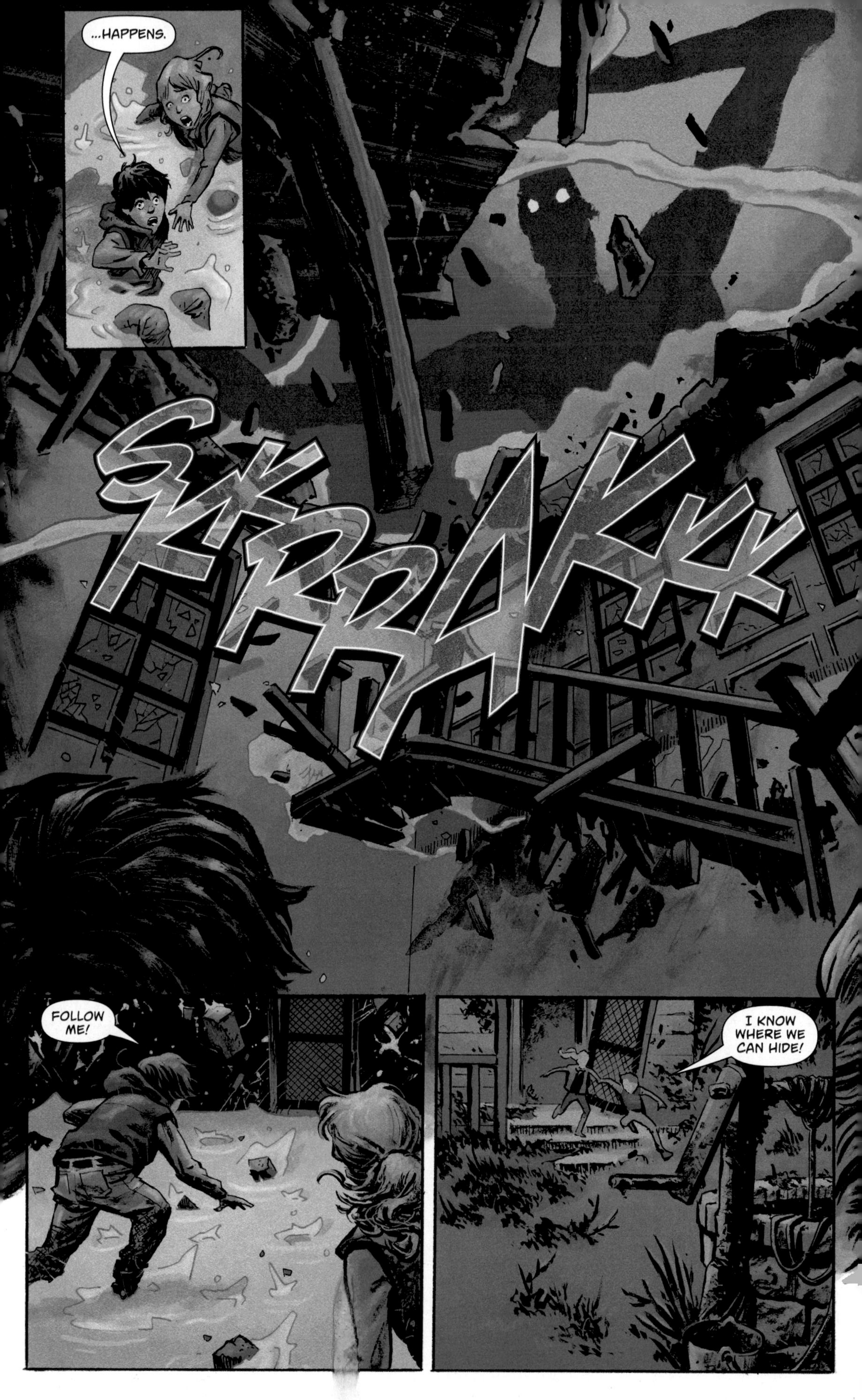
...HAPPENS.
SKRRAKKK
FOLLOW ME!
I KNOW WHERE WE CAN HIDE!

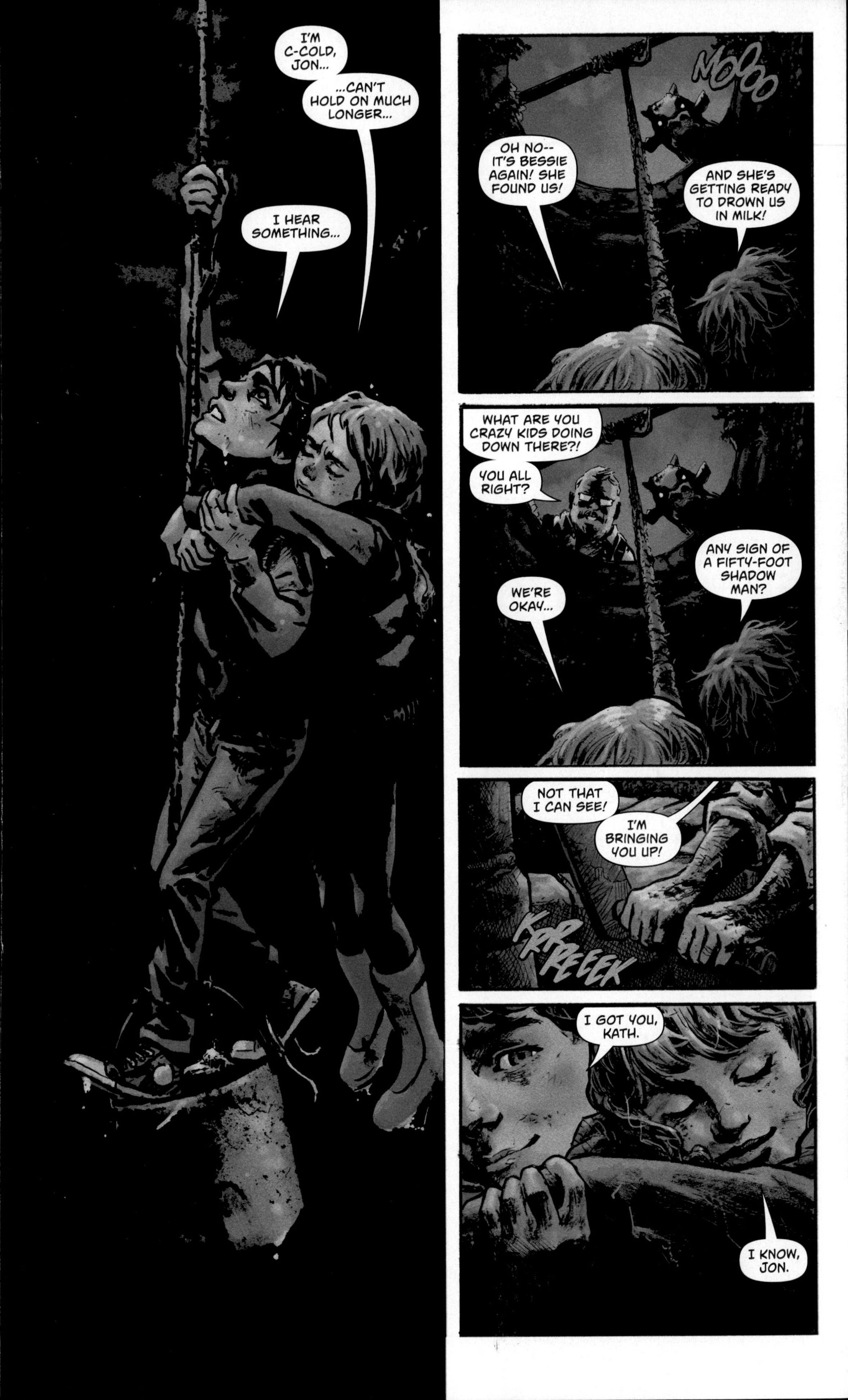
I'M C-COLD, JON...
...CAN'T HOLD ON MUCH LONGER...
I HEAR SOMETHING...
MOOOO
OH NO-- IT'S BESSIE AGAIN! SHE FOUND US!
AND SHE'S GETTING READY TO DROWN US IN MILK!
WHAT ARE YOU CRAZY KIDS DOING DOWN THERE?!
YOU ALL RIGHT?
WE'RE OKAY...
ANY SIGN OF A FIFTY-FOOT SHADOW MAN?
NOT THAT I CAN SEE!
I'M BRINGING YOU UP!
KRREEEK
I GOT YOU, KATH.
I KNOW, JON.

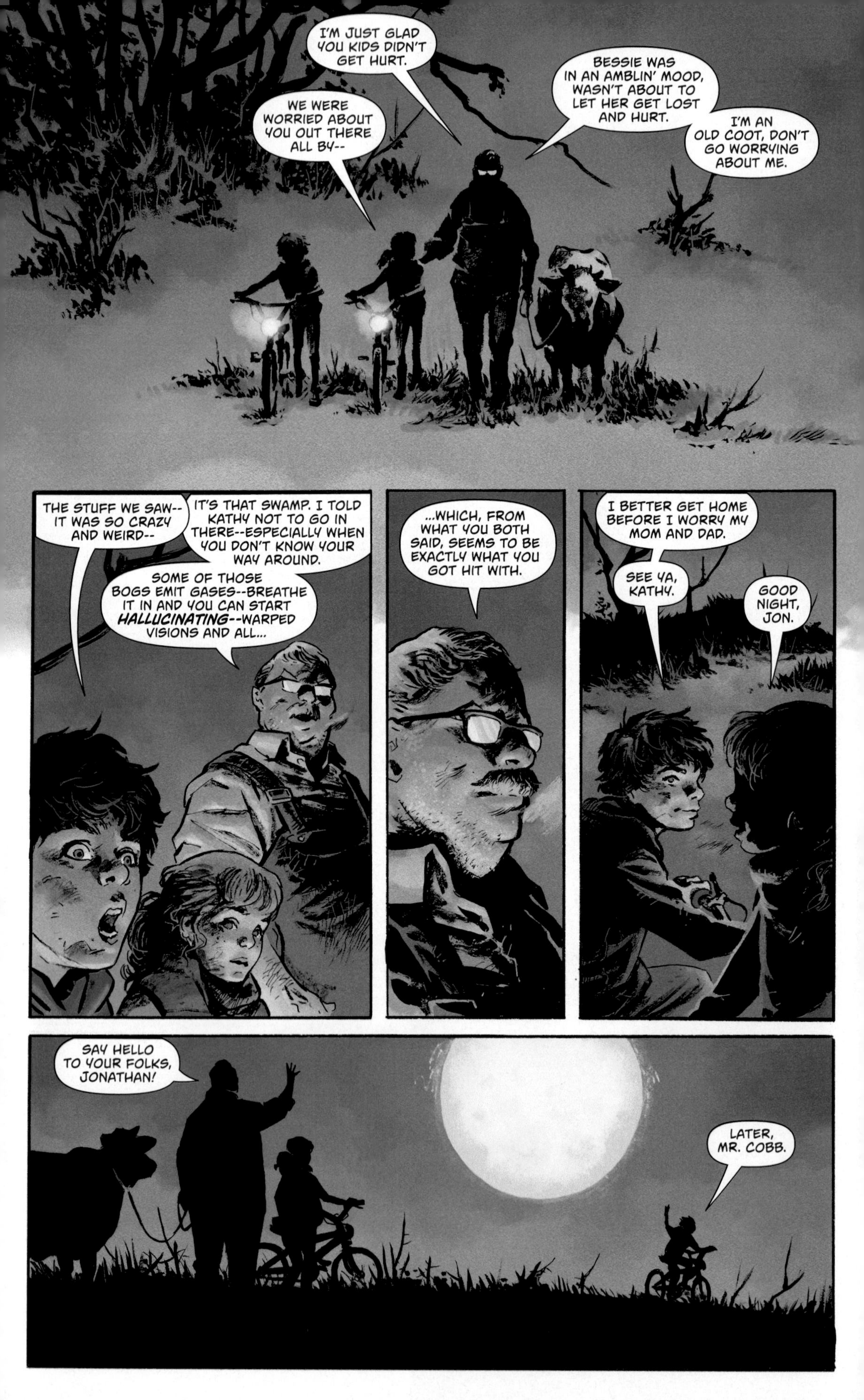
WE WERE WORRIED ABOUT YOU OUT THERE ALL BY--
I'M JUST GLAD YOU KIDS DIDN'T GET HURT.
BESSIE WAS IN AN AMBLIN' MOOD, WASN'T ABOUT TO LET HER GET LOST AND HURT.
I'M AN OLD COOT, DON'T GO WORRYING ABOUT ME.
THE STUFF WE SAW-- IT WAS SO CRAZY AND WEIRD--
IT'S THAT SWAMP. I TOLD KATHY NOT TO GO IN THERE--ESPECIALLY WHEN YOU DON'T KNOW YOUR WAY AROUND.
SOME OF THOSE BOGS EMIT GASES--BREATHE IT IN AND YOU CAN START ***HALLUCINATING***--WARPED VISIONS AND ALL...
...WHICH, FROM WHAT YOU BOTH SAID, SEEMS TO BE EXACTLY WHAT YOU GOT HIT WITH.
I BETTER GET HOME BEFORE I WORRY MY MOM AND DAD.
SEE YA, KATHY.
GOOD NIGHT, JON.
SAY HELLO TO YOUR FOLKS, JONATHAN!
LATER, MR. COBB.

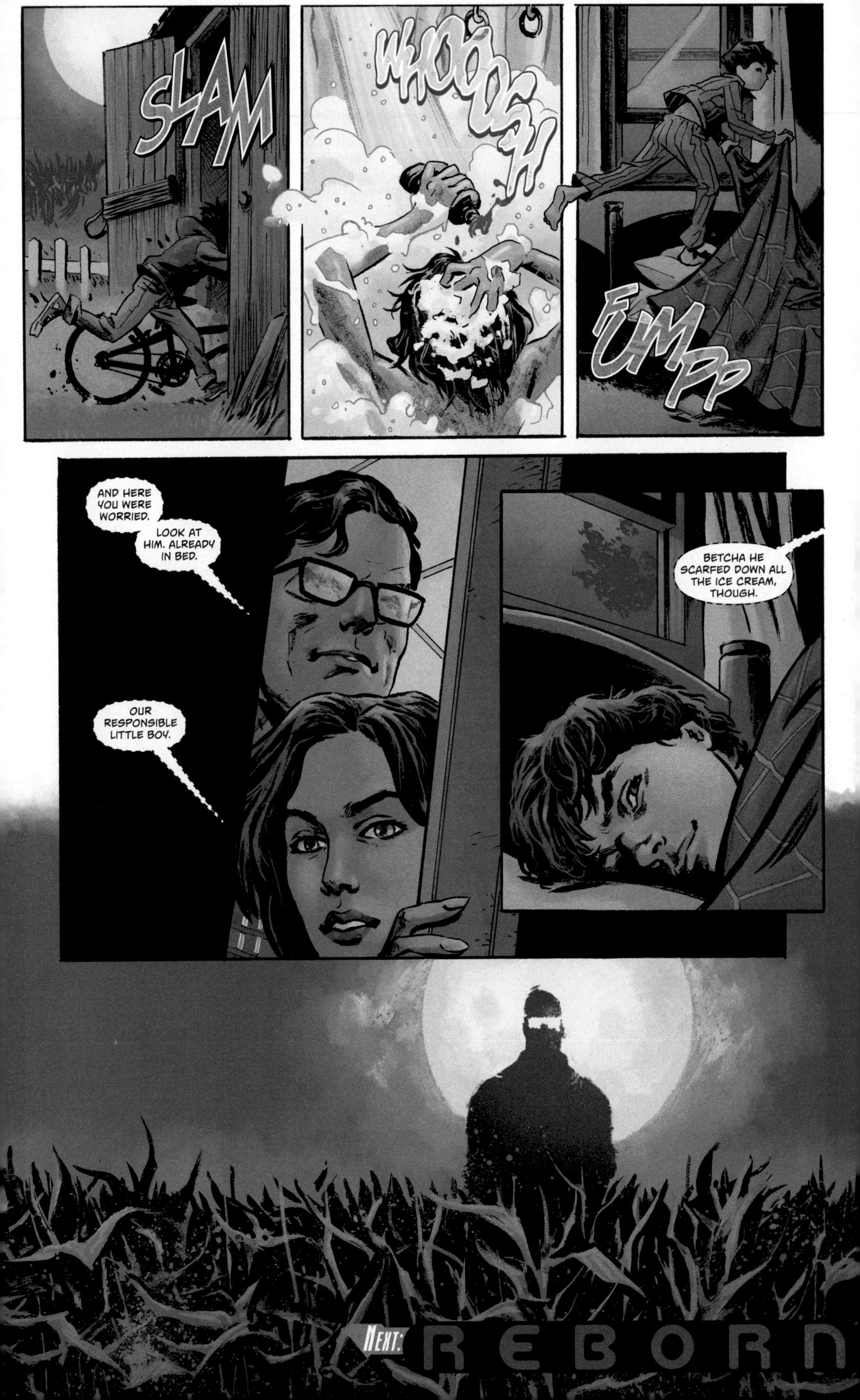
SLAM
WHOOOOSH
FUMPP
AND HERE YOU WERE WORRIED.
LOOK AT HIM. ALREADY IN BED.
OUR RESPONSIBLE LITTLE BOY.
BETCHA HE SCARFED DOWN ALL THE ICE CREAM, THOUGH.
NEXT: REBORN

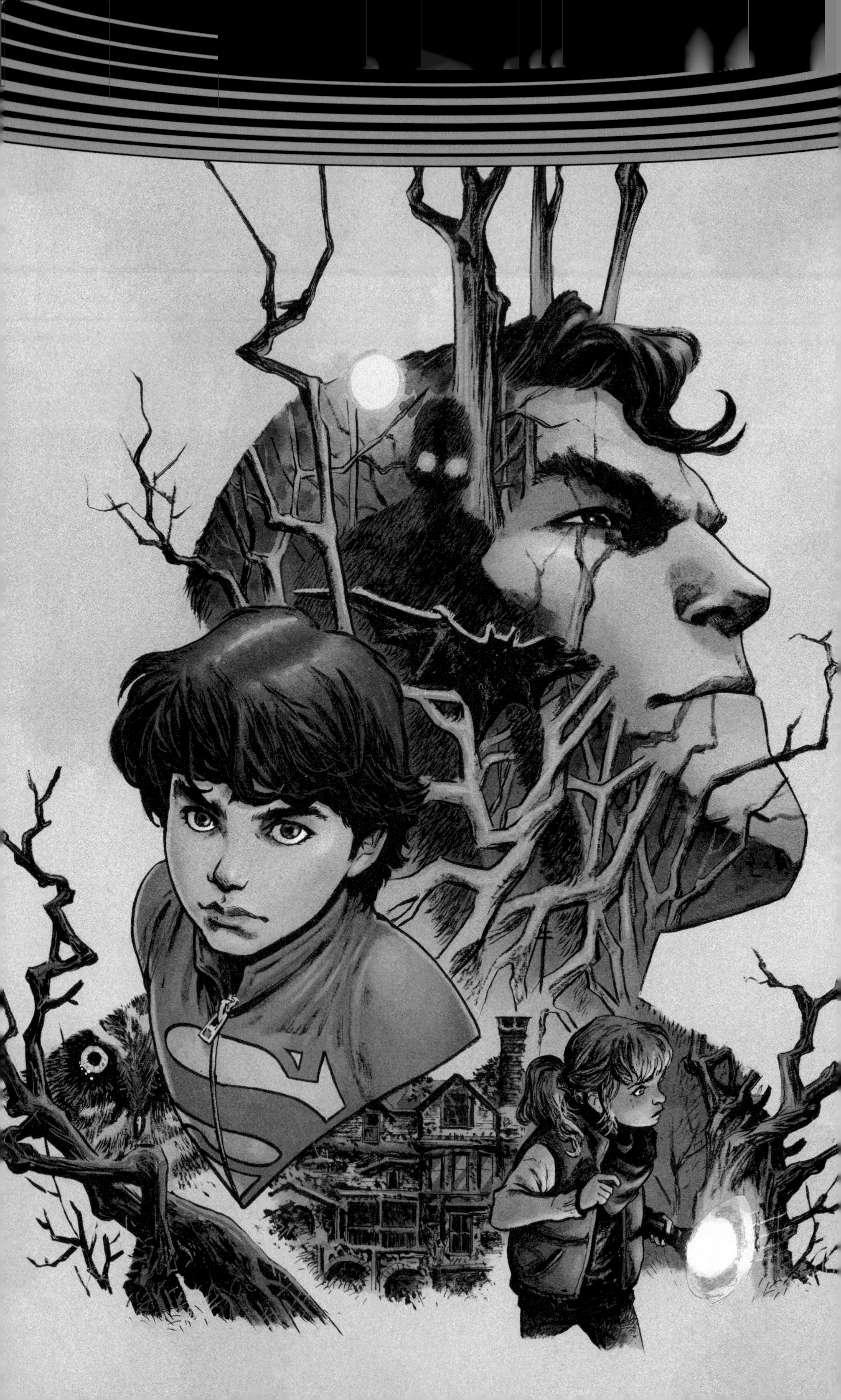

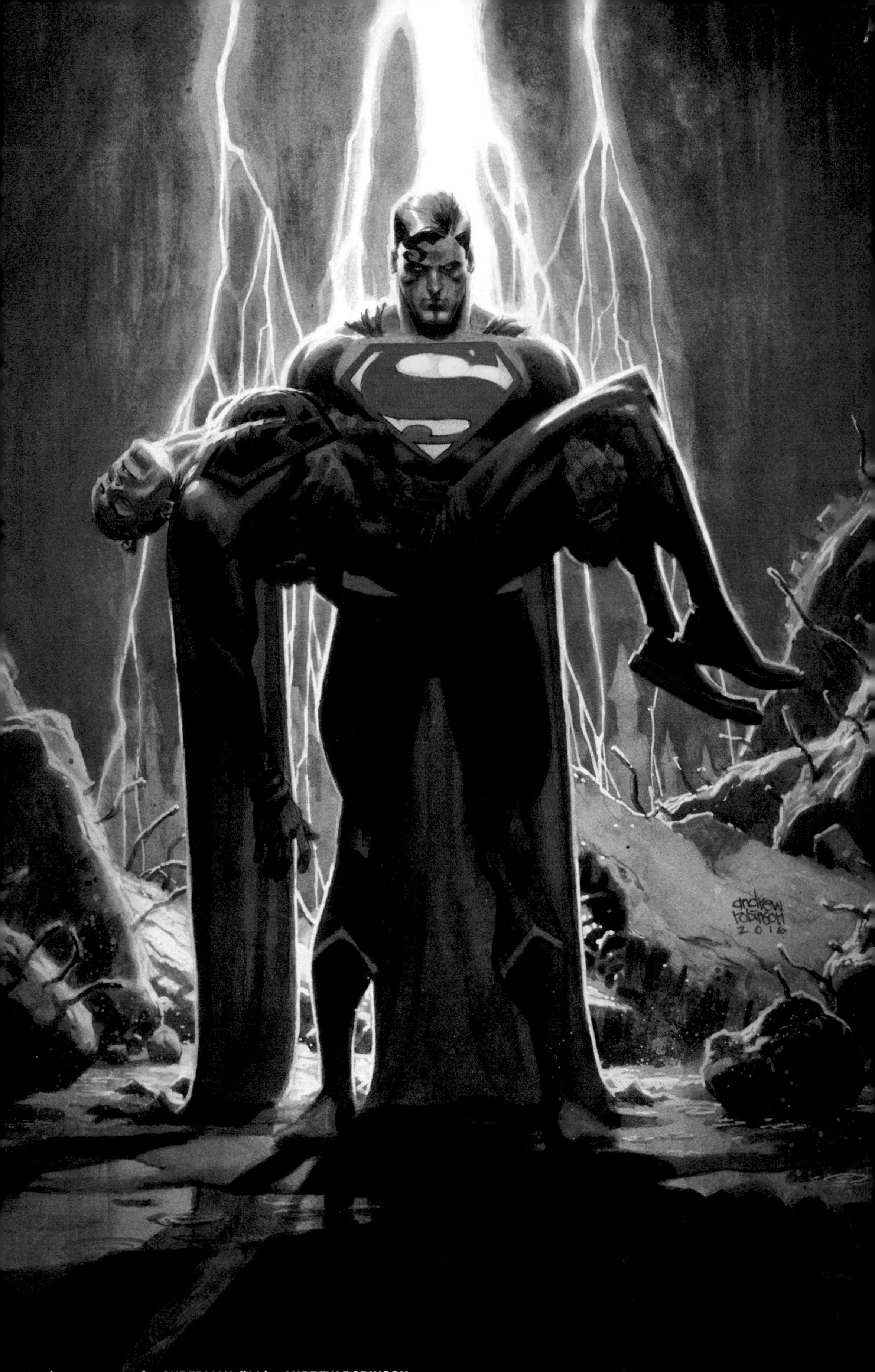
andrew robinson 2016

Variant cover art for SUPERMAN #14 by ANDREW ROBINSON

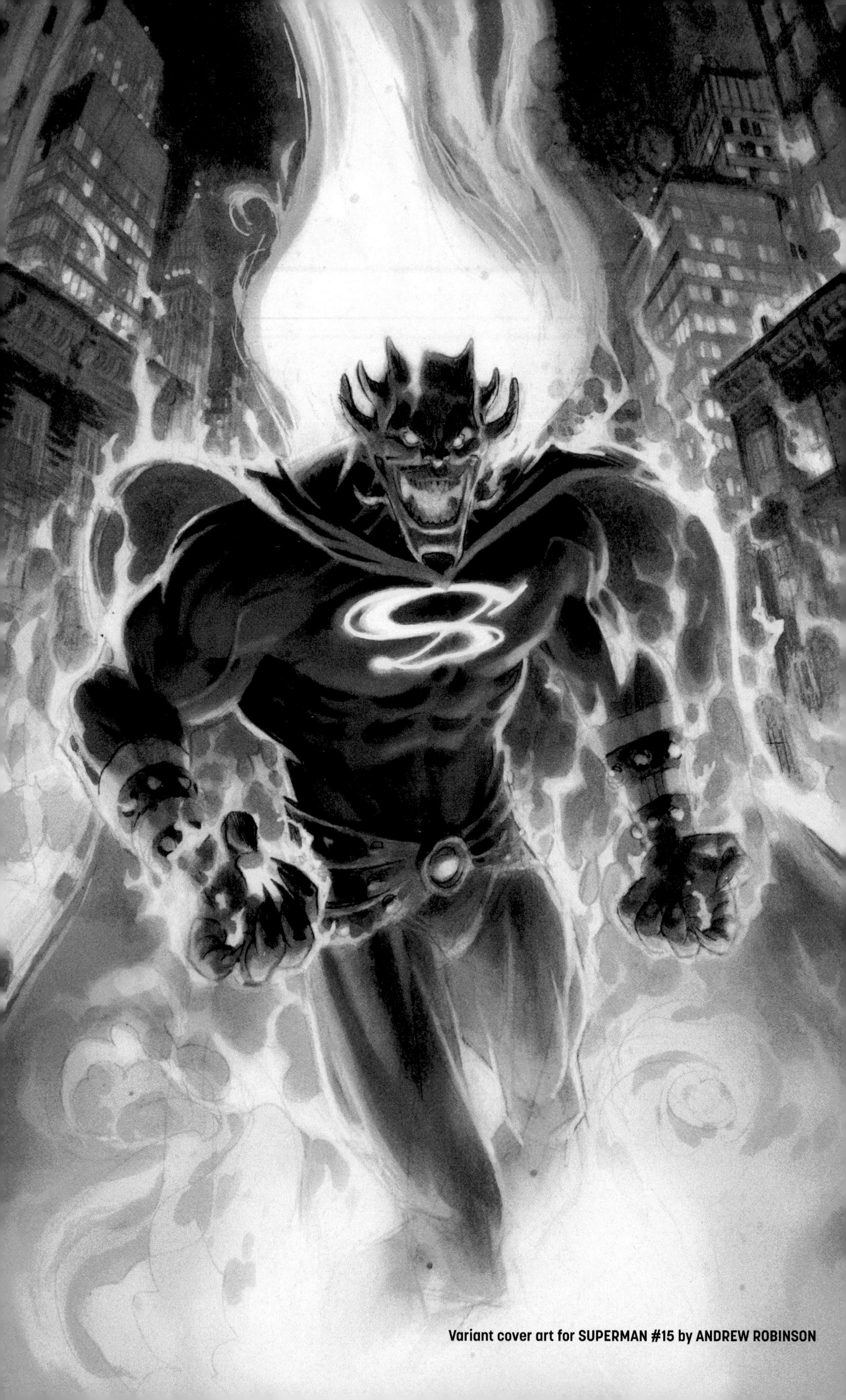

Variant cover art for SUPERMAN #15 by ANDREW ROBINSON

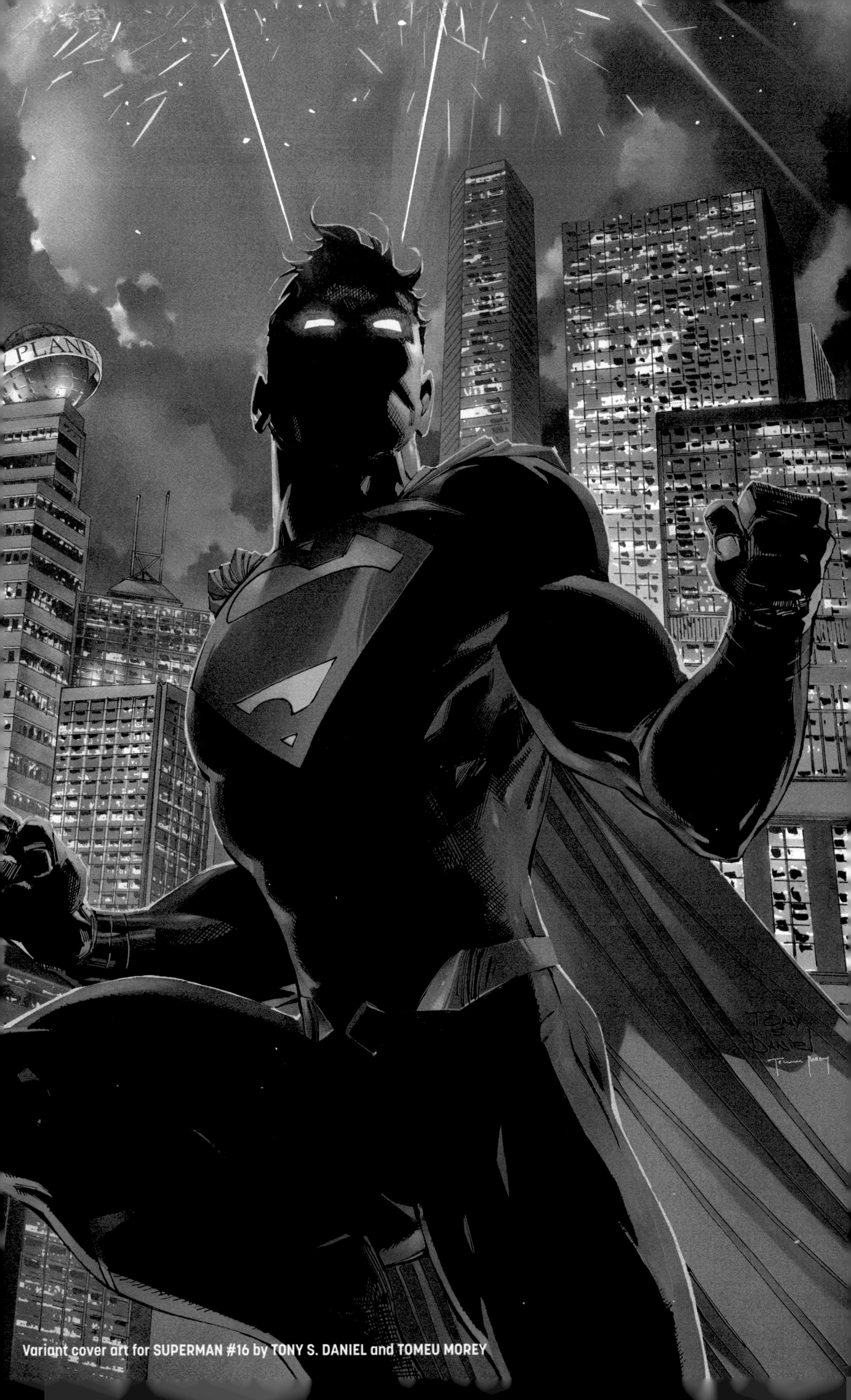

Variant cover art for SUPERMAN #16 by TONY S. DANIEL and TOMEU MOREY

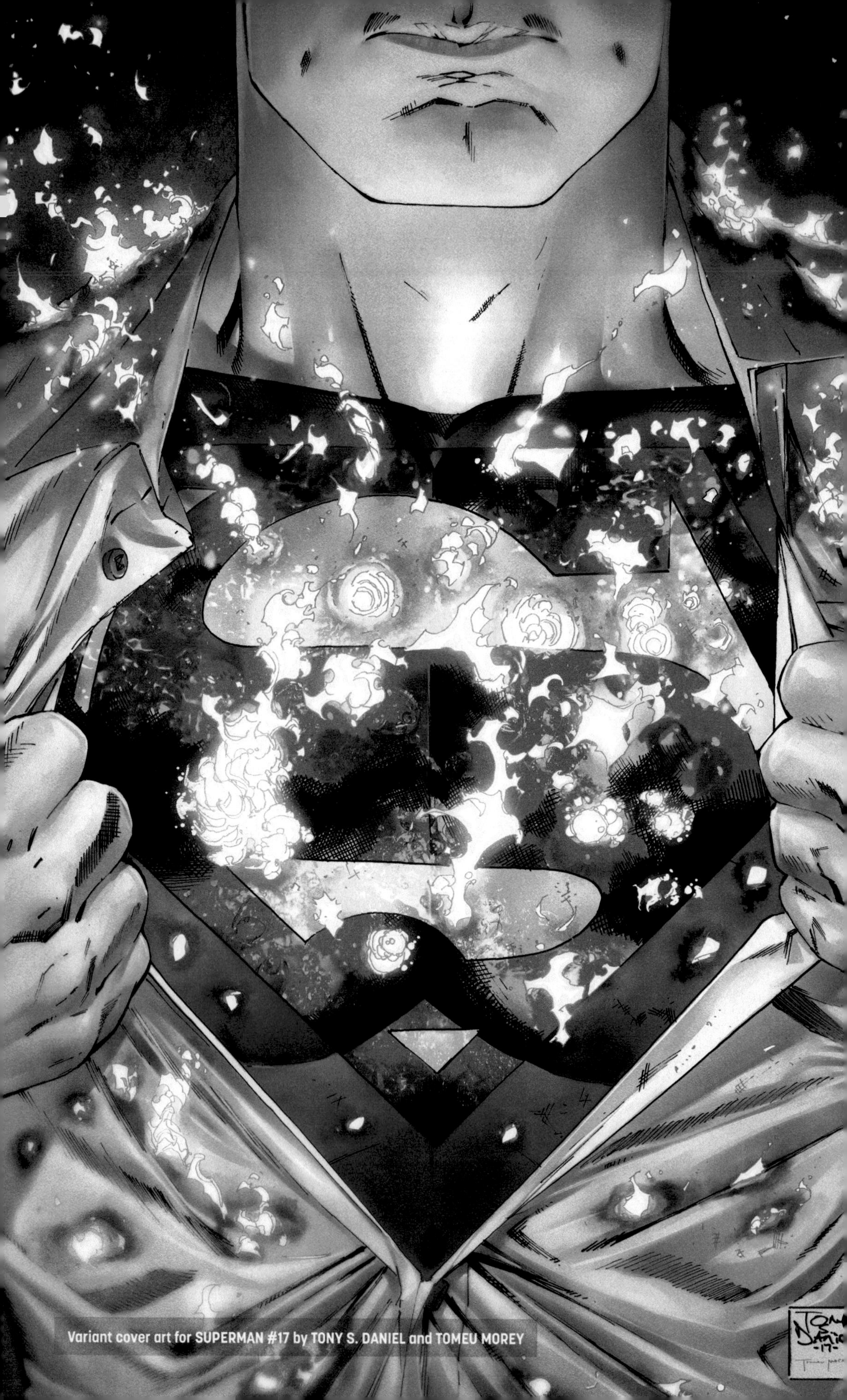

Variant cover art for SUPERMAN #17 by TONY S. DANIEL and TOMEU MOREY

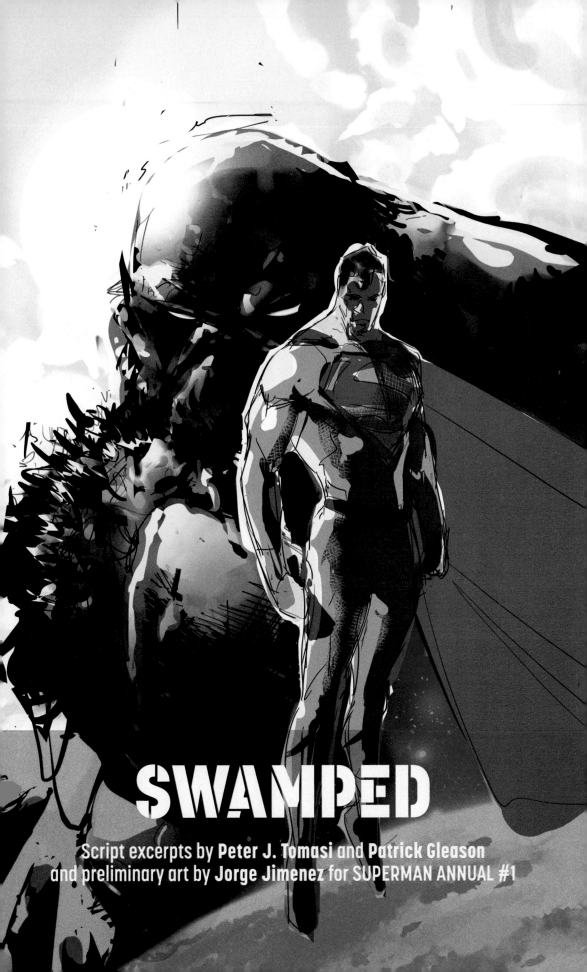

SWAMPED

Script excerpts by **Peter J. Tomasi** and **Patrick Gleason**
and preliminary art by **Jorge Jimenez** for SUPERMAN ANNUAL #1

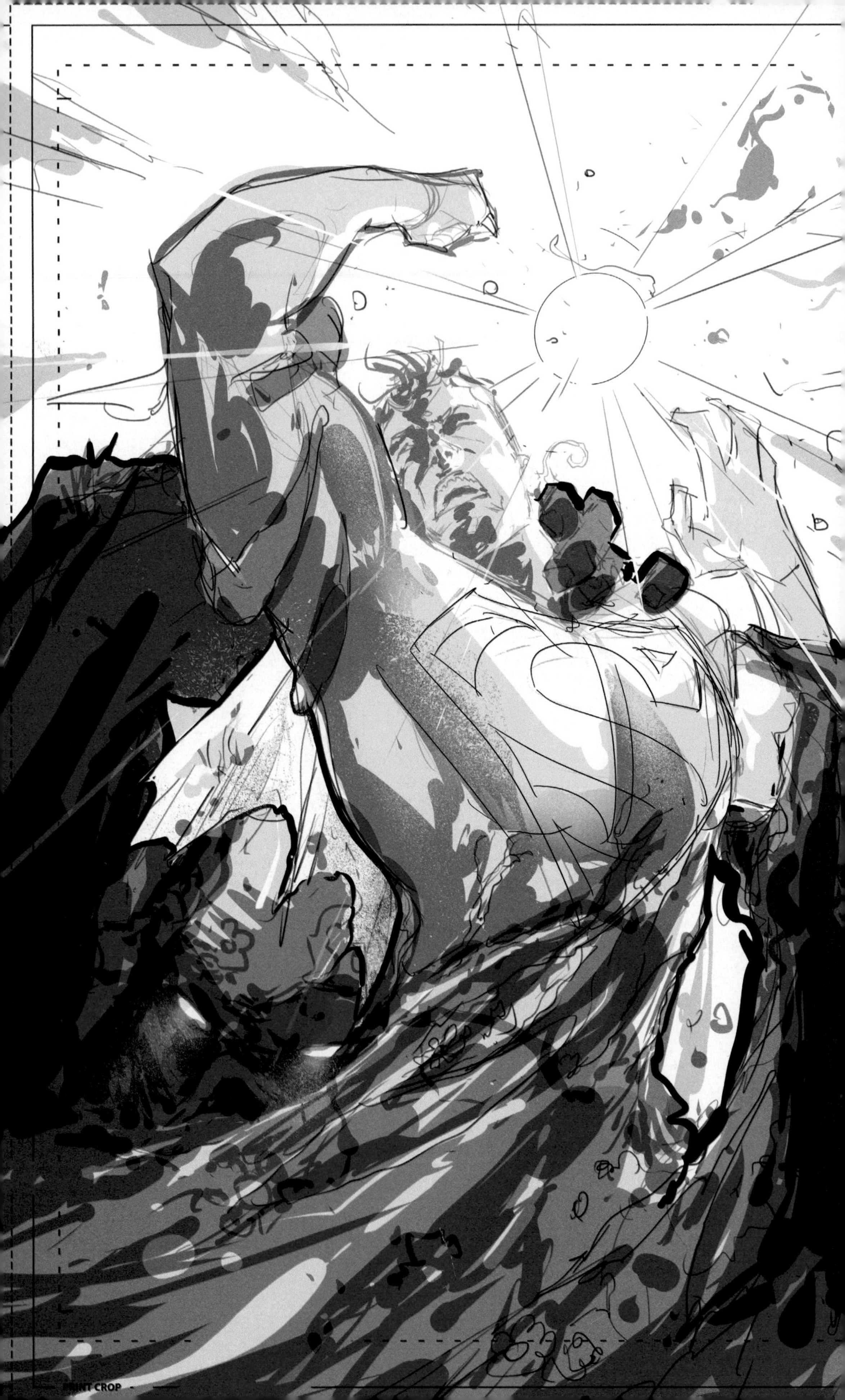
PRINT CROP

PAGE 1

Dawn. Open the story with a close-up on some DEAD LETTUCE in the ground. The following panels should then show us that we're in Hamilton County, the Smith Farm, as CLARK, frustrated, stands there alone in blue jeans, with a loose blue jean jacket over a red work shirt, and work boots. He's not too happy at the moment as he reaches down and pulls a head of lettuce from the dirt and examines it then tosses it to the ground amid the other dead heads of lettuce. He thinks aloud: "Pa made it look so easy." He doesn't understand why the fields need so much water lately. "We've had plenty of rain, why are they so brittle?"

PAGES 2 and 3

Clark takes off in a blur from the field, and as he flies at super-speed, we'd like to have him change within the speed blur into his Supes uniform. Now in his Supes uniform, he scans the ground below and sees several ponds and streams and lakes he's familiar with in the vicinity have drained almost completely, revealing assorted junk and random garbage at the mucky bottom, which we'll see more closely in a moment.

Supes stares hard, using his x-ray vision, and he can see that below/beneath the lakes are various sinkholes, which have resulted in them draining.

PAGES 4 and 5

Double page spread, Jorge. I'd shoot it from behind Supes so we can get the real scope and feel as the most disconcerting thing he sees is just under the ground, leaving behind a trail of raised dirt in its wake. Supes spots TENDRILS OF ORGANIC MATTER–SWAMP THING'S tubular vines–snaking like worms from all directions off the pages, rippling toward an empty lake below him in the center of the page. Think of it, Jorge, like the creature from that movie Tremors, except it's not just one creature, but dozens of vines the size of fire hoses.

In the middle of the page is the raised FACE OF SWAMP THING, YELLING AT SUPERMAN from the now largely empty muddy lake below. To help visualize what we're thinking of, Google FACE ON MARS and that'll give you the feel we're aiming for.

SWAMPY: YOU DON'T BELONG HERE ANYMORE, SUPERMAN! (Please use distinctive Swamp Thing lettering and balloon.)

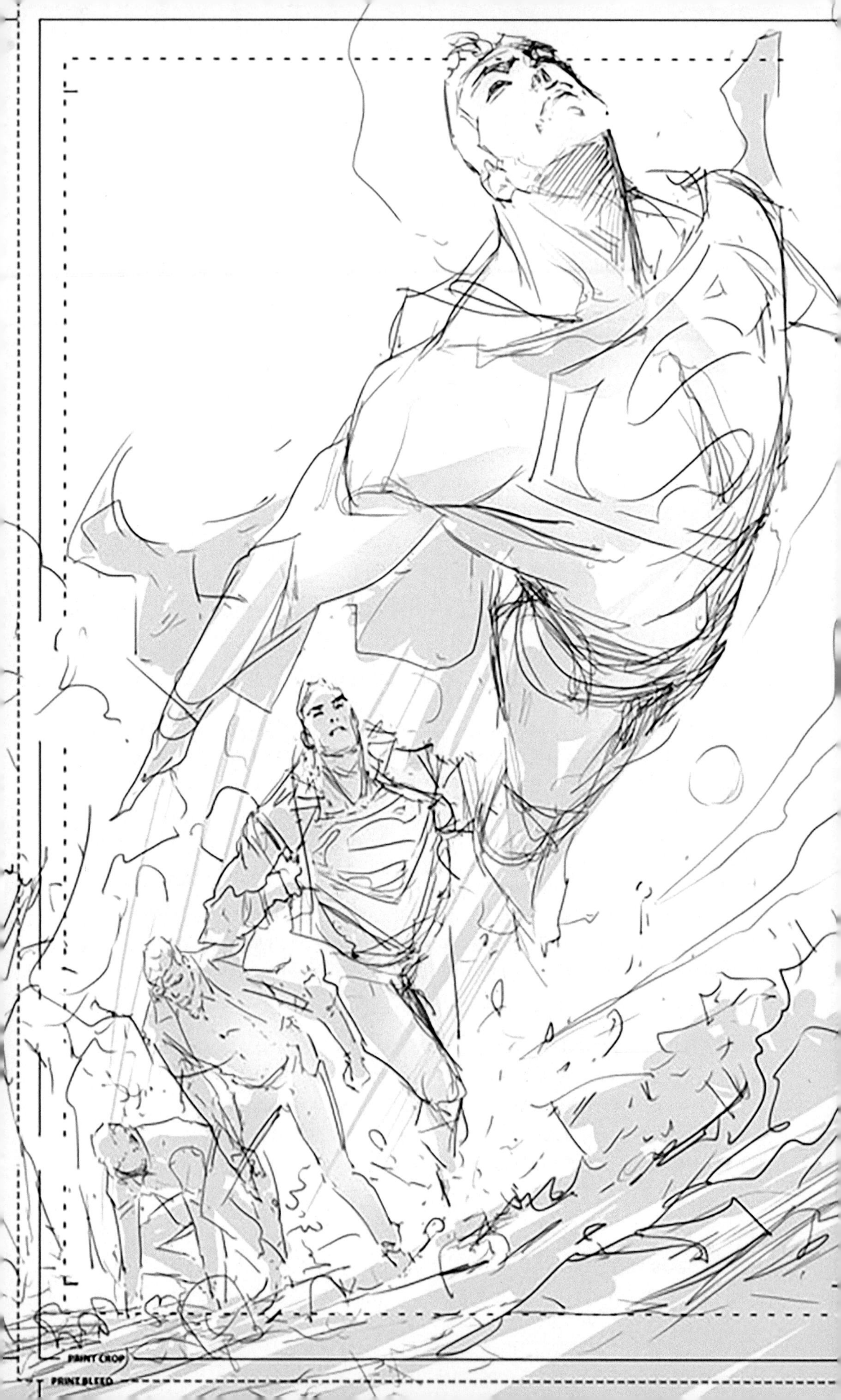
PRINT CROP
PRINT BLEED

PAGES 8 and 9

These two pages will get across some info, Jorge, so whatever you can do to spice up the camera angles would be great.

Supes asks, what did Swampy mean, and Swampy tells Supes that being the environmental elemental knucklehead that Swampy is, and tied into the Earth in such a distinct way, that he was drawn here to Superman in particular. Swampy tells Supes that something is out of whack–a vibrational aberration that is tied into the way he draws solar energy from the sun that is different from the previous New 52 Supes.

Supes thinks about the aspects of some odd stuff that's come up recently–for example, in Geoff's REBIRTH, the scene at the hotel, and of course our first issue where he left the blue hand energy outline. No need to flash back, Jorge, we'll cover it in dialogue as Supes relates these recent problems and the death of the New 52 Superman to Swampy.

Remember, the situation is still tense, but Supes tries to convince Swampy that there's nothing to fear from him, he's here to help, here to do what the New 52 Superman did. As Supes speaks, he rests his hand in a friendly gesture on Swampy's shoulder...

PAGE 10

...which leaves behind a BLUE HANDPRINT OUTLINE on Swampy's body...

...and in turn causes Swampy to start suddenly turning all blue, as the energy handprint outline spreads like BLUE VEINS all across his head and body, infecting Swampy and causing his WHOLE BODY TO TURN BLUE (except his eyes, which should remain red)...

PAGES 11 through 13

...and putting Swampy into a trance-like state as he suddenly starts speaking Kryptonian (think of that scene in *The Lord of the Rings*, when Galadriel, played by Cate Blanchett, goes into that weird trance) while blue vines from his body start shooting into the ground all around Supes like straws, trying to draw/suck elemental power from the Earth/dirt to keep the blue at bay.

As this occurs, Supes steps back, looking at his normal hand in surprise, trying to calm Swampy down as Swampy suddenly snaps out of the trance and lashes out at Supes, his arms growing as thick as tree trunks as he swings at Supes and knocks him around a bit at the lake bottom. The whole time Supes continues to try and help, taking hold of the blue vines snaking off Swampy's body and trying to use them to wrap him tight, control him and calm him, but it doesn't work as...

PAGES 14 through 17

...we go for a ride!

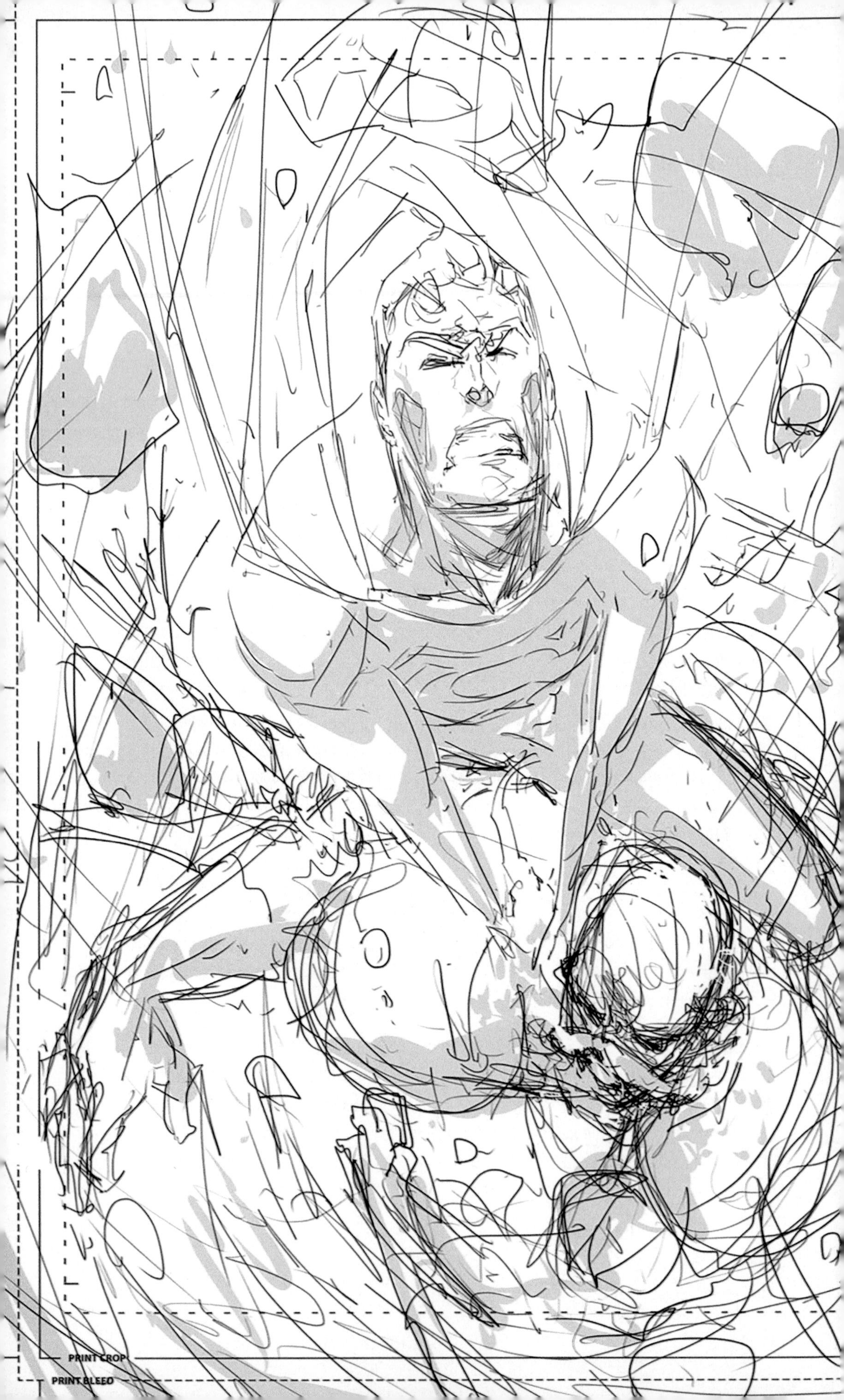
PRINT CROP
PRINT BLEED

PAGES 18 and 19
Cool shot as they explode out of the lake bed and Supes is knocked from Swampy as Swampy dives sideways under the ground.

Supes, all beat up, stands there waiting to see Swampy emerge, but instead, thick vines (no longer blue) shoot up from the ground and start wrapping around his legs and feet.

Supes uses his heat vision like a scalpel, trying not to burn Swamp Thing too much, as he attempts to cut away the vines, but it's too much and they really start getting a good grip on him, so let's have a lotta fun with Swampy's powers here as...

Supes takes to the sky, but the vines are still attached and trying to pull him back. He struggles as the vines wrapped around him start getting thicker and thicker, as do the ones from the ground. Think of it, Jorge, like Supes is trying to escape the clutches of the classic Beanstalk from Jack and the Beanstalk.

PAGES 20 through 27
We're doing comic books, right? So these next few pages should be insane, as we literally have Supes locked in a midair battle with Swampy as he fights the vines with his heat vision and also trades massive punches and whatever else you think could be cool, Jorge, as Swampy's body manifests itself in different vines and fights back as it tries to drag Supes down. In other words, think of, like, half a dozen of the vines looking like Swamp Thing's as the fight swirls around the clouds and some birds as they swoop in and even pull off food from Swampy to eat.

The sequence should end as Supes is really entangled by the vines that now turn into one big massive Swamp Thing hand (think of it like the size of King Kong's hand in the Peter Jackson movie) as it drops back to the ground where we once again see the FACE ON MARS SWAMP THING on the ground with its mouth wide open and the big Swampy hand FEEDING Supes directly into it!

The last image should be of Supes, entangled, wrapped tight, sinking into the black mud of Swamp Thing's mouth, the black mud like quicksand, pouring into Supes' open mouth as he slowly disappears under it until nothing remains but complete blackness.

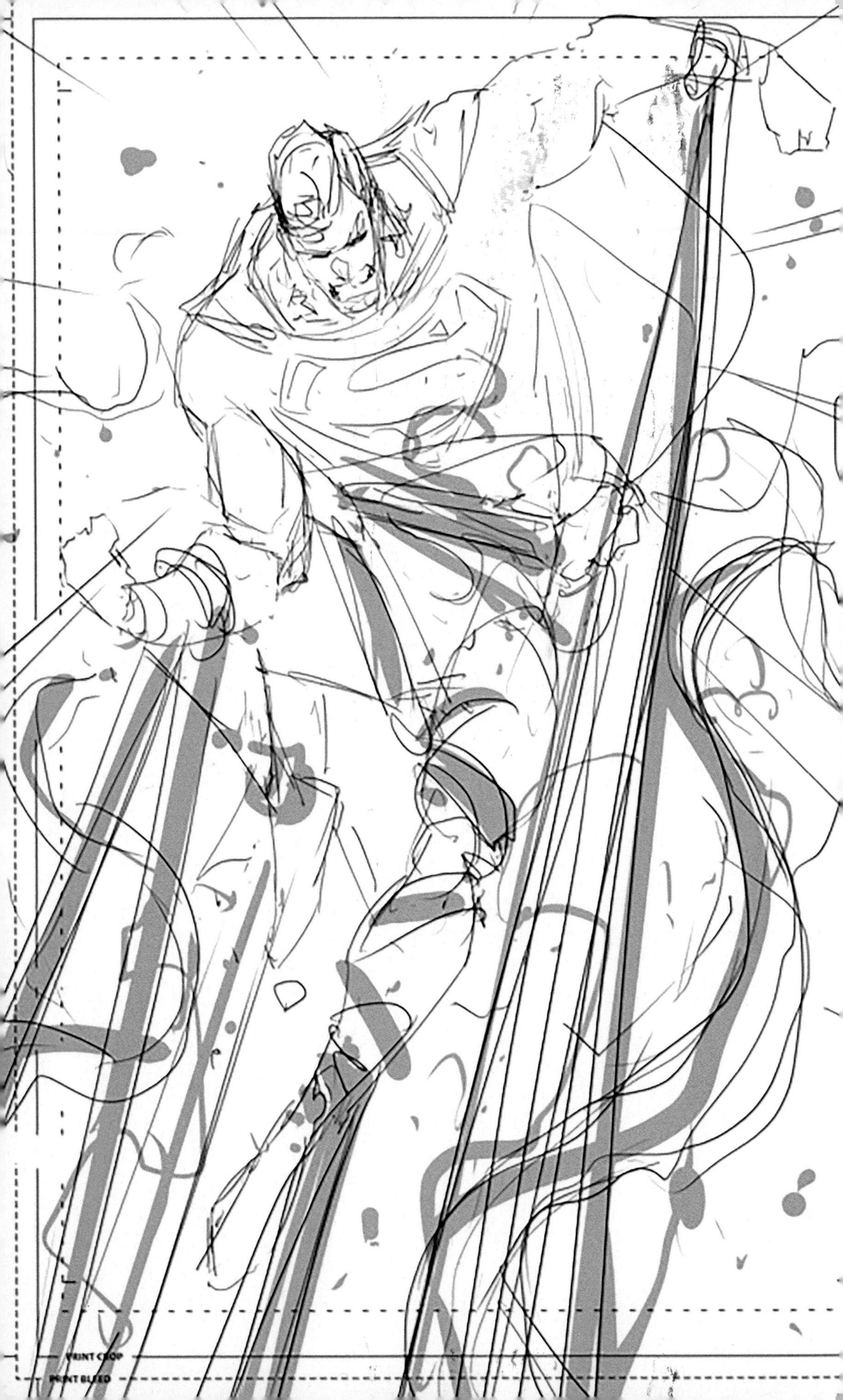
PRINT CROP
PRINT BLEED